THE GUINNESS BOOK·OF RALLYING

THE GUINNESS BOOK·OF RALLYING

JOHN DAVENPORT

GUINNESS PUBLISHING

JOHN DAVENPORT

ABOVE The author . . . with a friend.

In 30 years of direct involvement in motor rallying, John Davenport has been a co-driver, team manager, organiser, journalist and author.

He started navigating on British rallies while still at college in the late 1950s, writing reports on those events for *Motoring News* before becoming the paper's Rallies Editor, a post he held between 1963 and 1966. During that time, he continued to participate in rallies and this competitive involvement eventually inspired a return to freelance work, this time with *Autosport*. This gave him the chance to accept contracts as a co-driver with companies such as Triumph, Ford, Lancia, Alpine Renault, Fiat and BMW.

After a spell in 1976 of working for the RACMSA, he was recruited by British Leyland to run their motorsport department starting in the 1977 season. He guided their entries in both rallying and racing for just over ten years. Since leaving BL in 1987, he has concentrated on writing but still competes on international rallies and is also helping to organise historic rallies.

Editor: Charles Richards
Design: Steve Leaning
Picture Editor: Alex Goldberg

Published in Great Britain by Guinness Publishing Ltd, 33 London Road, Enfield, Middlesex

Typeset in ITC Garamond by
Ace Filmsetting Ltd, Frome, Somerset
Colour origination by Bright Arts, Hong Kong
Printed in Hong Kong by Imago

'Guinness' is a registered trademark of Guinness Publishing Ltd

British Library Cataloguing in Publication Data
Davenport, John
   The Guinness book of rallying
   1. Cars. Rallying
   I. Title

ISBN 0-85112-968-4

PREVIOUS PAGE The Californian Baha 1000. The style of this event and the kind of vehicles that participated had a strong influence on the creation of the Paris–Dakar in 1979.

OPPOSITE The scene is Wales, the year 1987 – and the spectators make good use of the terrain for a safe view of the rally.

CONTENTS

I should not have been a rally driver at all. When I was 13 years old, it seemed that my destiny was to become a ski-jumping champion. My father's business was making skis, and during the Finnish winter I was seldom off them. But then fate took a hand and I caught poliomyelitis.

It nearly killed me but thanks to a great deal of medical help and a bit of *sisu* – Finnish determination – I pulled through. It was clear that my skiing days were over. In fact, my legs were so weak that it looked as though I would never get to ride the motorbike that my grandfather had bought for me while I was in hospital. So to travel the 50 kilometres into Helsinki every other day for the therapy that was necessary, I was allowed to borrow the Jaguar MkI that belonged to my mother. I learnt to drive it really well and a year later I entered my first rally with it. We went off the road and someone else had to push us back on, as I still had iron supports on my ankles. But I now knew what I wanted to do.

It is history now that I got myself a Saab and that I won the 1000 Lakes twice in it, as well as three Finnish rally championships. I could drive that car so well with my weak legs because it had a freewheel which enabled clutchless gearchanges. I went on to drive for the Saab works team and then, at various times, with Triumph, BMC, Lancia, DAF, Peugeot, Fiat and Ford Germany. The important thing was that I had triumphed over a disaster and that rallying had helped me, quite literally, to find my feet again. Of course, the thrill of winning and of being rated in the

top 10 drivers in the world is tremendous, but I am pleased that I have been so lucky and that rallying has brought me so many new friends.

This sport which I love so much has taken me to nearly every part of the world. It is really noticeable that it creates situations in which restrictions can be swept away. When we did the London–Sydney Rally, they opened a border between India and Pakistan that had been closed for 10 years and subject to much fighting, and after the rally it stayed open. It certainly is a sport which seems to break down barriers and help international understanding. The current World Rally Champion, Carlos Sainz, is a Spaniard who drives for a Japanese team run by a Swede and operating out of Germany which uses British, Finnish, Swedish, Belgian and German people to pre-

ABOVE On his first major event, young Lampinen drove a Jaguar Mk I that officially belonged to his mother. The rally was the 1961 1000 Lakes, which he went on to win two years later in a Saab 96.

LEFT Simo Lampinen, triple winner of the 1000 Lakes Rally and now a FISA Steward and Member of their Rallies Commission.

pare the cars. You cannot do more for international co-operation than that!

I have enjoyed my 25 years of rally driving more than I can express in mere words. I am pleased that my companion on so many of those rallies should be the author of this book. I have shared with him quite a few successes, numerous adventures and occasionally the bitterness of failure.

I hope that by reading it, a wider audience will realise that rallying is a fantastic sport just waiting to be enjoyed.

Rallying is the most complex branch of motor sport.

This is a distinction gained only in recent years. It has long had undisputed claims to being the most complicated, since it has the problem of continual relocation in addition to those of time, speed and skill which it shares with other motor sports. Indeed, its possession of this 'fourth dimension' has often led to its rules being poorly understood by the competitors, and even, on occasion, by the administrators that penned them.

But in the 1980s, rallying embraced all those technologies that it had for so long ignored and which have done so much for the image of, and the interest created by, say, Formula One racing. At the same time, it has retained much of the appeal that saw it grow phenomenally as a sport during the 1960s and 1970s. It also managed to shed a tiny part of its complexity in the interests of standardising such things as route instructions and timing methods.

The result is that the challenge of rallying has shifted focus slightly. There is room now for the technical innovators alongside the skilled drivers and the logistics experts. A win on a major rally these days is dependent on all three. And the upsurge of engineering that has taken place in rallying has had a major effect on the vehicles that are sold for everyday use on the roads of the world.

A clear sign that the sport of motor rallying is vital and alive is that rallies themselves have continued to evolve during this period of technical change and whole new areas of healthy competition have grown up. Firstly, there are the Rallye-Raids, those long distance, off-road events that have the whiff of pure adventure about them. There were long distance events before them, but rallies like the London–Sydney and the World Cup were really just long versions of conventional rallies. It was Abidjan–Nice and Paris–Dakar that opened up the idea of having an off-road event over thousands of miles of uncharted territory. If there was any event capable of claiming ancestry of these new Rallye-Raids then it must surely have been the Baha 1000 in southern California.

Then there is the World Championship of Rallies which only started in 1973 with mainly European events, but now contains rallies in all parts of the world. These have common regulations and a driver or team from any country can go and do one of the WRC rallies without needing specialised local knowledge. The effect of this has been to bring drivers of several nationalities to the fore so that the results lists of the 1980s have featured top drivers from Germany, Italy, France, Greece, Sweden, Britain, Czechoslovakia, Poland, Finland, Spain, Portugal, New Zealand, USA, Australia, Argentina, Uruguay, Kenya, South Africa, Brazil, Canada and Japan.

Finally, there is the phenomenon of historic rallying, where thousands of people new to the sport

have discovered its lure through their interest in cars that are more than 25 years old. Taking part in rallies catering specifically for older cars gives the owners a chance to do more than just admire their cars. At the beginning of the last decade, one would have been hard pushed to find any truly competitive event run for this type of vehicle. Now there are literally hundreds, especially in Europe, and they will surely spread to other continents before long.

Rallying is a complex business requiring a number of very different skills to be brought together in order that a car and its crew may be successful. It might have been thought that this was something which would count against it in the popularity stakes, but in fact this appears to be its main strength. The reason is that if one participates in a sport that is complex, subtle and requires understanding, then it is far more rewarding.

ABOVE Some headgear is essential when driving an open Triumph but it is down to personal taste rather than rules when one is competing on an historic rally that is not a special stage event.

This is as true for the individual as it is for the team, for the private owner as much as for the factory équipe, and for the spectator as for the participant. And because rallying takes place to a very large extent on public roads and eschews formal settings, everyone can feel involved in it because they have access to the cars and competitors that is simply unrivalled. To go spectating on a rally is an adventure almost comparable with the fun of doing the event, though with fewer personal thrills.

The object of this book is to reveal what rallies are all about, to trace their history and to look at some of the people, the cars and the events that constitute the sport and make it the adventure that it undoubtedly is.

JOHN DAVENPORT
March 1991

CHAPTER 1

THE STORY SO FAR

Once you realise that it is impossible to provide a simple, one-line definition of a motor rally, the task of explaining the attraction of rallying becomes much easier.

Like any other branch of motor sport, rallying is part of the love affair between man and the motor car. As with some of man's other relationships, the thin line between love and hate is crossed, and there are times, as in the current decade, when the motor car, or rather the internal combustion engine that propels it, is far from popular. But the ability to move freely over the land mass of our planet and to experience speeds far in excess of those at which our own muscles can propel us has proved to have an appeal that just cannot be denied.

To try and define exactly what sets rallying apart from motor racing is not easy. It can be stated that the unique feature of rallying is that it involves the use of roads, but then so do several motor races, not least of which is the annual 24 Hours of Le Mans. And there are rallies, principally those which are now called Rallye-Raids, which must pass over deserts and other places where there is no road in the normal sense. And yet it is that use of ordinary roads, or what passes for them in the particular part of the world where the event is taking place, that does characterise motor rallies.

It is also possible to say that, in rallies, there are two or more crew members in the vehicle, but even then there are exceptions such as the Ronde Cevenole in France, now no longer held, where only a driver was needed. There is certainly no mileage in claiming that the practice of setting cars off on a common route with a fixed time interval between them is unique to rallying, since many early events that can only be described as races, and subsequently many classic races such as the Targa Florio, operated on a system by which cars were started at regular intervals on the same route.

However, if one combines all these elements then some kind of picture starts to emerge.

For an event to be a rally at least part of it needs to take place on the ordinary road in normal traffic conditions where the competing cars have to obey all the laws relating to the use of normal vehicles. Thus the cars have to be equipped with all that one would expect to find on a road car, such as lights, mudguards, windscreens, and bumpers. And, almost without exception, the competing car has to follow a specified route and pass through controls where the time of passage will be recorded. Since it may have to keep going for periods well beyond the endurance of a single driver, two people are considered as being the minimum crew.

To go further, this crew and the car are undertaking an adventure, or, at the very least, an exploit, where a very great variety of things may befall them which would be unlikely to happen to a driver participating in a race. It may require them to pass through a border control between two countries without vary-

PREVIOUS PAGE Even now that it has hundreds of miles of forestry tracks on which to run its special stages, the Lombard RAC Rally still runs some tarmac stages on the first day to provide safe viewing for a larger number of spectators.

RIGHT On an African rally – this is the 1974 Moroccan Rally at the start of the Rich special stage – the conditions can vary between the arid and the positively damp.

ing too far from their schedule. Or they may have to rebuild their car's broken suspension with wire taken from a roadside fence. Or dig their way out of a snowdrift. Or take a detour to avoid conflict with a herd of elephants occupying the correct road.

Of course, not all of these are likely to happen on the same event, but the rally competitor leaving the start must be prepared for anything to happen within the range of possibilities that the particular event has to offer. His ability to improvise in both driving skills and other areas will govern his performance in the rally. This is the challenge that separates the motor rally from its companions in the motor sporting stable.

When the motor car first started to be used for competitions, such distinctions were impossible to draw. The first event that sought to provide a formula by which drivers and their machines could be compared was the Paris–Rouen Reliability Trial of 1894, which is worth examining in some detail since it provided most of the key elements in what came to be known as motor rallying.

The Paris–Rouen was the brainchild of Pierre Giffard, the editor and owner of a Parisian newspaper called *Le Petit Journal*. Prior to his announcement, on 19 December 1893, of the proposal to organise the event, various people had been trying to gain publicity for their vehicles by undertaking solo runs between various French cities, although none of these was in any sense competitive. There had also been an event organised by a magazine called *Vélocipède* in 1887, held locally in Paris, which had unfortunately only received a single entry. This was not to be the fate of the Paris–Rouen which, once its

ABOVE Crowds were attracted to the earliest events, like the Paris–Rouen of 1894, by the very novelty of the vehicles rather than the possibility of watching them at speed. The same is still true today with some of the more exotic forms of rally car.

details were announced, received 102 entries.

It was quite clear from the regulations published by M. Giffard that this was not a race. Indeed, the winner was to be the car which, in the opinion of the judges, all of whom were staff members of *Le Petit Journal*, most closely adhered to their ideal of *'d'être sans danger, aisément maniable pour les voyagers, et de ne pas coûter trop cher sur la route'* (being safe, comfortable and cheap to run). There was no element of beauty in this judgement since it was clearly stated that the finish of the car was immaterial. The idea was to allow the Trial to assess the practicality of the cars entered in it.

In order to be accepted, each car and driver had to subject themselves to a qualifying run in which they had to cover 50 kilometres in three hours, implying an average speed of some 10.42mph. This was thought to be too high by many of the prospective entrants and was therefore reduced to 50 kilometres in four hours, equivalent to 7.81mph. The need for this qualifying test is made clear when one reads through the list of applications and considers some of the fanciful methods of propulsion listed therein. The aptly named Victor Popp of Paris had a four-seater driven by compressed air while several others revealed that their transport was to be driven by a system of pendulums. Two Parisians, seemingly anticipating the arrival of the modern rocket, gave their motive force as *liquides combinés*. And then there

TOUR DE FRANCE 1923

Les plus hautes récompenses sont attribuées à

LA QUADRILETTE

Peugeot

la seule grande triomphatrice
de la formidable randonnée (4.000 kilomètres)

qui enlève toutes les Coupes réservées aux Cyclecars :

COUPE CHALLENGE DU TOUR DE FRANCE — COUPE INTERNATIONALE DE TOURISME
COUPE CHALLENGE DES CYCLECARS — COUPE DE LA REVUE MOTOCYCLISTE

4 quadrilettes engagées **4** classées **premières** ex-æquo

La seule équipe de cyclecars
(CYLINDRÉE 750 cm.)
**rentrée au complet
et sans pénalisation**

Ce résultat démontre une fois de plus les qualités
d'endurance et de régularité de la *Quadrilette Peugeot*,
le véhicule à deux places le plus économique du monde

Consommation : Moins de 5 litres aux 100 kilomètres
Impôt : 100 francs par an

EN VENTE ICI

ABOVE Down the years, the principal reason for taking part in motor sport has been the chance to exploit success in advertising. Note Peugeot's keenness to emphasise their low fuel consumption.

were the hydraulics, the gravity engines and the amazing Baricycle that was moved by the weight of its passengers.

It was less than amazing, therefore, that by the beginning of June not all these 102 vehicles were ready to undertake the 126km/80-mile route to Rouen. By a democratic vote, it was decided to postpone the event from 7 June until 22 July to allow for more preparation and testing. A grand exposition of the vehicles was organised for 18 July in the suburb of Neuilly, quite close to the start venue. Only 26 were initially on display and, when the qualifying trials started on 19 July, only 17 came up to scratch. Of these, only 13 qualified. For these qualifying runs five routes were chosen so as to satisfy the public demand to see the cars. In fact the exposition had proved so popular that it had virtually constituted a public disturbance as people strove to see the cars and the cars attempted to gain entry to their own exposition. A second series of runs was organised for Friday 20 July when six cars started and all finished successfully. A further session was held on Saturday when two more qualified bringing the number of

accepted starters up to 21.

Thus it was that on Sunday 22 July, at 8.01am promptly, the first competitor started from Neuilly towards Rouen over a route that went via Nanterre, Saint Germain, Mantes, Vernon and Pont de l'Arche. On board each car, apart from its appointed driver and passenger, was an observer who was either an engineer or one of the judges appointed by M. Giffard. They were flagged off at 30-second intervals which meant that the entire ceremony took just over 10 minutes. The vehicles kept more or less in convoy until mechanical or other troubles began to beset some of them. There were compulsory stops, the longest and most important being for lunch at Mantes, when the observers took the opportunity to swap vehicles and exchange views on the cars in which they had been travelling.

A careful note was made of the arrival times at Mantes and Rouen, but such was the nature of the compulsory stops and the haphazard re-starts that the actual times taken can only be regarded as the most gross approximations. It would appear that the steam tractor of the Comte de Dion was actually the fastest vehicle over the distance, hotly pursued by various Peugeots, but the jury, meeting on the Monday morning, decided that the first prize should go equally to the Peugeots and the Panhard-Levassors. Their deliberations were mainly on the technical innovation and reliability of the respective cars though the performances realised were, of course, taken into consideration.

This was a classic event and foreshadowed all the rallies and races that were to come later. It had nearly all the elements by which a rally would be recognised as such today. The cars travelled a common route on which they set off at fixed intervals and timing, albeit of a rudimentary nature, was seen to be important. The driver was accompanied and there was a spirit of adventure in taking part and achievement in having completed the course within a reasonable time. The use of an observer in each vehicle was not to be a long-term feature of rallying, though it was employed frequently in events prior to the First World War. It has more recently been used on Economy Runs where it is necessary to check that the driver is not saving fuel by freewheeling.

The popularity of the event with both spectators and competitors surprised nearly everybody and it became inevitable that there would be more of its kind. One very interested spectator at the start of the Paris–Rouen had been James Gordon-Bennett, the man who owned the *New York Herald* and who was subsequently to sponsor the famous Gordon-Bennett races that did so much to promote worldwide interest in motor racing in the early years of the twentieth century. Indeed his interest in what was happening in France led to the *Chicago Times-Herald* sponsoring a contest between cars in November 1895. This comprised a road race which was undertaken in the most unfavourably snowy condi-

Deuxième année. — N° 31. Huit pages : CINQ centimes Dimanche 30 Juillet 1899.

LE PETIT MÉRIDIONAL

Supplément Illustré du Dimanche

ABONNEMENTS

SIX MOIS | UN AN
France, Algérie, Tunisie. 2 fr. · 3 fr. 50
Étranger (Union postale). 2 fr. 50 6 fr. ·

Direction, Rédaction, Administration : Rue Henri-Guinier, MONTPELLIER

ANNONCES

POUR LA PUBLICITÉ S'ADRESSER
A Montpellier : Rue Henri-Guinier.
A Paris : 135, rue Montmartre.

Le départ des automobiles pour la Course du tour de France

ABOVE Rallying and racing were indistinguishable in the early days. This is the start of the 1899 Tour de France which, in its time, has seen both.

tions, a laboratory test which purported to measure engine output and mechanical efficiency and a test of the maximum pulling force that each car could exert.

In Europe, the Paris–Rouen spawned every kind of inter-city event that could be imagined, with distances and speeds constantly rising. The timing became more and more important as it was realised that here was a criterion that gave a result without recourse to committees, judges or juries. This resulted in competitors designing their cars for speed only and resorting to a full-scale reconnaissance of the route to improve their performance. Since this 'reconnaissance' was usually undertaken in a vehicle similar to the competition vehicle, if not the competition vehicle itself, in order to discover how it stood up to the roads, the nuisance caused by these events was increased by a very large factor. This nuisance could be due to anything from clouds of dust to the slaughter of domestic animals unused to any form of transport that was not pulled by a horse at a suitably sedate speed.

In six short years from the Paris–Rouen the average speed of the winning cars went up from 11mph to 44mph, with the top speeds increasing proportionally. In an attempt to offset some of these problems, timing systems had become sufficiently sophisticated that they could be used to neutralise sections across major towns or cities and confine the really quick motoring to the countryside and villages. An early way of doing this was to have the arrival time of the car at the outskirts of the town written on a card which was then transported to the out-control on the other side of the town by a cyclist. The cyclist was not supposed to be passed by the competing car on its way to the out-control, but frequently he was, the competitor using the delay until the out-of-breath cyclist arrived with the time card to work on his car.

Eventually, a system of timing boxes was adopted. These were fitted to each competing car and were a kind of sealed postbox into which each control officer dropped his card recording the car's number and time of arrival at the control. These cards thus arrived at the finish with the competing car and results, queries and even protests could be settled quickly. It

did not, however, remove the problem of cars being worked on in controls or of competitors speeding through towns to make time for such work. It was these elements of timing and of restriction on the work allowed on the cars that finally created the break between what we know now as motor racing and motor rallying.

Up until 1902, the great road events progressed unchecked. Their zenith was probably the Paris–Vienna of that year which was a superb event won by the remarkable Marcel Renault in a tiny 16 horsepower car made in the factory he owned with his brothers. The Renault was only 18th at the end of the first section, Paris to Belfort, but as the event progressed through Switzerland and onto the rough alpine roads of Austria, his little car made up so much time on the more powerful but ponderous Panhards, Mercedes and Mors, that he won by a comfortable margin. It would have been greater if he had not arrived in the stadium at Vienna and made a wrong approach to the finish line. He was then forced to go out of the stadium and approach once more, this time coming to a halt facing the right way. This whole manoeuvre cost him some 15 minutes! Perhaps even more remarkable was the story of his brother Louis, also competing in a Renault, whose car was struck by the Mercedes of Baron de Caters while waiting to check in at the Salzburg control. The damage was limited to several broken spokes in one of his car's front wheels. This would normally have spelt retirement as spare tyres were carried but not spare wheels. However, his extremely resourceful mechanic found a supply of wood and used a knife to create new spokes which were strong enough to enable the car to cross Austria and finish the event.

Successful though the Paris–Vienna was, two things were in the offing which would bring about the downfall of such inter-city events. The first was that the competitors did not like the time controls and there was often a great deal of dispute about them. When the Belgian Automobile Club announced that it was to run a long-distance race without a single time control, it received a great deal of interest. In July 1902, barely a month after Paris–

Vienna, it ran its first Circuit des Ardennes over a course of some 53 miles, starting and finishing at Bastogne, which each competitor would attempt six times. Any stopping for work on the car would lengthen the competitor's lap time and thus act as a penalty in its own right. Timing was simplicity itself since only one timekeeper was needed who could sit by the start-finish line and record the passage of all the cars. It worked remarkably well apart from the problems entailed in having to pass slower cars in the dust and having to contend with the odd spectator driving round the circuit to get a good view of the competitors. The winner was Charles Jarrott, a professional, English driver, who on this occasion was working for Panhard. His 70 horsepower, 13.67 litre car averaged 54mph for a total time of 5hr 53min which represents a considerable advance in performance from that obtained in Paris–Rouen just eight years earlier.

The more serious blow came when in 1903 there were several fatal accidents involving cars in competition. The first occurred during the Nice Speed week when Count Zborowski was killed at the wheel of his Mercedes while participating in the La Turbie hill climb. This was no unskilled amateur making a silly mistake as he was the man who had nearly beaten Marcel Renault in the Paris–Vienna. His death shook the motor sport world. It also gave the French authorities food for thought as they had in front of them at the same time the requests for permission to use public roads for the forthcoming Paris–Madrid, the big race of the year. They did not, however, dare to stand in the way of an event that had received the sanction and blessing of King Alfonso of Spain. He had already signed the order permitting racing between the French–Spanish border at Irun and the capital, Madrid.

The event started from Versailles on Sunday 24 May at 3.45am. There were 275 entries and thousands of spectators gathered along the route which

RIGHT Early competition cars, such as this Panhard et Levassor, were bereft of creature comforts. The event was the 1904 Circuit des Ardennes in Belgium.

LEFT Some idea of the task facing the competitors in the 1902 Paris–Vienna can be obtained from this map showing the four stages of the event. Very few of these roads would have been tarmacked and the event would have been much more like a modern Safari rally without the deep mud and exotic animals.

LE CIRCUIT DES ARDENNES EN 1904. — M. TESTE, 2e SUR VOITURE PANHARD & LEVASSOR, MUNIE DE *Pneumatiques Michelin*

lay through Chartres, Tours, Poitiers, Angoulême and Bordeaux. As the dawn turned into full day, speeds rose and on one of the sections of road before Chartres, cars were being timed at over 90mph. Between Poitiers and Angoulême, Marcel Renault was lying third behind Charles Jarrott, this time driving a De Dietrich, and his brother Louis Renault who was leading the event. Then he came up to pass a slower car, ran two wheels into the ditch, spun twice and inverted the car on top of himself. He died almost immediately. On the approach to Bordeaux, Barrow went off the road trying to miss a dog. His De Dietrich hit a tree and his companion, Pierre Rodez, was killed instantly. In another incident, Stead, also in a De Dietrich, left the road while dicing with another car, was trapped under his car and suffered broken ribs with internal injuries. Lesley Porter had his Wolseley go out of control on the approach to a level crossing and in the subsequent accident, his riding mechanic, Nixon, was thrown from the car and killed, while the car itself burst into flames.

Most serious of all, however, was the accident that befell Tournad driving a Brouhot. He drove into a crowd of spectators while attempting to avoid a child that had run out into the road and succeeded in killing a spectator and his own passenger as well as the unfortunate child that had provoked the incident.

There were many other accidents with far less serious consequences, so that at the control in Bordeaux, there was a consensus between the organisers, the authorities and the competitors that the race should be stopped. Almost simultaneously, the government in Paris issued an edict forbidding all further racing on French soil. The Paris–Madrid would not be visiting Spain. Indeed, so great was public feeling in Bordeaux that the owners were not allowed to drive their cars away from the town. They had to be towed behind horses to the railway station and every car then went back to Paris by train.

The success of the closed racing circuit in the Ardennes and the terrible events of the Paris–Madrid had a profound effect on the evolution of motor sport. France had always been the home and the inspiration of competitive events and now her roads were banned for such use. In fact, the blanket ban did not last very long and events – we should now properly call them races – were allowed, but only on relatively short circuits and in relatively uninhabited parts of the country. The Circuit des Ardennes went from strength to strength, the Gordon-Bennett Trophy races saw competitions organised on a national basis, the Florio Cup started in Italy on a circuit based in Brescia, the American Vanderbilt Cup saw serious motor racing on a circuit at Long Island and even the English managed to get in on the scene by holding their Gordon-Bennett eliminating trials

LEFT On a thoroughly modern rally, there is no requirement for the car to be timed with the co-driver out of the car. On the Coupe des Alpes of 1968, Jean-Claude Andruet's diminutive lady co-driver 'Biche' is about to print the time on their card and then leap into the Alpine Renault A110.

RIGHT An artist's impression of the fatal accident to Lorraine Barrow's De Dietrich on the Paris–Madrid of 1903.

ABOVE In the early events, such as Paris–Vienna and the truncated Paris–Madrid pictured here, the lightweight Renaults proved that muscle is not everything. Sixty years later, Erik Carlsson and the Saab were still proving the same point.

on the Isle of Man. And before three years had passed, the French were running the first Grand Prix on a circuit at La Sarthe just outside Le Mans.

Such events had several important features that represented a great advance over the shortcomings of Paris–Madrid. Firstly, the roads could be closed to other traffic. Thus any other vehicles that one might encounter during the race were also competing and were all going in the same direction. Secondly, the public – and their animals – could be kept off the roads comprising the circuit. Indeed, spectators could be accommodated in places of safety from where they could watch the racing in comfort. They could also see the cars more often than they would have been able to with an inter-city event. Finally, the surface of the roads could be improved and, with the advent of tarmacadam and other sealing methods, the problems of dust and flying stones could be practically eradicated.

So where was rallying in the post-1903 era?

One has to admit that its evolutionary trail becomes exceptionally weak at this point – the fossil record does not show very much at all. In Britain, the legal requirement to have your car preceded by a man walking on foot and carrying a red flag to warn the populace of your approach had been repealed in 1896. To celebrate this astonishing piece of forward thinking by the British Parliament, a smart entrepreneur by the name of Harry Lawson organised an event called the Emancipation Run from London to Brighton. He basically conceived it as a way of promoting various products in which he had a financial interest. It may have been successful in that respect but it was otherwise deemed to have been a flop. However, it must have had something going for it, since it was subsequently adopted by the Royal Automobile Club and survives in a very healthy form to this day.

The Automobile Club of Great Britain and Ireland was created in 1897 and received its royal patronage in 1907 from Edward VII. It was responsible for organising an event called the 1000 Miles Trial in 1900. Such events could not make use of raw speed as the British laws did not allow for the kind of legal dispensations that had permitted public roads to be used for the inter-city events. They had to content themselves with demanding set average speeds from the competitors and these were varied to suit the terrain. It is important to remember that, outside the main towns and cities, few roads were tarmacked and road maintenance was not as highly developed as it is today. The 1000 Miles Trial set some average

ABOVE The end of the beginning . . . Louis Renault arrives at Bordeaux leading the 1903 Paris–Madrid to learn that his brother is dead and that the event will go no further.
LEFT Competitors on the 1907 London to Brighton Run take refreshment at Crawley while their motors cool down.

RIGHT Early success in trials with a Panhard persuaded CS Rolls to start manufacturing cars of his own. He is seen here at the start of a promotional non-stop drive from Monte Carlo to London in 1906.

speeds close to the 12mph permitted maximum speed for motor vehicles, which prompts thoughts of the Liége–Sofia–Liége 50 years later that used to run average speeds of 98kph on the Yugoslav *autoput* where the maximum speed allowed was . . . 100kph. The 1000 Miles Trial also had timed sections over mountain roads in the Peak and Lake Districts as well as a proper speed test on private roads in the Welbeck Estate. This too foreshadows the special stages on private land that make up so much of the modern RAC Rally.

The idea of trials soon caught on. They were distinguished from the inter-city races by having time controls whose function was to prevent people going too fast rather than just seeing who was going quickest between them. In Germany, the well-known painter Hubert von Herkomer lent his name and influence to a series of trials starting in 1904. They were the Herkomer Trophy events and the first was a great success as a social event even if few of the competitors could understand the complicated time schedules to which they were required to adhere. The 1906 event saw the advent of professionalism and many more entries coming from factories which had interpreted the rules governing modifications to the cars quite freely. When, at the end of six days with tests in the Alps, the whole thing was decided on a speed trial held in a park in Munich, interest died despite the fact that the winner would have his portrait painted by none other than Herr Herkomer. But one competitor in the 1906 event was Prince Heinrich of Prussia, brother to the Kaiser, Wilhelm II, and he could see the benefit of such motor trials to the German state and its young automobile industry.

Thus in 1908 was held the first of three Prinz Heinrich *Fahrten*. Loosely based on the format of the Herkomer Trophies that had preceded them, they were an instant success and the first event received 144 entries. The fact that this popularity attracted the same professionalism that had sunk the Herkomer events without trace was only to be expected, and when neighbouring Austria swept the board with its Daimlers in 1910, the Germans decided that the event should be given a rest. But these German trials had clearly established that a competition could be run on the roads without racing and since, in the early part of this century, there were very few race tracks, it was clear that these examples would be followed elsewhere.

Austrian success in the Prinz Heinrich Fahrt led to the establishment of a major event in that country. It was in 1910 between 26 and 29 June that the Austrian Automobile Club organised its first *Internationale Alpenfahrt*. It had, close at hand, some of the most severe alpine passes and thus was able, in a route of some 520 miles, to throw enough difficulties at the competitors that it would take them three full days to tackle it at an allowance of 12 hours' driving a day. As with all these trials, there were plenty of rules and a system of handicapping the large engined cars. Penalties were handed out, for instance, for stopping on the mountain sections or for having to raise the engine cover and administer cooling balms to the overstressed engine. In fact, so steep and rutted were some of the passes that only one or two of the competitors were able to climb them unaided. The nub of the action in that respect was the infamous Katschberg Pass which was still featuring in Alpine

Trials right up to 1939.

The *Alpenfahrt* continued up until 1914, gaining a formidable international reputation and greater severity as it did so. After the First World War there was no more Austro-Hungarian Empire, the socio-political body from which this event had sprung, but so strong was the event's reputation that it was revived by a combination of Austrian, Swiss, German, Italian and French automobile clubs during the 1920s as the International Alpine Trial. This too grew from small beginnings into one of the most important motoring events of the period, although since each country took it in turns to organise the event consistency was not one of its strong points. Indeed, in 1935 it was cancelled by the French, whose turn it was to organise and host the rally, because, they said, the Germans couldn't pay their entry fees, or, as the Germans said, because the entry fees were enormously high. Be that as it may, the Alpine Trial survived such problems, including the Second World War, to be revived a second time by the *Automobile Club de Marseille-Provence* as the Coupe des Alpes. The final demise of the event after the 1971 rally was due to its own success in promoting the use of the motor car in the mountains – too many private motorists made it impossible to use the classic roads for rallying.

The *Alpenfahrt*'s English translation was 'the International Alpine Rally', though it is possible that this translation came along after the *Société des Bains de Mer de Monaco* gave their patronage to an event, first held in 1911, called the *Rallye Automobile*

ABOVE The Prinz Heinrich *Farhten* introduced the German and Austrian motor industries to a new way of promoting their products. When Ferdinand Porsche, shown here on the 1910 event, was too successful with Austro Daimlers, the onus passed to the Austrians to start organising competitive rallies.

RIGHT The last Austrian Alpine Rally to be held was in 1973. Among the competitors on that occasion were Harry Kallstrom and Claes Billstam in this Volkswagen 1302 S prepared by Porsche Austria.

Internationale Monaco but far better known today as the Monte Carlo Rally. The idea of 'rallying' was that of Antony Noghès, son of the President of the *Sport Vélocipédique et Automobile de Monaco*. He had been asked to come up with some ideas to promote the use of Monaco's facilities – hotels, casino, bathing etc. – in the off-season, namely January and February. He first thought of having a kind of Tour of Europe starting and finishing at Monaco, but then modified his idea to have a multiplicity of starting points and a single finish at Monaco. The idea was that he would award points according to the distance travelled. It wasn't a big step from there to having time controls to make sure that no one went too fast and, before long, the Monte Carlo Rally was in existence.

Like the Herkomer Trophy, it was initially designed for 'ordinary' motorists and their cars, bearing in mind that at that time such people were from the richest strata of society and that they were quite likely to employ a chauffeur to drive them to Monaco. The most important aspect of the rally was the Concours at the finish, and the winner on the inaugural event, Henri Rougier, scored maximum points on the speed test and for the comfort of his 25 horsepower Turcat-Mery. Other categories for scoring points were the turnout of the car, the number of people on board, and the distance driven.

The Monte Carlo Rally eventually became one of the toughest events around, but only after a gentle evolution from this hedonistic start. The main thing going for it was the weather that could be expected in January which was likely to make a hard test of even the easiest of routes. The early rule that connected points with distance driven persuaded people to choose starting points that were ever further away from Monaco. In 1911, Berlin to Monaco was the longest route, but it was not long before the choice of St Petersburg (modern Leningrad) had almost doubled that original 1700km. In its turn, this was followed by John O' Groats, Tunis, Athens, Sundsvall, Palermo and Uméa but, before people could start nominating cities in even more remote locations, it was decided to nominate a fixed number of starting points and try to have the same length of route from each to Monaco. This system started in the 1930s, and at the same time the special tests, whether they were regularity sections up in the mountains or driving tests on the promenade in Monaco, took a much bigger part in deciding the ultimate winner.

In order to try and even things out between the powerful and not-so-powerful cars, the Factor of Comparison was introduced. This was applied to the times achieved on the classification tests and comprised, in the early 1960s, for example, a rather nasty

LEFT The cars and the people may change but the backdrop of the Riviera is an ever-present feature of the Monte Carlo Rally.

RIGHT Even today, the Monte Carlo Rally maintains its traditional convergence of competitors on Monaco from a selection of starting places. The ski resort of Sestrières has become the main jumping-off point for Italian teams. Shown here is the Lancia 037 Rally of Markku Alen and Ilkka Kivimaki on the 1984 event.

formula. The car's cylinder capacity in litres was divided by eight times the capacity plus one. The square root of this was then taken and multiplied by a further factor depending on the tuning category into which the car had been entered. For standard saloon cars the factor was 1, for tuned saloon cars it was 1.03, and for GT cars it was 1.06. This comparison factor led to the odd result of 1961 where three Panhard PL 17s took the first three places overall. They were so unknown that most of the newspaper photographers did not have a picture of them. The factor was highly unpopular with competitors and, as the rally evolved away from the regularity and driving tests of the pre-war events and put its faith in pure special stages on the winter roads of the Alpes Maritimes, it became patently unnecessary. The severe conditions in which the rally of 1965 was held did away with any lingering sentiment for such mathematical adjustments and from then until today it has been run on a scratch basis.

So, by the time that Europe entered into the First World War, rallying had been given its name and there were at least two major international events that would represent it well into the latter half of the century.

In the wake of the turmoil caused by the war, it was only natural that the motor industry should take some time to return to normal. The European manufacturers felt under threat from the Americans, who had continued to build cars during the war years. New car registrations in the US topped 5.5 million in 1918 compared with just over 1.6 million in 1914, and now US manufacturers could benefit from the lifting of the tariffs that had protected Europe before 1914. It is little wonder that the European manufacturers concentrated on producing cars that they knew would sell. The proportion of sporting cars produced at this time was consequently very small. But then came the American recession with new car registrations in the US dropping back to 1.6 million in 1921. The paranoia of the European car makers gradually dissipated, though it was not helped by the American driver, Jimmy Murphy, who won the first post-war Grand Prix in 1921 at the wheel of an American Duesenberg. In any case, it was not until 1924 that the Monte Carlo was reinstated on the international calendar, and even then it could raise only 30 entries. The Alpine Trial was even later, its first appearance coming in 1928 with an event that started in Milan, finished in Munich and attracted 90 entries.

The rally which emerged soonest after the war was in fact the Polish Rally. This made its debut in 1921 with an event of 450km based on Kracow which was won by T Heyne in an American Dodge. The Polish Rally was held consistently through the 1930s until

the outbreak of the Second World War. Its route quickly grew to some 3000km and while it was well supported by the Germans and Austrians, it never quite achieved the wider appeal of the Alpine Trial.

There were many other events that started honourable careers during the 1920s of which the Marathon de la Route was one. The first event for cars under that title was organised by the Royal Motor Union of Liège in 1927 over a route that went from Liège to Biarritz and then back to Liège. As in Poland, the majority of European countries had a major rally of one kind or another which tended to model themselves either on the Monte Carlo Rally or on the Alpine Trial. Unlike the Marathon de la Route, they were not tough events in the sense that we would understand that phrase today. They were very much what would now be classified as touring assemblies where neither the route nor the time schedule presented any grave problems. The early RAC Rallies, based on the old 1000 Miles and Scottish Trials, were quite undemanding events provided that the weather did not turn nasty. In fact, the principal requirement on such rallies as far as the crew were concerned was to be able to keep awake for long periods.

With the honourable exceptions of the Alpine Trial and the Marathon de la Route, nearly all rallies of this period were decided on a limited number of tests, most of which were concentrated towards the end of the event. The 1930s saw the advent of the infamous 'wiggle-woggle' test on the *Quai Albert 1er* in Monaco

which, despite all the best efforts of the Monte Carlo organisers to have a winner decided on the road sections, only too frequently provided the result of the whole rally. In his personal recollections of competing in the 1937 Monte Carlo Rally, the Dutch driver, Maurice Gatsonides, explained how he and his co-driver had taken a week to reach the starting point at Uméa on Sweden's Arctic Circle with their Hillman Minx. That journey alone involved a 24-hour period with the Minx walled up in a Danish snowdrift. They then drove through equally bad conditions some 3000km to reach Monaco which took four days and four nights. The last 100km into Monaco were done as a regularity test where secret controls monitored their adherence to a set average speed and they, like many others, arrived at Monaco with no penalties. It was then down to the test which that year was more of an acceleration and braking test. They finished second in the up-to-1500cc class to Gigi Villoresi in a Fiat 1500 but would have been denied that if the Riley Sprite that was classified behind them had not been penalised two points for having a rear-view mirror that was fractionally too small.

Such rallies called for exceptional endurance of both car and driver but, with their final result decided on such a small part of the whole event, it is easy to see why the harder events drew the more daring drivers whose results meant more to the purchasers of sporting cars. The Alpine Trial of the 1930s was hard for the cars and required high standards of driving, but it did at least give the competitors almost every night in bed. A night section was introduced on the 1930 event and remained a regular feature, but more normal was a decent stop such as the one in 1932 at Stresa where the Mayor entertained the drivers in a paddle steamer on Lake Maggiore. The Alpine was run almost entirely on open roads and was able to do so because of two things: the minuscule traffic density on the mountain roads even in midsummer and the whole-hearted co-operation of the police. It was in 1929, one should remember, that Benito Mussolini made possible the first Mille Miglia in Italy by suppressing all speed limits for the duration of the race. This same *laisser faire* attitude prevailed well into the 1960s and enabled both the Coupe des Alpes and the Marathon de la Route to survive when other rallies, including the Monte Carlo, had already gone over to closed road special stages.

A typical Alpine Trial was decided by the reliability of the car while being asked to maintain quite respectable average speeds over unsurfaced and precipitous roads. The emphasis was on the unaided performance of the crew. The Hon. Mrs Victor Bruce, who competed on the 1928 event in an AC, would have been awarded a Coupe des Glaciers for an unpenalised run had her car not been struck while unattended by a non-competing vehicle. Because she needed help from other competitors to make her car mobile again, she could not be awarded the coveted trophy, but the organisers did give her a special gold plaque.

Even more evocative of that era was the story of ex-racing driver Felice Nazzaro who was entered in a factory Fiat on the 1929 Alpine Trial. Entering Merano at the end of the third day's run, he was misdirected by a policeman and chose to hit a wall rather than an oncoming lorry. The accident ripped out the front axle and the spring mountings so that both would have to be replaced before the car could continue in the rally. He limped into *parc fermé* that night and, had he been competing in a modern rally, would have slept happy knowing that a team of mechanics were going to fix the car for him in the morning. As it was, the no-assistance rule applied and Nazzaro, aided only by his mechanic, had to change the parts. It took them one hour and ten minutes after leaving the *parc fermé* to change the front axle and fit a new spring and damper. They then had to drive like the devil to make up the time lost working on the car. In the course of doing so, they set second fastest time behind their teammate, Salamano, up the test on the Passo di Stelvio. This story had an unhappy ending for they had a near miss with another lorry outside Bergamo which caused them to skid on the wet surface and they went off the road again. This time they broke a rear spring which they laboured to fix within the maximum time allowance, but were too late into the main control at Lugano and were thus eliminated.

On the Continent the move to special stages was much slower, as the population density in the Alps

LEFT Not so many spectators on the Col de Braus in 1953 as Ian Appleyard and his wife tackle the regularity section in their Jaguar. Appleyard went on to become one of only three drivers ever to win a Coupe d'Or on the Alpine Rally.

ABOVE The Harrisons from Yorkshire were redoubtable competitors with Fords during the 1950s and 1960s. Their winter tyres seem out of place on dry tarmac as they enter Monaco in 1959, but they would have proved their worth on the run down from Stockholm.

was not so great as that of the Pennines or the Trossachs, but by the beginning of the 1960s the strain was beginning to be felt in France, at least. For the 1961 edition of the Monte Carlo, the first special stages appeared and, although they were subject to the Factor of Comparison, that too had but a short time to live. The Coupe des Alpes maintained its open-road nature right to the end with the majority of the route comprising difficult but achievable *selectifs* with only 13 *épreuves*, mainly hill climbs, on properly closed roads.

The Marathon de la Route was even less amenable to change, but then it was different in every way and adored by the competitors. To start with, it retained its format of a trans-Alpine event going down through Germany and Austria, then through the Dolomites to Rome and returning to Belgium via the French Alps. By this time, Switzerland had developed an antipathy to all forms of motor sport on its roads, excepting only the most pedestrian of transfers across its territory. Its own major international rally, the Geneva, started and finished in that Swiss city but, apart from a couple of hill climbs on the west side of Lake Geneva, it was held entirely in France. Thus the Marathon de la Route had to skirt the 'milk chocolate' mountains on both outward and return journeys. The roads to Rome became less friendly in the wake of the Mille Miglia disaster in 1955, while the French Alps were frankly being overused by their own national rallies plus the Monte Carlo, the Geneva, the Tulip and any other rally that passed that way. Thus for 1961, when the RAC and the Monte were adopting special stages for the first time, the Marathon de la Route discovered the empty roads of Yugoslavia and Bulgaria and changed the event to the Liège–Sofia–Liège.

This version comprised four days and nights of non-stop motoring with a rest halt of one hour in the Bulgarian capital at half-distance. And the motoring was such as to give rise to quite considerable penalties. The way the organisers did it was to set times for the sections that were totally legal and probably quite easy to achieve. Then on another piece of paper were the times at which the controls opened and closed to individual competitors. It was ruefully observed by one entrant on the 1963 Marathon that, if he stuck to the times set for each section and ignored opening and closing times, then he would arrive back in Liège some 24 hours after the prize-giving! The fact that such a device was able to be used owes much to the complicity of competitors and the ignorance of authorities in the countries through which the rally passed.

Systems gradually evolved for organising time controls and special tests whilst the idea finally dawned that perhaps normal traffic should be prevented from proceeding down timed test routes up which rally cars were coming. As the cars and the roads both improved, these tests began to assume an even greater significance in the format of the rallies. Certainly they enabled the organiser of any rally to have a clearly defined winner. It was a fault clearly evident in the early Marathons de la Route that, even as late as 1939, it was sometimes impossible to differentiate between two or more cars which tied on road penalties.

After the Second World War, motor sport got back to normal fairly quickly. The technology of motor vehicles had not been as drastically improved by the necessities of war as had that of aeroplanes and ships. In the first global conflict, the replacement of the horse had been the most urgent step, especially when the majority of the fighting had been land-based. The advent of electronics and the truly world-wide nature of the second war had seen the biggest

LEFT Before studded tyres and snowploughs had taken charge in the Alps, Peter Harper heads south in his Sunbeam Talbot during the 1955 Monte Carlo Rally.

RIGHT The post-war Monte Carlo Rallies were extremely popular and received entries of well over 300 or so cars. A British Austin A40 is about to be overtaken by a Finnish Skoda on the 1962 rally.

BELOW No shortage of snow or ice when rallying moves into the Arctic Circle. This is Leo Kinnunen in his Porsche 911 on the 1972 Finnish Arctic Rally.

advances made in machines that could cover the oceans or deliver weapons at long range. That is not to say that such devices as the tank got overlooked, but developments in that area did very little for the sporting motorist. Motor cars were eventually to benefit from the general improvements in technology, but in the immediate post-war years, it was sufficient to roll the old cars out of the garage and pick up where the sport had left off in 1939.

As proof of the competitiveness of the pre-war cars, in 1949 the Monte Carlo was revived and Jacques Trevoux won in the same type of Hotchkiss he had triumphed with in the 1939 event. The Coupe des Alpes, this time adopted 100 per cent by the French, had returned in 1947 with a route that stuck largely to France with just a brief excursion into Italy. The Marathon de la Route started up again one year after the Monte Carlo. But the real development in the early 1950s was that literally dozens of major and minor rallies appeared all over Europe, most of which were getting sizeable entries. The Swedish, the Acropolis, the 1000 Lakes, the Polish, the Tour de France, the Tour de Corse, the Sestriere and the RAC Rally were all part of a massive increase of interest in rallying. Perhaps the freedom granted by the motor car was a powerful symbol of a free Europe and the re-opening of frontiers. Whatever the reason, rallies were the thing to do in a liberated Europe.

In 1949 the Monte Carlo had 203 starters, which grew to 282 the following year, to 337 in 1951 and 404 in 1953. The RAC Rally was able to attract 242 starters in 1952 and it rarely had less than 200 for the rest of that decade. These were not all rich amateurs or

ABOVE Gravel roads are in plentiful supply in modern Scandinavia, and their existence helped the Finns and Swedes to become a dominant force in rally driving. This Audi Quattro is driven by Michele Mouton, sampling the Finnish 1000 Lakes Rally on her way to second place in the World Drivers' Championship in 1982.

TOP LEFT In 1975, the Monte Carlo Rally tried an experiment with some special stages in Italy. They found snow, but the Italian spectators preferred to travel and watch the event in France.

LEFT The Acropolis Rally has the reputation of being one of the toughest in Europe. Hard landings are frequent, as Henri Toivonen is about to discover on the 1984 event.

works entries, but were largely people who looked for adventure and excitement after the fear and deprivation of the war years. It was their enthusiasm on which the rallying explosion of the 1950s was based.

To start with, the rallies were like the cars in that they were not very different from the pre-war events. The important catalyst for change was supplied by events in Scandinavia where the practice of closing whole sections of road for use in a speed test or as a special stage was common from the outset. The reasons for this were not hard to find. The police in Scandinavian countries were far less tolerant of the motor car than those in, say, Italy or France. When the pre-war Monte Carlo Rallies used to pass through Denmark, the cars were marshalled into groups of eight, each with a police car at its head, and then convoyed through some 450 miles of snow-covered roads to ensure that the 40mph speed limit was not broken. Even today, the principal function of policemen on Scandinavian rallies seems to be to exercise the latest in radar speed detection equipment.

In addition, Scandinavia has few mountains so that most of the roads lack hairpin bends and steep gradients. This makes for an unchallenging event if you are only allowed to set average speeds of 30mph or so. The Finns and the Swedes managed to persuade the authorities to allow much higher average speeds to be set over roads that were totally closed to other traffic. It wasn't a unique idea, as the Welbeck Estate test had shown on the 1000 Miles Trial and the parallel sport of hill climbing had always been able to close Continental roads. But the concept of special stages timed to the second with a set time under which the

competitor was not penalised emerged, without doubt, from the woods of Scandinavia.

When the Scandinavian drivers, raised on special stages conducted on either gravel or snow-covered roads and linked by very easy road sections, came out of their own countries to compete in other European events in the late 1950s, they brought their ideas with them. In many countries they were eagerly received, as the organisers of events that had sprung to fame on the post-war boom were now discovering that the increase in car ownership meant considerable competition for the occupancy of the roads, even the remote ones so beloved of their rallies.

In Britain, the organiser of the RAC Rally was Jack Kemsley, who had been brought in to toughen up the event in 1959. That particular event, though well received by the competitors, had suffered badly from the weather and from the difficulties of running competitive sections on public roads, even when they took place at night. Kemsley, determined to find a solution, adopted the concept of special stages. Since public roads could not be closed in Britain, he had the inspiration to tackle the Forestry Commission and asked to use their tracks as special stages. That became a reality in 1961 and the rally has benefited, as has all rallying in Britain, from the use of those roads ever since.

Sadly, the Liège–Sofia–Liège lasted only four years before the conflict of road usage between the influx

of tourists to Yugoslavia on the one hand and the rally competitors on the other led to the authorities declining permission for the rally to continue. The Royal Motor Union of Liège was not prepared to seek a compromise and, having run out of new territory within 48 hours' drive of their city, they took their Marathon to the Nurburgring in Germany and ran five events there under the sub-title 'The 84 hours of Nurburg' before their enthusiasm faded altogether.

In almost every country in Europe, the special stage rally was able to survive and indeed thrive. Those that could, still kept some difficult open road motoring in their events and the rallies held in the Eastern European countries became quite famous for that feature. The Polish Rally of 1967 was sufficiently severe in both its choice of roads and its foggy weather that just three cars survived from 67 starters. Its sister events in Czechoslovakia (Rallye Vltava), Hungary (Three Cities Rally – Munich/Vienna/Budapest), Bulgaria (Rallye Zlatni Piassatzi) and Romania (Danube Rally) also ran hard open road sections combined with a selection of special stages. They were able to do so because they enjoyed a traffic density that was 30 years behind that of Western Europe.

The same could initially have been said of the Acropolis Rally in Greece and the TAP Rally in Portugal. They too made best use of their remote areas to run difficult sections without having to go to the trouble and expense of closing them to other traffic.

LEFT The De Dietrich of Lorraine Barrow pictured on a wet Route Nationale prior to the start of the 1903 Paris–Madrid.

RIGHT Early RAC rallies were short of competitive sections thanks to the impossibility of closing public roads for special stages, so they used traditional hill climb venues, such as Prescott.

BELOW Sometimes – such as here on the Hong Kong to Peking Rally of 1987 – the business of rallying can become a complete washout. Did someone mention a Chinese laundry?

BOTTOM RIGHT There are few pure snow rallies left in the World Rally Championship, and in 1990 global warming even caused the Swedish Rally to be cancelled through lack of snow. Sometimes the Monte Carlo makes up for it, such as here in 1984, with François Chatriot in his Renault R5 Turbo 2.
LEFT As the East African Safari evolved, the one element that did not change was the severity of the gravel roads. The Nissan 240 RS is being driven by five-times winner of the Safari Shekhar Mehta during the 1984 rally.
BOTTOM LEFT Argentina has a regular event in the World Championship and the exploits of drivers like Jorge Recalde, seen here in a Mercedes 450 SL, have helped to popularise the sport.

But, in time, they suffered from the very popularity of rallying, as spectator control became a problem for them in those very areas where they had felt safe. Closing the roads for use as special stages was the only way to avoid major problems. Portugal, of course, was the unwilling host to the worst rally accident of modern times when a Ford RS 200 crashed on a tarmac special stage outside Lisbon in 1986. The resultant withdrawal from that rally by all the factory drivers was a major factor in increasing the control of spectators at rallies. Though this particular incident did not happen on an open road, the general discussion of rally safety which it spawned means that there is now no rally left in Europe where the organisers demand high speeds away from special stages.

Until the 1950s, the amount of rallying that had taken place outside Europe was tiny. The Peking–Paris of 1906 was not really a rally in the sense that we would understand it, since there were but two controls – start and finish. There were plenty of speed events in North America like the Mount Washington hill climb, held on the dirt road up to the summit of that mountain in New Hampshire, but until they invented the TDS (time, distance, speed) rally in the same period that the rally explosion was taking place in Europe, there was nothing on which you could really hang the label 'rally'. The TDS rallies were run on the basis of total regularity where average speeds, often specified to two places of decimals, were varied from junction to junction so that the co-driver had to navigate and keep track of the car's progress to a very precise degree. Secret controls tested the crew's

accuracy from time to time and there was rarely any call to be in a hurry except to make up time after navigational errors.

The shores of Lake Michigan had played host to one of the earliest motor vehicle competitions in America back in 1887 when Frank Duryea, driving a car of his own make, won the Chicago Times-Herald event based loosely on the Paris–Rouen. In 1949, the Michigan peninsula saw the first running of the Press On Regardless Rally organised by the Detroit Region of the Sports Car Club of America (SCCA). On that first event, the main source of penalties came from dealing with heavy traffic near the cities, but it gradually evolved into one of the toughest rallies on the North American continent. Its use of gravel roads in late October made even TDS sections demanding for the driver, and the car was known to suffer on them as well. A race around the houses was introduced in 1954 as well as special tests on an airfield. It was in 1958 that the endurance aspect was introduced with a 1400-mile route. To diminish the problems with local traffic, scarce at the best of times, the rally became nocturnal with two 12-hour sections through consecutive nights.

Its claim to be America's oldest, richest, longest, meanest car rally was well founded and in 1970 the SCCA entered it on the international calendar. The following year, it was observed by FISA for inclusion in their new World Rally Championship and was one of the events in the inaugural WRC of 1973. For two years it held that status but the rally of 1974 attracted works teams from Renault, Fiat, Lancia, Porsche, Alpine Renault and British Leyland. The disruption to the quiet life of the Upper Michigan peninsula proved a little too much for a couple of the elected sheriffs. The problem lay in the fact that it was impossible to formally close roads, even when they were just logging trails, and thus the co-operation of the local police was needed to 'advise' non-competitors not to use the roads while the rally was on. The professionals from Europe, used to being able to service after a special stage and then rush madly to the next one, alienated the police and thus the days of America's contribution to the WRC were numbered. Fortunately, the Press On Regardless has survived as a major North American rally and prospers today as a counter in the US national championship.

In the 1950s, rallying came to the African continent. There had been informal events such as the 1936 Nairobi to Johannesburg race and various attempts on the record from Cape Town to Algiers, but nothing that could really be called a rally. To celebrate the accession of Queen Elizabeth II to the British throne in 1953, her loyal subjects in East Africa devised several kinds of event, one of the most significant being a motor rally called the Coronation Safari. Originally conceived as a tour round Lake Victoria in homage to the new Queen, this had to be abandoned when it was discovered that the various ferries involved were not up to the task of handling 50 or so cars. Eventually they settled on three starting points in Tanzania, Uganda and Kenya with a finish in Nairobi. Despite their sticking to fairly major roads, the conditions on these were bad enough to reduce the entry by half at the finish.

From this ambitious start, the Safari grew annually, becoming an international event in 1957 and changing its name to the East African Safari in 1960. By then, the roads used were much more difficult than in the early events and, if there was bad weather, often extremely difficult to pass. This led to Safaris like the notorious ones of 1963 and 1968 when only

LEFT DR Lloyd and GH Robins tackle a hill climb in Brighton during the 1939 RAC Rally in their Riley.

TOP RIGHT A combined RAC and RSAC Trial in 1908 saw this scene at a control in Kirkby Stephen as the competitors queued to depart.

seven cars finished despite there being a generous time allowance before late runners were excluded. Since 1974, the Safari has been run entirely in Kenya but still retains its open road nature, though the common regulations recently imposed on the events counting for the World Rally Championship have forced it to time some sections to the second rather than the whole minute, and to provide spectator stages. These have not yet diminished the challenge of the Safari nor indeed of its imitators like the Ivory Coast's Bandama Rally or the Egyptian Rally of the Pharaohs, but even in Africa there must be an eventual limit on open road rallying.

Similar events to the Safari were run in Australia at about the same time. These went under the name of Round Australia Trials and were sponsored at various times by Redex, Mobil and Ampol. Like the Safari, they were hard, endurance events run on open roads in territory where stray animals were a more frequent hazard than non-competing motorists. But today they are just not possible and the Australians have turned to the two acceptable faces of modern rallying. The Rally Australia is a new event held for the first time in 1988 and quickly promoted to World Championship status. It is a modern special stage event with properly closed roads, organised service areas and with everything done to facilitate the access of spectators to safe viewing points. The Australian Safari, of which more in a later chapter, is a modern

marathon taking four-wheel-drive vehicles and motorbikes onto tracks and deserts.

By the start of the last decade of this century, motor rallying has made its mark in just about every country in the world with the exception of Albania. At the last count, every year 70 countries run international rallies and more are joining in all the time. FISA now sets out clear rules for running international rallies in its annual Year Book of Automobile Sport, known as the Yellow Book. It even goes into the precise details of running time controls and how the route should be set out, and also defines what types of cars are eligible for rallying and what modifications may be carried out on them. This standardised approach has done a great deal to popularise rallying though it did meet with a lot of initial resistance. What it means is that a rally car from one country can be accepted in another with a minimum of fuss, while a competitor from abroad finds road books and control formalities much the same as in his own country, albeit in a different language.

With a Japanese car manufacturer employing a German company run by a Swede to enter its car for a Spanish driver to win the World Championship in 1990, it can be seen that rallying does more than just cross physical boundaries between countries. While the United Nations is only just finding its way towards international co-operation, rallying has long since achieved it.

CHAPTER 2
THE RALLY CARS

It would be nice to be able to say that people initially used standard cars for competing in rallies and their participation led to a steady technical progression that has culminated in today's high-powered, four-wheel drive, specialised rally cars. The truth is that technical progress has frequently been hindered by rally regulations governing the type of vehicle entered and what may be done to it. These regulations have swung, sometimes violently, between encouraging the off-the-peg rally car and the bespoke vehicle.

Such swings have been the result of a tension between the general desire by rally organisers to have standard production cars used on their events, and the opposing need of the competitors to be able to modify things if their cars were going to perform well. This interaction has been present throughout the history of rallying, and while on occasion it has produced spectacular developments, more often it has stifled them.

A very early example was the first Austrian *Alpenfahrt* where, in common with most of the competitors, Ferdinand Porsche discovered that his Austro-Daimlers were over-geared for the gradients that they were expected to climb. By 1912, this had been rectified by altering the gear ratios and the final drive. No less than four Austro-Daimlers reached the finish unpenalised, which was more than could be said for James Radley's 7.9 litre Rolls Royce. This lone Englishman could not climb even the first pass on the rally's menu, the Tauernpass, but he saw what had been done to the other cars and in the spring of 1913 returned for some tests of lower ratios. The result was that a Rolls Royce won an Alpine Cup that year and Radley himself won another in the 1914 event.

Realising that these modifications were not available to just any aspiring entrant, the *Alpenfahrt* organisers sought to preserve some measure of equality between the competitors and started to insist that these items were at least listed as being available in the manufacturer's catalogue. Similar expressions of good intent have been made down the years in an attempt to keep the results of rallies meaningful to the general public and to have a fair contest between the entrants. When homologation (*see Chapter 5*) was introduced to define what constituted a particular production car, and it was understood that it should be granted on evidence being received that a minimum number of identical cars had been made, it was also recognised that a limited number of parts could be recognised on a smaller production basis. For the old Group 2, based on 1000 production units and valid between 1966 and 1974, it was possible under the rules to have parts as fundamental to the performance of the car as the cylinder head recognised on the basis of 100 units, and even those did not have to be fitted to cars. The consequence was that some fairly mundane cars were soon competing in rallies equipped with twin-cam cylinder heads and large double-barrelled carburettors. To continue the analogy of the swing, once this got out of hand, new rules were introduced and the cars changed yet again.

The cars competing in the very earliest of events were subject to few rules. The technology of the internal combustion engine and the production of gears and shafts was not sufficiently advanced for there to be anything other than major reliability problems. But as we saw with the Austro-Daimler effort on the *Alpenfahrt*, manufacturers were ready to respond

LEFT The cockpit of Ian and Pat Appleyard's Jaguar, showing the very minimal changes demanded by post-war rallying. The twin Smiths clocks reflect the emphasis on timekeeping.
RIGHT The Volvo PV 544 made a fearsome reputation for itself in the hands of Gunnar Andersson, Tom Trana and Carl-Magnus Skogh, thanks to its strength and good handling. This is Skogh on the 1964 RAC Rally in Dovey Forest.
PREVIOUS PAGE The 1965 Lombard RAC Rally, with Tony Pond on his way to third-place in a four-wheel drive metro 6R4.

with any necessary improvements that were highlighted by the severe strains imposed by the rallies, and they brought out models incorporating those improvements, sold as 'Alpine' or 'Prince Henry' models.

In the inter-war years, the cars that were successful in rallying became ever more sporting. A look at the results of any of the major rallies of the time would indicate that, gradual though the process might be, the saloon car was being edged out by the sports car with its better handling and greater power-to-weight ratio. The success of Donald Healey's 4½ litre Invicta in both the Monte Carlo Rally and the Alpine Trial is a good example, while Morgans, Triumphs and Frazer-Nash-BMWs dominated the last RAC Rallies held before 1940. Generally speaking, the same situation pertained when rallying started up again in the 1950s, but a couple of things had changed.

Previously, there had been a class system whereby rally cars competed in classes defined by the cubic capacity of their engines and no notice was taken of whether they were sports or saloon cars. It is true that the RAC Rally did differentiate between 'open' and 'closed' cars, but seeing as in 1939 a Morgan 4/4 won the small open class while a Morgan 4/4 Coupé won the small closed car class, it did not seem to make a great deal of difference. In the post-war era, it was soon decided that sports cars, or Grand Touring cars as they were to be known, should have classes of their own whether they had hard or soft tops, or even none at all. With this segregation in place, it was not long before organisers of events such as the Monte Carlo Rally decided to handicap the more powerful GT cars by applying some form of correction to their test times. For rallies like the Coupe des Alpes, the GT cars had shorter times for the road sections and stiffer penalties for the tests.

The result was that saloon cars became more successful, a situation that largely remains today, though for a different reason. Now it is because to be active in rallying, the car manufacturer needs to have built 5000 identical cars of the specification that he wishes to use and this nearly always means that the rally car is based on a high production volume car, which is inevitably a saloon.

The other change that had occurred which was ultimately to favour the saloon car was that rallies had become more difficult, either in terms of weather conditions or in the length of time that the crew had to spend at the wheel. The modern saloon car was able to offer decent heating, good visibility and comfortable accommodation. There were still brave types competing in open cars during the 1950s but to see one on a major event in the 1960s was equivalent to finding a four-leaf clover. During the period when Hannu Mikkola was contracted to Peugeot in the

1970s, he was persuaded to drive a 402 in the Historic Monte Carlo which took place in April. To his horror, he discovered that it was an open version and that there was a night section in the Alps. He maintains that he has never been so cold, even when rallying above the Arctic Circle.

Sports cars were still successful during the 1960s but it is fair to say that this was mainly on rallies like the Marathon de la Route where they suffered no artificial handicap. Indeed the Marathon was amazingly liberal in its attitude to the vehicles that could be entered on it. It was said that provided the vehicle had four road wheels and two headlights, it would be passed by the scrutineers. Certainly, it was a tough enough event for them not to have to worry about a few extra modifications here and there. The Austin Healey 3000 won that event twice, in 1960 with Pat Moss and Ann Wisdom and again in 1964 with Rauno Aaltonen and Tony Ambrose, but elsewhere, while it drew the crowds, it did not always take home the spoils of victory. This could not be blamed on imposed handicaps intrinsic in the rally regulations, since the big Healey failed to win the RAC Rally, on which there was no such handicap, after 1959. Its record of fourth (1959), third (1960), second (1961), second (1962), fifth (1963), second (1964) and second yet again (1965) was a proud one, but as a classic sports car with leaf springs and limited suspension movement, it was doomed to be left behind by the new breed of saloons. These boasted coil springs, hydrolastic or hydropneumatic systems with considerably more vertical wheel movement than had ever been possible on earlier cars.

Sports cars were still able to play a rôle in rallying, as the results through the 1970s can show, but the Alpine Renault, the Porsche 911, the Lancia Stratos and its successor the Rallye 037, were all fixed-head coupés and benefited from modern suspension sys-

ABOVE Pauli Toivonen takes his Porsche 911T through a typical section on the 1968 Acropolis Rally. The 911 ultimately proved to be versatile as a rally car, equally at home on tarmac, gravel or snow.

BELOW Before four-wheel drive, the most successful cars were those with the engines over the driven wheels. Porsches proved particularly successful in winter rallies, with Leo Kinnunen winning the Arctic Rally in this 911.

RIGHT Saab were one of the leaders of rallying's front-wheel drive revolution in the 1960s. They continued to be successful on certain rallies – this is Per Eklund on the 1971 RAC Rally – thanks to the excellence of their competition department and their drivers.

ABOVE The British stuck to traditional sports cars well into the 1960s. This example is a Sunbeam Alpine, driven by the then Editor of *Autosport* Gregor Grant, on the 1963 Monte Carlo Rally. The version of this car fitted with the American Ford V8 engine, the Tiger, came out too late to keep the front-engined sports car alive in rallying, though the Datsun team had some success with their 240 Z.

LEFT Purposeful and purpose-built, the Lancia Stratos revolutionised rallying when it was introduced in 1973. It brought words like 'supercar' into the rallying vocabulary.

tems. Indeed, the Porsche 911 was at one time homologated as a saloon car, since its rear seats and headroom plus its large-scale production enabled it to qualify as such. Its stable-mate, the humble four-cylinder 912, even managed to gain recognition as a Group 1 saloon car on the basis that over 5000 of them had been produced. So it was that during the latter part of the 1960s, Porsche had one of their 900 series cars homologated in each of Groups 1, 2 and 3.

As well as seeing hard times for sports cars, the 1960s heralded the success of front-wheel drive cars in just about all kinds of rally except the endurance events. It was clearly a benefit to have the engine over the driven wheels and as the 1970s saw the front-wheel drive cars falling behind once again, it was still cars adhering to that particular design feature that

ABOVE Herald of yet another Lancia supercar was this turbocharged Lancia Beta Monte Carlo, driven by Markku Alen and Michele Alboreto on the 1980 Giro d'Italia. From what was learnt with this prototype came the supercharged 037 Rally model.

defeated them. The only difference between them and the rear-wheel drive cars that had previously dominated rallying was that they were cars with rear engines driving the rear wheels.

The 1980s saw the greatest struggle yet between the rally regulations and the car manufacturers. In the seventies, using the low production quantity needed for recognition of a special series GT car – 400 examples produced during one year – Lancia had created their Stratos which carried all before it, winning three World Championships on the trot. Other people soon realised that you did not have to be building a sports car to benefit from this loophole and soon Fiat had their 131 Abarth, Ford the Escort RS 1600, Opel the Ascona 400 and Talbot the Sunbeam Lotus. All of these vied with the Stratos for supremacy and rallying was very competitive again for a while.

Lancia had plans to replace the normally-aspirated V6 Stratos with a new sports car featuring a supercharged version of the engine that had worked so well in the Fiat 131 Abarth. This was the Rallye 037 which, though not the first forced induction car to appear in rallies, was thought by Lancia to represent a distinct advantage for them. It was the Audi factory that stole the march on them however, as they intro-

duced for the 1981 season their startling Audi Quattro, whose five-cylinder engine was turbocharged and which put its power to the road by means of four-wheel drive. When the rear-engined, rear-wheel driven Lancia 037 came on the scene over a year later, it was outclassed as a car and it is only to the very great credit of the team and its drivers that it was able to carry off the 1983 world title before succumbing to the superiority of the Quattro.

The advent of the Audi Quattro coincided with discussions at FISA involving all the manufacturers as to what technical rules were needed to replace the old system of Groups 1 to 7 which covered racing categories as well as those eligible for rallies. Few manufacturers imagined that they would be able to produce four-wheel drive cars on the scale of Audi and thus a powerful lobby grew up which resulted in their being two rallying Groups for the 1984 season which were to be called A and B. Group A was to be based, as ever, on high volume production of 5000 cars per annum, but Group B only required there to be 200 identical cars produced during the same period. This was the passport to four-wheel drive rally cars that the majority of manufacturers needed and, to be fair to FISA, a great number of them immediately started work on a limited production run of new cars to fit this formula.

Some got there earlier than others. Audi merely re-homologated its Quattro into the new category and by the end of 1984, it had been joined by the revolutionary Peugeot 205 T16, with its transverse turbocharged engine and gearbox, which promptly won three World Championship rallies. In 1985, the Peugeot added seven WRC rally wins to take the 'double' of World Championship titles for both manufacturer and driver, in this case Timo Salonen. By the end of that year, Citroen, Ford, Austin Rover and Lancia had joined Audi and Peugeot with state-of-the-art, four-wheel drive machines and this influx of high-powered, technically innovative and exciting machinery was making rallying more popular than ever with the general public. Regrettably, this popularity and the sheer speed of the super-cars led to several fatal accidents involving spectators and two involving the competitors themselves.

The reaction of FISA was to announce immediately a ban on Group B cars in rallies, which would start from the end of the 1986 season. Like most decisions taken at a time of high emotion, it was flawed, if only in detail, and led to seemingly endless recriminations from those manufacturers who had expended large sums of money on creating special cars. In fact, what the decision meant was that those manufacturers who were serious about being involved in rallying had to go back to the drawing board and design a car with Group B transmission and a turbocharged engine that they could produce in quantities of 5000

per annum. In short, FISA had raised the stakes needed to play at the rally game. At the time, it seemed like a very poor idea and the instant departure of the Group B cars from the international rally scene at the end of 1986 saw an alarming drop in spectator interest. Within two years, however, the number and variety of Group A cars had increased and their development had made them almost as competitive as the old Group B cars. Thus, by the end of the decade, the sport was as lively as ever and showing signs of becoming yet more popular with spectators worldwide.

It seems a very far cry from the modern four-wheel drive cars to look back at the ponderous vehicles that took part in the early rallies. But they were very much limited by existing technology. The principle of coil springs was known but who was to prepare the steel and wind them? The fact is that the vast majority of cars used leaf springs right up until the 1950s when coil springs became easier both to manufacture and to incorporate in car suspensions. The leaf spring was active in rallying much longer than one might suspect, since the Lancia Fulvia Coupé was supported on three of them. The front suspension comprised a transverse leaf spring acting directly on double unequal length wishbones, while at the rear,

BELOW The Ford Escort was conventional in every way, but it kept Ford on the winners' lists right through the 1970s. This is Hannu Mikkola on his way to victory in Portugal in 1979.

ABOVE After one stab at an unconventional car with the RS 1700T, Ford produced the revolutionary RS 200. The crowded engine compartment is dominated by the double coil spring/damper units.

a live axle was suspended on two semi-elliptic leaf springs and further restrained by a Panhard rod. This lay-out won the Monte Carlo Rally as late as 1972 so it would not pay to scoff too much at the leaf spring. There were leaf springs too on the rear axle of the Ford Escort RS that proved competitive right into the 1980s and won the World Rally Championship for Ford in 1979.

The real problem with leaf springs is that the maximum vertical movement of the axle is limited by the length of the leaf spring itself. If it were possible to fit a leaf spring that was two metres long, then a vertical movement of some 30cm would be a practical possibility but the idea of trying to incorporate such a spring in a car with independent suspension just never appealed to any car designer. If cars needed large wheel movements plus the benefits of independently suspended wheels on the same axle, then leaf springs were out. They had a further difficulty, encountered by both Lancia and Ford, which was that they were not easily changed nor did they allow the ride height of the car to be adjusted quickly. For the Safari, Lancia used to add a leaf to the front spring of the Fulvia, which had the effect of raising the spring rate as well as the front ride height of the car. At the rear, as on the Ford, it was a question of swapping blocks between the spring and the axle to

achieve an increase in ride height.

It is almost impossible to talk of road springs without mentioning dampers at the same time. The British tend to call them shock absorbers, which is entirely wrong. The absorbtion of energy due to hitting a bump is done to a very large extent by the spring which in a typical case would take about 70 per cent of the energy. The rest would be absorbed by the damper and turned into heat. The energy stored in the spring is also converted into heat in the damper when the suspension resumes its original position. Basically, the damper is there to damp the oscillations which result from the displacement of the suspension and, in doing so, to dissipate the energy from the movement of the car which has been transferred to the suspension.

Early dampers worked on a friction principle with two or more plates clamped together, often with an adjustable wing nut so that they could be tightened up to increase the damping when the going got tough. They were an ideal partner to leaf springs, since their scissor-like design meant that they could be fitted in front of or behind an axle and thus not restrict its upward or downward movement. They were eventually superseded by the telescopic damper in which a piston drives oil through a valve to provide the damping for the spring. The problem with the telescopic damper is that it works best when mounted directly to the axle and is in a roughly vertical position. If the wheel movement is going to be increased, then the overall length of the telescopic damper is also increased and room needs to be found above the axle in which to mount it. The Saab 96, one of the revolutionary front-wheel drive cars that came to dominate rallying in the 1960s, typified the approach of combining coil springs with telescopic dampers. Like the Fulvia, its front suspension comprised an unequal length double wishbone arrangement, but the spring and the damper were mounted above the top wishbone leaving the way clear below for the drive shaft. The Saab front wings were high so that they and the wheel arch were able to contain a 15-inch diameter wheel and tyre as well as the suspension. The compliance of the Saab's suspension gave it an immediate advantage over its contemporary rivals on all but the smoothest roads.

The final step was to take the coil spring and telescopic damper and combine them into a single unit. This was most commonly done by using a patented design known as a MacPherson strut, where the coil spring is concentric with the damper and the damper body forms the main suspension element. Only a single wishbone or track control arm is required at the lower end and a single mounting at the top which normally incorporates a bearing. These struts first appeared in rallying on cars such as the Cortina 1500s entered on the 1963 Safari, but were soon to become standard equipment on just about every make of volume production car. They were cheap to incorporate in production cars and they had several advantages for rally cars. If bent, they could be changed quickly, as a complete new unit could be fitted within minutes by skilled mechanics. It was possible, by making the lower spring platform adjustable, to regulate the ride height of the car in seconds rather than minutes. And last but not least, it was a relatively quick job to change one coil spring for another of a different spring rate.

It is true to say that the advent of the suspension

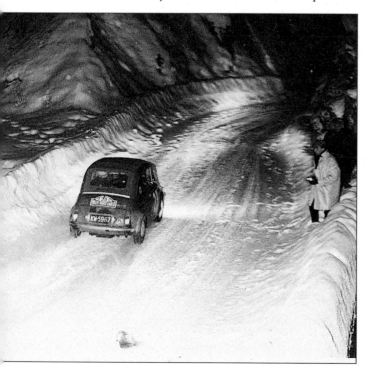

LEFT Often ridiculed for its tiny size, the Steyr Puch proved to be a mini-Porsche for Polish driver Sobieslaw Zazada during the 1960s. Such a small car does make the road seem considerably wider.

ABOVE After several years of limited success with their big cars, Ford moved to rallying their Anglia 1200 in the 1960s. It proved, as here in the hands of Anne Hall and Val Domleo on the 1960 RAC Rally, to be a useful competitor, and what was learnt from it contributed to the later success of their Cortinas.

strut enabled the manufacturers involved in rallying to develop their suspensions faster and more scientifically than had been possible before. The ability to alter the lower spring platform to adjust ride height was useful in testing as well as on the rally. In the 1970s, first Datsun came with their 240 Z which had suspension struts at all four corners, and then Fiat introduced the 131 Abarth which had struts that could be detached from just above the hub carrier. This meant that either the damper or the spring, or both, could be changed even more rapidly, and with them, of course, the ride height of the car. Such suspensions are now the norm in rally cars, except where the designer has opted to keep his springs and dampers separate as on the rear of the Lancia Rallye 037.

It was realised fairly quickly that good dampers made a major contribution to the performance of a rally car's suspension. In the 1960s, it was sufficient merely to make the telescopic dampers stiffer for

LEFT Time and again
Lancia seem to be able to
come up with a rally-
winning package. This
Lancia Delta, being
driven to fourth place on
the Lombard RAC Rally of
1988, is just the latest of
a long line of winners
stretching back to 1965.

competition use, which was the equivalent of turning
the screw on the early friction dampers. But then the
advent of the strut brought new considerations. The
body of the damper in a strut is actually a structural
part of the suspension and has to take bending and
shock loads as well as performing its duties of controlling the spring and dissipating the energy
absorbed by the suspension as heat. The damper
body therefore had to be substantial in thickness and
was certainly thicker than was necessary merely to

contain the pressures of the fluids. This meant heat
retention and soon the materials of the valves were
failing when rally cars were travelling over
unsurfaced roads at high speeds.

The answer seemed to lie with the gas-filled
damper where inert gas loaded under pressure
above the damping fluid, usually oil, prevented it aer-
ating and ensured that the heat generated in the oil
was passed to the body of the damper most effectively. The early ones were invented by Dr De Carbon

whose French company supplied them originally to the Lancia Fulvia and to certain Renault models. But then the German firm of August Bilstein was licensed by De Carbon to make gas-filled dampers and they took the art to new heights. The major advance that Bilstein incorporated into their design was to turn the strut upside down so that the piston rod was attached to the wheel hub. This meant that the sliding bearings between the two operating parts of the strut could be much larger in diameter and thus, even under the high bending loads present in the strut, were less likely to stick and cause the strut to bend. They also discovered that the rates at which the damper could be compressed (bump) and extended (rebound) should be different for the best suspension performance. They combined these discoveries with the ability to make extremely light and strong damper inserts for struts so that it was not long before

they were supplying all the major European teams such as Porsche, Ford, Opel, Lancia, Fiat, BMW and Peugeot.

Of course, there were other suspension systems, often unique to the particular manufacturer or to one of his cars, that provided sophistication before the gas-filled strut became almost universally adopted. Citroen had their hydro-pneumatic suspension on the highly successful ID and DS front-wheel drive saloons. Apart from having large wheels and significant suspension movements, the big Citroens seemed to be able to soak up rough going much better than the sports cars that they were pitted against in the rallies of the late 1950s and early 1960s. They also had the tremendous advantage of being able to regulate the ride height of the car from the cockpit while in motion. Thus the car could be raised for a rough section and then lowered to make it handle

LEFT The workhorses of many British successes during the late 1950s were the Triumph TR2 and 3 sports cars. Here a TR2 takes Paddy Hopkirk to his first Alpine Coupe in 1956.

RIGHT This man and this car, or variations on it, came to symbolise the Coupe des Alpes in the 1960s. This is Jean Rolland with Gabriel Augias in an Alfa Romeo on the Col d'Izoard during the 1961 event. They missed their Coupe by a single minute on this occasion but went on to win a Coupe d'Argent in 1963, 1964 and 1966.

LEFT There were still British troops in Trieste when Stirling Moss did the 1954 Monte Carlo Rally in this Sunbeam Talbot. It was in this model that Moss won his Coupe d'Or on the Alpine Rally.

better when the tarmac was regained. In the same era, the BMC Mini came with first the Alec Moulton rubber-in-compression suspension and then his hydrolastic suspension based on a similar idea but with the units linked hydraulically. Indeed, so successful were the Mini and its Cooper derivatives that this type of suspension is still used today on the Metro produced by the Rover Group.

Suspension testing started on factory rally cars during the 1970s and is today a highly developed technique. Its purpose is not the same as the testing undertaken by racing teams, since the rally driver is looking for something slightly different from his rally car. The fact is that, no matter how many times he may practise a road which is to be used as a special stage, he is unlikely to have same completeness of knowledge about it that a race driver will have of the corners on a racing circuit. In addition to that natural

uncertainty, there can be any number of others ranging from snow, ice, water, gravel or even oil on the surface, not to mention some other change than may have been wreaked on the road between reconnaissance and the event. Thus the rally driver wants his car to be able to respond quickly and safely to a last-second change of mind on his part.

This means that while the race driver is seeking to make his car hold the road better, so that he can brake later and go even faster round the corners that he knows so well, the rally driver is looking to make his car handle well. Good handling and good roadholding are not the same thing, but nor are they complete opposites and it is success in this difficult area of setting up cars for events that brings results in modern rallying. The thing to remember is that a car adjusted to achieve its maximum grip around a corner probably feels unpleasant to drive. Such a set-up

ABOVE The classic features of a classic rally car – the Alpine A110 was underpowered in its early years and rather unreliable, but once it discovered the 1600cc Renault engine and the suspension was properly developed, it became a winner everywhere but the Safari and the RAC Rally.

could not be considered by a rally driver, for if he were called upon to improvise by virtue of a change in the road condition or an imperfect reconnaissance, the car would simply not react correctly or quickly enough. Thus while good roadholding is sought by engineers setting up rally cars, it is not the ultimate goal, and they have to retain good handling characteristics. It is a difficult task and there will often be suspension and transmission changes carried out during a rally, as a driver tries to adjust his car to give him the feel that he requires.

Apart from a general technological improvement, transmissions had not seen a major revolution in rallying until the 1980s when the four-wheel drive cars came into their own. The limited slip differential and the five-speed gearbox that gradually became standard for rally cars during the 1960s were the major innovations to the pre-war rally cars. Rear-wheel drive cars had the most to gain from a limited slip differential, especially when engines were not over the driven wheels. The BMC team tried them in the big Healey as early as 1963, but a failure cost Donald and Erle Morley a Gold Coupe des Alpes and it was not until more reliable units started to come in from the USA that they became generally accepted. For

front-wheel drive cars they were even more problematical, as the torque reaction across the front axle made the steering wheel kick and jump in the most unpleasant fashion. Lancia Fulvia drivers of the early seventies like Harry Kallstrom, twice winner of the RAC Rally, had to live with the fact that large blisters on the hands were part of the price that had to be paid for performance. Later, when four-wheel drive cars had to have limited slip differentials in both axles, it was discovered that the fitting of power steering took out a lot of the shock and kick-back between the road wheels and the steering wheel.

The advent of power steering is perhaps the most beneficial development as far as the driver is concerned, but first the steering rack had to evolve and become a common fitment on production cars. The pre-1960s cars frequently had steering boxes that were either provided with a worm and pinion or recirculating balls. Because of the various limitations imposed by front leaf springs, friction dampers and chassis rails, the amount of lock available to the early rally cars was somewhat limited. Reports of the Alpine Trials suggest that reverse gear was often needed in the middle of a hairpin bend to enable it to be successfully negotiated. One of the reasons that

HJ Aldington decided to become an importer of BMW cars in 1936 was the ease with which they were able to negotiate sharp bends thanks to their superior lock.

Steering boxes were prone to ice up in winter and anyone doing a Monte Carlo Rally was advised to fill them with a thinner oil. Steering racks were, of course, known from pioneer days, but until manufacturing techniques were sufficiently sophisticated to produce the enclosed modern steering rack with sufficient strength to be able to resist the tendency of the front wheels to point in different directions, the dreaded boxes stayed. Again, the Lancia Fulvia was one of the last successful rally cars to have a steering box rather than a rack, though the highly successful Datsun rally cars – the 1600 SSS, and the 160 J – continued to use steering boxes up until 1985 when the Nissan 240 RS Evolution 2 was introduced.

Long before then, Citroen had steering racks on their DS models, complete with power assistance, and used them to good effect with Paul Coltelloni winning the Monte Carlo for them in 1959. But for the majority of rally drivers, power steering was something found on big American cars that gave you no feeling of what was happening down where the tyres meet the road. To a certain extent that was true, but the need for power steering soon outweighed the prejudice once four-wheel drive and 400-plus bhp arrived on the scene in the mid-1980s. It was simply not possible to drive cars like the Audi Sport Quattro unless there was some assistance in moving the front wheels. Once adopted and developed so that there was both speed and feel, rally drivers took to it like ducks to water. They found that it enabled them to place a car with greater accuracy on both tarmac and gravel roads, and to recover from situations where their strength alone would not have been enough.

As with their racing counterparts, one cannot hope to understand the performance of modern rally cars without appreciating the amount of progress that has been made by the tyre companies over the last twenty years. Before the Second World War, improvements were made to tyres so that competitors in a Monte Carlo could at least think in terms of carrying only two spares – and those normally fitted with chains for deep snow. Winter treaded tyres were developed for Scandinavian countries and then adopted more widely to cope with bad going, but they were not initially recognised as being useful for gravel roads when there was no snow around.

ABOVE Attempts to win rallies with conventional cars included those of the Leyland Cars team, who had some limited success with V8-engined Triumph TR7s driven, as here, by Tony Pond. Better suited to practised rallies, the burly Triumph had its best results on tarmac events.

Michelin brought out the first radial road tyre, the eponymous Michelin 'X', in 1953 and this proved to be a major step forward for rallying. Indeed, much of the success of French cars in the years that followed could be directly attributed to that type of tyre, which gave better grip and feel on nearly all surfaces. Dunlop followed with their Duraband, and Pirelli with their Cinturato, and both enjoyed equal success.

The idea of improving grip on icy roads by fitting metal studs to the tyre came, not surprisingly, from Scandinavia. The first studs were quite literally bolted through the tyre's tread and a cap of hardened steel protruded a few millimetres. Soon studs were developed with tungsten tips mounted in aluminium frames. These were fired by compressed air into holes drilled part-way into the tread and retained there by the grip of the rubber on the stud frame. The knowledge of how to drive on such tyres, and which types of stud to choose for particular conditions, was a skill which enabled the Scandinavian drivers to dominate the Monte Carlo Rally results for almost ten years after their introduction. All kinds of studs and other devices were tried in order to ensure success on that rally. When Timo Makinen won in 1965 amid the blizzards, his Cooper S was using an ice racing tyre which had 600 knife blade type 'studs' extending some 12mm or more from the surface of the re-moulded tyre. It made the car almost impossible to drive on a tarmac road devoid of snow and ice, but gave the most fantastic performance on fresh snow.

It was the Scandinavian drivers who also introduced the idea of using a winter pattern tyre on gravel roads at any time during the year to improve the grip. The coarse pattern coped better with the fine dirt or sand, while the sharp corner of the tread made it steer much more positively.

At about the same time, and stemming from the BMC team, came the idea of using racing tyres on tarmac stages. A racing tyre in those days was a traditional cross-ply tyre, but it was normally wider, had no tread pattern, and the sidewalls were less of a compromise in an effort to achieve low road noise. The consequence was that when the Cooper S's of the team started to use them on tarmac tests, they were able to beat more powerful machinery whose drivers had not caught on to the use of such tyres. Of course it did not take long for that to happen and soon it was the Porsches, Lancias and Alpine Renaults that had racers and were leaving the Cooper S's behind. Michelin and Pirelli came quickly with radial racing tyres which proved to be better still than the cross-ply, and such tyres are still in use in today's rallies. The latest gambit, again borrowed from the racing teams, is to have tyre warmers – electrically heated blankets – to pre-heat the tyres before they are fitted to the rally car.

The most frequent source of dissatisfaction that a rally driver has with the tyres fitted to his car comes when they puncture. He either has to stop and change the wheel or has to proceed slower than he would like to the end of the special stage. To be fair to

LEFT The winning car from the RAC Rally of 1953 was the Appleyards' famous XK 120, seen here among the stunning scenery of the Lake District.

BOTTOM LEFT When is a flat tyre not flat? When it has Michelin ATS inside it. This particularly good example is from the Acropolis Rally of 1989 and the writing on the tyre (in white) tells that it was used by Didier Auriol's Lancia on the 14th special stage.

the tyres, the damage is often inflicted by the driver either failing to miss some part of the scenery or making contact with a rock churned into the road by the passage of an earlier car. Punctures were a nuisance but not a problem until the advent of special stage rallies where a stop to change a wheel was a disaster. Self-sealing compounds were often tried, but without great success until Michelin perfected their ATS (*Appui Temporaire Souple*) which was introduced in the late 1980s. This comprises a mousse-foam which is fitted inside the tyre and, under the normal pressure of the tyre, say 30 pounds per square inch, does not fill the air chamber. But should that pressure disappear, as when a puncture occurs, then the mousse-foam expands to fill the entire chamber and plug the gap. Thus even if a large piece of the tread or sidewall is ripped out, the tyre will not deflate entirely. It is a true run-flat tyre, but the teams that use it do have to pay a small penalty in carrying the extra foam and chemicals as part of the unsprung weight of the car.

Allied to the improvements in the grip provided by tyres came improvements in the braking systems on rally cars. In the very beginning, the driver was lucky to have brakes at all since the normal arrangement was to have the brake pedal act on some form of transmission brake. This feeble drum was later backed up by a hand-operated brake lever which applied two further drums attached to the rear wheels. Mercedes took to using a second foot pedal for these extra drums, but it was not until well into the 1920s that it became standard practice to have drum brakes on all four wheels actuated by a single foot pedal. All these methods of retardation depended on some form of mechanical linkage and it was not until the 1930s that cars even appeared with hydraulic operation to all four wheels.

The disc brake was developed during the Second World War for use on aeroplanes and soon made its debut on racing cars, first in Formula One with BRM and then in sports cars with the C-type Jaguar, both in 1952. By the 1960s, most competitive rally cars had disc brakes fitted to the front wheels and drum brakes on the rear. The creation of left-foot braking techniques by the Scandinavians and their adoption by nearly all rally drivers in the 1970s caused enormous problems. This was largely due to the amount of extra heat generated and the fact that the disc had little time to recover between applications of the brake pedal, since it was nearly constantly in use. Very quickly, ventilated discs were substituted for

solid ones and the rear drum brakes were replaced by discs. The search for better ways to get rid of the heat led to the adoption of alloy wheels, which were able to provide a better heat sink and could also be designed so as to allow as much air as possible to reach the calipers and discs.

In the 1980s, the tyre manufacturers and the suppliers of brakes had a common cause in trying to increase the diameter of the road wheels used on rally cars. The tyre maufacturers wanted bigger diameter tyres so that they could use softer compounds yet still persuade the tyre to last as long. With a bigger diameter, each block of rubber has a longer 'rest' before it is presented once again to the road. And the brake men wanted to fit larger diameter discs to provide a greater mass into which heat could pass from the pad and caliper. Gradually, the 10-inch wheels of the Cooper S gave way to 12-inch versions, while more recently with other cars 13-inch wheels have been left behind as the works teams have gone to 15, then 16 and now to 17-inch road wheel diameters. All of which has also provided a new phenomenon for spectators to watch at night, when the disc brakes of rally cars can be seen glowing cherry red through the

ABOVE The Mini Cooper reigned for six years in European rallying, but by the time Adrian Boyd came to do the Scottish Rally in 1969 with this example, it was being left behind by more powerful newcomers.

wheel centres as the cars descend long special stages. Fortunately, at the same time as all these other improvements were being made, the scientists were able to supply brake fluid, seals and friction material that stood up to the temperatures, with the result that a modern rally driver can count on his brakes no matter how much abuse they have received in his attempts to set a fastest time on a special stage.

Because so much rally driving takes place at night or in bad weather conditions, the demand of rally drivers for better lights has always been a major force in introducing new developments. When fog lights were introduced in the 1920s, their design and testing was done with rally cars on actual events. There was no universal agreement on where such lamps should be fitted for best effect and photographs of cars from that period show them fitted to roofs, windscreen pillars and, more conventionally, to the front of the car on a lighting rail which also supported the headlights. The post-war lamps and bulbs were big improvements, and double-filament headlamp bulbs were supplemented by two spotlights and a fog light mounted on or near the front bumper. From Scandinavia came the swivelling spotlight or roof-light which was fitted to the centre of the roof and controlled by the co-driver to point where the car was to go. This was very important when one was sliding about on icy roads and there could be no guarantee that the car was pointing where the driver wanted it to go next!

Legislation soon banned the use of roof-lights – except when the car was stationary – but there were two further developments on the way that were to improve the night-time performance of rally cars dramatically. The first concerned the actual supply of electricity. This had been guaranteed by a dynamo whose output was not normally able to feed all the electrical accessories should they be used at once. It was no good having six spotlamps if, when they were on in conjunction with the headlamps, windscreen wipers and electric de-mister, the dynamo cried 'enough'. Enter the alternator, which made its first appearance on rallies with the works Citroens whose equipment was supplied by Paris-Rhone. Lucas were not far behind and the Cooper S owed much of its success to the fact that an alternator had been made that was small enough to fit inside its already crowded engine compartment.

With the arrival of almost unlimited electricity, the way was open for the automotive version of the halogen bulb. This technology had been in use for commercial lighting for some time and was also used for aircraft landing lights, but it was a great consumer of power. Once its miniaturisation had been perfected, it teamed up with the alternator to create a revolution in night-time visibility from fast moving cars. Almost at once after its arrival in 1964, everyone in the rally world had to have them and now they are standard fitments on nearly all road-going vehicles.

As far as normal instrumentation goes, rally cars have probably been influential in reducing this over the years. The description of a Frazer-Nash from the Alpine Trial of 1934 reveals that it had in front of the driver an ammeter, oil pressure gauge, oil temperature gauge, water temperature gauge, fuel tank pressure and rev counter. The speedometer was fitted well out of the driver's direct gaze in front of the co-driver. A modern rally car would have warning lights for most of the fluid systems, an electronic rev counter, a speedometer, an oil pressure gauge and, if a turbocharger is fitted, then perhaps a boost gauge as well. A fuel gauge is not always fitted as it is sometimes difficult to get reliable information from the inside of a foam-filled safety tank. The substitute for a gauge in such circumstances is a dipstick which can be used to plumb the fuel tank at service stops.

RIGHT Lights may have been the reason for the disqualification of the Cooper S's on the 1965 Monte Carlo, but here on the 1967 rally Timo Makinen is more concerned about being blinded by the photographer's flash.
BELOW RIGHT The original Halda Speedpilot, the co-driver's best friend. It was capable of measuring distances very accurately and expressing the distance travelled as a gain or loss of time against a specified average speed.
BELOW LEFT The modern rally car – this one a Lancia Delta S4 – has a cockpit full of technology ranging from digital fuel gauges through circuit breakers to electronic odometers. Michael Eriksson is at the wheel.

There might be many more switches than in a normal car, but that is inevitable when you fit half-a-dozen spot and fog lights and want to be able to use them in different combinations. One major advance that arrived with the Lancia Stratos is the light-pod. This is a fibreglass or carbon-kevlar addition to the front bodywork which contains all the additional spot and fog lights. It is fitted to the existing bodywork by quick-release fasteners while a multi-way plug and socket supplies the electricity. The advantage of this is that while normally if the additional lights or their permanent mountings are damaged in an accident it is very difficult to replace them, with a pod, provided that the service car has a replacement, it is the work of a minute or two to restore normal lighting.

One cannot leave the subject of instrumentation in rally cars without dwelling on the co-driver's best friend, the trip meter. Back in the 1930s, the Dutch driver Bud Bakker Schut, who won the Monte Carlo Rally for Ford in 1938, invented a clock which had two concentric dials. The outer dial was connected to the speedometer drive and was so geared that it would make one revolution for every 50km covered by the car. The inner one was driven by a conventional clock mechanism and rotated once every hour. It was possible to set two arrows on each dial to be opposite one another when you started and then, provided that you drove at 50kph, they would stay pointing at one another. Any variance from this aver-

age speed could be read off either in minutes on one dial or in kilometres on the other.

It is not surprising that such devices became very popular with co-drivers who were required to keep the cars to set average speeds on regularity sections where secret controls could suddenly crop up and hand out penalties for either early or late arrival. In 1956, the Swedish company of Halda produced something called the Speedpilot that was forever to endear them to the rally driver. Halda were a company which made taxi meters, and indeed still do under their new name of Haldex. Their

Speedpilot contained a clock and an odometer requiring connection to the speedometer drive of the car. Here resemblance to the early Dutch device ceased, for there were two dials alongside each other. On one was set the average speed that was required. By simply turning a knob, the co-driver could get any average speed between 40kph and 150kph. Arranged as part of that display was a regular distance recorder, measuring in 100-metre increments up to a total of 999km, which could be easily zeroed. The other dial was the clock, but this one had three hands. The normal hour and minute hands were supplemented by a red hand which was driven by the odometer via the average speed regulator. The red hand could be moved by the operator to coincide with the minute hand. From that instant, if the car was being driven at the average speed set on the other dial, then the red hand would keep pace precisely with the minute hand. Any variance would show as the difference between them and could be read off directly in minutes.

These wonderful devices, of which over 56 000 were sold in the 22 years that they were produced, were indeed the rally driver's best friend. Apart from their use on strict regularity sections, they were useful on ordinary road sections where they could tell the co-driver at once whether he was ahead of schedule or behind. And they provided for almost the first time a really accurate odometer which in its turn led to accurate road books and the kind of detail preparation for rallies that is commonplace today. On endurance events where one of the crew had to sleep while the other drove, they were often mounted on a swivel so that the man that was driving could turn the Halda Speedpilot partly towards him and keep an eye on his progress without having to indulge in calculations.

There were a couple of things that could not be done with a Speedpilot and these caused Halda to bring out their Tripmaster in 1958. If the tyre diameter was changed during the rally, then the odometer could not be correctly adjusted without some difficulty. Also if the wrong road was taken and the car had to retrace its steps, then the Halda could not be disconnected temporarily or put into reverse. The Tripmaster could do all of that. The change of gearing was achieved by a simple swap of gears in the side of the machine while the mechanics changed the tyres, while a knob on the front acted like a gear lever and was able to stop it counting or to go into reverse. What it did not have was the clock to tell how the average speed was progressing, but as that became less important in international rallying the Tripmaster and its stablemate, the Twinmaster, took off in a big way. In 30 years, 144 000 were sold to rally drivers all over the world.

It was inevitable that electronics would eventually be used to carry out these functions, and in 1980 Halda brought out their Rally Computer which does just about everything except drive the rally car for you. Its two digital readouts can display the states of

ABOVE When strict adherence to average speeds became less of a concern, Halda produced their best seller yet, the Tripmaster, which enabled accurate road books to become standard on just about every rally in the world.

TOP The private Alpine A110 of 'Sirocco' on the 1975 Acropolis Rally. The light weight of these fibreglass cars made them agile over even the roughest roads.

RIGHT It took Toyota a while to get their Group A Celica GT4 working well, but they had not had the benefit of using a four-wheel drive car during the Group B years. This is Juha Kankkunen on the 1988 Lombard RAC Rally.

three separate odometers and a clock. The odometers can be idling or reading up or down independently, and when tyres are changed a new ratio can be punched in from the keyboard. The Halda Rally Computer takes its input from the speedometer but could just as well take it from a pulse generator on the wheel hub or the propeller shaft. It has had many emulators but its place in rallying technology is fairly secure. For 19 years, with the advice and help of Gunnar Palm, Haldex has given an annual award called the Golden Halda to the person it considers the most deserving co-driver of the year.

Of all the technical developments that have come to prominence and acceptance due to rallying, none is more outstanding than the use of four-wheel drive. The concept was in use from the very earliest days of the motor car. In America, the Twyford Motor Car Co. of Brooksville, Pennsylvania sold a rather crude five-seater with open bevel gears driving all four wheels between 1902 and 1908. In Europe, the Dutch Spyker company revealed a 50hp six-cylinder model at the 1903 Paris Show which had drive to all four wheels, but despite the interest it caused it was never put into production. It was certainly never rallied and neither was the other American four-wheel car, launched in 1908 and called the Badger. This was produced in Clintonville, Wisconsin by the Four Wheel Drive Auto Co. but never caught on and the company went into the truck manufacturing business. The first real pro-

duction four-wheel drive vehicle for sale to the general public came from the Russians. It was the GAZ 69, an all-purpose four-wheel drive vehicle powered by a 72bhp four-cylinder engine.

In the years following the Second World War, a great number of what might be described as Jeep or Land Rover type vehicles were produced but none seemed suitable for rallying. It was left to the Americans to show the way with Gene Henderson winning the 1972 Press On Regardless Rally in a Jeep Waggoneer. At the end of that decade, the Volkswagen/Audi Group won the Paris–Dakar with a Volkswagen Iltis driven by Freddy Kottulinsky. This was a four-wheel drive vehicle based on a military design, but what the rest of the world did not know was that it was also a test bed for a normal production car. It is of interest to note that when VW-Audi engineers made a key presentation of the saloon version of their four-wheel drive system, they chose as a venue the Turrache Hohe pass in Austria which had been one of the toughest tests on the original *Alpenfahrt*. When it was announced that the Audi factory was going to rally its new turbocharged, four-wheel drive Quattro starting in 1981, scepticism was rampant. It was silenced after the Quattro had first won the Janner Rally, then set fastest times on the Monte Carlo Rally before crashing, and finally won the World Championship Swedish Rally on only its third outing. WRC titles followed in 1982, 1983 and

LEFT Kitty Brunel's Talbot shows little in the way of special preparation for this 1920s Monte Carlo Rally. The only additional light is the tiny spot on the driver's door pillar which must have been used for reading signposts.

1984 and it was quite clear to everyone that, in future, four-wheel drive was going to be an essential feature for any car that wanted to win rallies.

The Group B era which lasted from 1984 to 1986 enabled many manufacturers to develop four-wheel drive technology themselves at a cost not very much greater than that of experimental cars. A considerable amount of knowledge was gained quickly as a result, so that when Group B was cut off in its prime at the end of the 1986 season, a large number of manufacturers were ready to mass produce four-wheel drive cars. Several European manufacturers had grabbed the chance provided by the Group B regulations to try their hand at the new concept, and both Peugeot and Lancia showed that they could outdo Audi when given their head. It is interesting to note that the Japanese manufacturer Subaru had run a Hatchback 4x4 on the Safari Rally in 1980 and brought it to the finish in 18th place, first in the standard car category. When the change to Group A came at the beginning of 1987, it was no surprise to find Japanese manufacturers emerging with competitive four-wheel drive rally cars based on mass production vehicles.

Before leaving the subject of rally cars and how they have evolved alongside technological progress in the automotive industry, it is necessary to look at the specialised things which have been done to them in the name of safety. On looking into a modern rally car, the most obvious safety item is the roll cage. This is a complex arrangement of metal tubes welded and bolted into the shell of the car so as to protect the crew in case of an accident. Such cages were first used in American stock car racing but until the mid-1960s nothing was fitted to rally cars to prevent the superstructure collapsing on the crew in the event of the car rolling onto its roof. This was acceptable for cars like the Saab 96 which seemed to be designed to be rolled in perfect safety, but when designers started increasing the glass areas and reducing pillar thicknesses to improve the styling and the driver's visibility, then they needed something to protect the crew. To start with, the *Commission Sportive Internationale*, the ruling body at the time, would have none of these roll-over bars or cages in rally cars. It was, they said, an attempt by the manufacturers to stiffen the bodyshells and make them more able to stand up to bad roads. Fortunately, better sense prevailed and as rallying entered the 1970s it became compulsory to have at least some form of roll cage fitted to rally cars for international events.

As rally car preparation became more sophisticated in the late 1970s, so did the roll cages become more and more an integral part of the bodyshell. Indeed, it has been said of the very latest cars that if the bodyshell were removed then the car would work just as well, since all its strength resides in the roll cage. Certainly, wherever possible the suspension and major components are mounted directly onto it. There is no question that this liberality has resulted in a very safe vehicle in terms of protecting its occupants during an accident, but it is equally clear that full use has been made of the opportunity to strengthen the car at the same time.

Also compulsory now on rally cars are plumbed-in fire extinguishing systems that can be operated either by the crew or by someone outside the car. There were experiments with systems triggered by a heavy shock, such as would be generated by an accident, but since rally cars were frequently being subjected to such shocks by bouncing off the scenery, the drivers who were the subject of these trials got fed up with being choked by extinguishant. Seat belts were compulsory in rallying long before they were in road cars and, indeed, their use in rallying helped to have them accepted as being a positive step. Only a very few rally drivers eschewed their use once roll cages were adopted, since it made good sense to stay inside the protected area rather than being flung from it as the car rolled over.

One driver who never wore seat belts was Jean-François Piot who was always adamant that, in an accident, he liked to be able to move inside the car and not be strapped in, possibly unable to get to the release mechanism, when the car was on fire. Sadly, he died during a Rallye-Raid in Morocco when he was thrown out of a Land Rover 110 which then landed on him. But the fear of being strapped in when the car is on fire is a very real one. Rauno Aaltonen had an horrific accident on the 1962 Monte Carlo in a Mini Cooper when he inverted it on the Piera Cava road down from the top of the Col de Turini. The car caught fire and he was half unconscious and unable to release the seat belt. This had to be done by his courageous co-driver, Geoff Mabbs, who was quite badly burnt in the process, but succeeded in getting the pair of them clear of the blazing car.

There have been fatalities among the crew of modern rally cars but they have to be considered as almost freak events, since the physical protection offered to the crew is much better than one can find in the majority of racing cars. The problem with fire is that, unlike racing, there is no marshal's post on every corner and if the crew cannot put out the fire themselves or get away from it, then they are in a very bad situation. The deaths of Henri Toivonen and Sergio Cresto in the 1986 Tour de Corse shook the rally world to its foundations. Their Lancia Delta S4 left the road for an unexplained reason and tumbled a fairly modest distance before coming to rest on its roof among some rocks. At this point, or shortly before, it caught fire and, either because of the intensity of the fire or because the position of the car prevented them from opening the doors, the crew were unable to extricate themselves or attempt to control the inferno and died where they sat. So unique were the conditions of this accident that nothing like it has happened before or since, but it was a grim reminder that extreme danger does lurk amid the fun and general exuberance of rallying.

CHAPTER
3

RALLYPERSONS

There is no stereotype for a rally driver. Whereas a boxer might be recognised by his broken nose, an athlete by his slender build, or a ballet dancer by his calves, there is nothing to distinguish the top performers of rallying by sight alone. Indeed, this is hardly surprising, since they come from all walks of life and a variety of backgrounds.

Take, for instance, the protagonists on that pioneering event, the Paris–Rouen Reliability Trial of 1894. The Count Albert de Dion was born in 1856 as the first son of a French aristocrat. He took a great interest in things mechanical and in 1883 founded the company of De Dion-Bouton with the object of building steam-powered vehicles. He was in partnership with Georges Bouton and his brother-in-law M. Trépardoux, and it was with one of their highly successful products that he competed in the Paris–Rouen. It is perhaps inaccurate to classify him as a driver, for the vehicle was an articulated semi-carriage drawn behind a four-wheel steam car. The Count rode in the carriage, but was certainly in charge of what went on. He was later to be founding father of the *Automobile Club de France* and became Marquis de Dion in 1901, by which time the De Dion-Bouton company was producing petrol-engined cars and tricycles. The latter were successful in competitions and the company flourished up until the First World War. After that it went into decline, finally closing its doors in 1932. The Marquis survived until 1946, which was all the more surprising since his other hobby had been that of duelling.

Matched against him in the Paris–Rouen, and indeed on the Paris–Bordeaux–Paris of the subsequent year, was the entrepreneur Emile Levassor. Born in 1844, he became co-owner together with Rene Panhard of the woodworking business of *Perin et Pauwels*. In 1886, his friend Edouard Sarazin bought the rights to exploit the Daimler patent in France, but Sarazin died in 1887 and the rights passed to Levassor when he married Sarazin's widow. They started designing and making cars and the first one was on the road in 1891. By 1894 it was good enough for Levassor to take one to joint first place in the Paris–Rouen, but his greatest triumph came in the Paris–Bordeaux–Paris of 1895.

The Paris–Bordeaux–Paris started from the Arc de Triomphe at 9.00am on the morning of Tuesday 11 June. Levassor was start number five in his two-cylinder, 4hp, two-seater Panhard. By Tours at 8.45pm he was the leading car on the road. Like the others, he drove through the night with only the beams generated by two oil lamps to guide him. At Ruffec, where he was supposed to change driver, the man in question was still fast asleep so Emil drove on into the night. He reached Bordeaux at 10.40am and promptly set off back for Paris. He was now some three and a half hours ahead of the next car, but so worried was he that another driver might make an error and lose the lead he had built up that he stayed at the wheel all the way back to Paris where he

reached the finish at the Porte Maillot at 12.57pm on Thursday 13 June. His longest stop on the way had been for 22 minutes. It was a truly epic drive and yet, because a two-seater car could not be acknowledged as the winner, he was credited with second place. But the endorsement of the car's performance was sufficient and, thanks to this success, in 1899 the car manufacturing company of Panhard and Levassor was born. Sadly, while competing on the Paris–Marseille of 1896 – and leading it by a margin of some two hours – Levassor ran into a dog and overturned his Panhard. He was pretty badly shaken but continued to Avignon where another driver took over. The car eventually finished fourth but Levassor was more badly hurt than was imagined at the time. He died on 11 April 1896, whereupon a public subscription was immediately started and the money used to erect a monument to him at the Porte Maillot in Paris, the scene of the finish of his famous non-stop drive.

Emil Levassor was the kind of rally driver that would easily be recognised – and welcomed by professional teams – today. He was a perfectionist who knew his cars from the chassis bolts to the cylinder head. He knew that to win, one must first finish, and under his guidance the Panhards that came from his factory were some of the most reliable cars of their generation. He also realised that there were no half-measures in tuning engines and, second to reliability, he always looked to get the most out of his car. Finally, since he and René Panhard had done most of the development work themselves, he knew the value of testing, and his rigorous validation of components would meet with approval from a rally engineer of the 1990s. It is no surprise that the Hon CS Rolls won the 1000 Miles Trial of 1900 with a Panhard from the Ivry factory and then went on to found a firm whose name is now a synonym for reliability and excellence.

Considering the very temperamental nature of the early motor cars and the need to understand their weaknesses, it is hardly surprising that so many of the early rally drivers were engineers. No better example could be found than Dr Ferdinand Porsche. Born in 1875 in Hafersdorf, Bohemia, he worked initially as an electrical engineer and got involved with cars in 1898 when he was employed by the Austrian car maker Jacob Lohner of Vienna, to design him a new electric car. This featured a separate electric motor on each front wheel, thus dispensing with the need for transmission. It was known as a Lohner-Porsche. The same company also made cars where a petrol engine drove a generator which in its turn powered the electric motors that drove the wheels. Lohner entered examples of this model in races, with Porsche as the driver.

When Lohner discovered that electric cars, though practical, could not be commercially competitive with pure petrol engined vehicles, he sold out his patents. Porsche stayed with cars and in 1905 became the senior manager of Austro-Daimler, originally the

PREVIOUS PAGE Even the professional man's professional can let his hair down once in a while . . . Miki Biasion and Tiziano Siviero make with the Moët waterfall at the end of the Costa Brava Rally in 1983.
RIGHT Ireland's favourite son, Paddy Hopkirk, whose winning ways have spanned the period from the late 1950s to the historic rallies of the present day. The unchanging factors are his smile and the Cooper S.
BELOW Rauno Aaltonen was European Rally Champion in 1965 at the wheel of a Cooper S. He brought a highly technical approach to the business of driving a rally car – plus sartorial elegance.

Austrian off-shoot of the German Daimler company but which became independent in 1906. He immediately set about persuading them to build a new series of cars, based on his design, to replace the old PD which was merely a copy of the German design. Mercedes and Benz had taken all the prizes in the first Prinz Heinrich Fahrt of 1908 and Porsche was determined that his Austrian car should displace them. He had to wait until 1910 when Austro-Daimler unveiled the 22/80 PS model, with five valves per cylinder – one inlet and four exhaust – and a streamlined body, which was called the Prince Henry Tourer.

Ferdinand Porsche took the wheel of one of the factory cars himself, and as mechanic he chose a young man called Joseph Brosch, later to become Marshal Tito of Yugoslavia. For the first four days, there was little to choose between the Opels, the Benzs, the Mercedes and the Daimlers, and the majority of the factory drivers were effectively unpenalised on the speed tests. A critical factor was the reduction of the service time allowed to just one hour per day. This worked to the advantage of Daimler, who had Porsche and Brosch as well as other technicians who had been entered as drivers of other competing Daimlers. The event came down to a final test on some particularly bad roads near Colmar where Porsche set an average speed of 81.7mph and went into a lead he was never to lose. His Daimler finished first ahead of two other Daimler

team cars and the best of the rest was Herbert Ephraim in an Opel. This result turned out to be a Pyrrhic victory for the Austrians, since Germany promptly announced that there would be no more Prinz Heinrich *Fahrten*, while the general public was scared by all this speed and, when buying a new motor car, stuck to the more sedate models.

Porsche was not daunted, and when the Austrians developed their own *Alpenfahrt* in 1910 he got Daimler involved with that event, with himself again at the wheel. In the 1911 event he drove one of the new 16/25 PS Daimlers and won an Alpine Cup for an unpenalised run. For the 1912 event, he had a special version of the same car called an Alpine and was again rewarded with an unpenalised run. As were his team-mates, Count Schoenfeld and the Prince of Parma, though none of them were too happy when it was discovered that Fiat had won the team prize, the top award, as Daimler had not entered the three of them as a team!

Dr Porsche went on to work for Steyr, Mercedes and Auto Union before designing the Volkswagen and starting a car company under his own name in 1948. When one considers how his early success as a designer and manufacturer of cars was buttressed by his own efforts in competition, it is little wonder that the Porsche factory has had such a dedication to motor sport for the past 40 years.

When the First World War was over, Europe had changed politically while the motor car had emerged

ABOVE Andrew Cowan's success as driver and team manager have contrived to overlap in his duties for Mitsubishi. In the same year that he drove a Pajero on the Paris–Dakar, the Galant VR4 won both the 1000 Lakes and the Lombard RAC Rally.

TOP LEFT The Audi team take a mineral refreshment during the 1987 Acropolis Rally. Walter Rohrl (right) and Hannu Mikkola flush the dust with the inevitable Perrier.

RIGHT With a career as a film stunt-man, Jean Ragnotti tries to avoid spectacular accidents when he is driving on rallies. He is a faithful adherent to Renault and has won many of the major rallies for them.

from a period of rapid development the like of which, sadly, only armed conflict seems able to create. Gradually during the 1920s, the old rallies came back and new ones started. The rally drivers were a different breed, however. There were still engineers, but the increase in reliability of components and accuracy of assembly meant that it was not essential to know everything about the car to know how to drive it. The two decades between the World Wars was also a period of wealth and *joie de vivre*, when it was accepted that risk gave a certain spice to life. It was no surprise to find that daring young men of independent means were easily attracted to rallying.

Perhaps typical of the new men was the Honourable Victor Bruce who, accompanied by the famous motoring photographer of the day WJ Brunell, won the Monte Carlo Rally in 1926. He had competed for the first time the previous year, just 12 months after the Monte Carlo's post-war resuscitation, finishing 12th overall but winning the 2-litre class in the 80km mountain trial that was the rally's crowning glory. His car was an AC two-seater powered by AC's renowned six-cylinder, single overhead camshaft engine. It was possessed of a soft top, open side-screens, a single windscreen wiper and a single tiny spotlight fitted to the driver's side windscreen pillar. Apart from two spare wheels and tyres, that was it. He and his co-driver had to drive 2641 kilometres in something like three days – an average speed of 23mph – through snow, sleet and fog from the northernmost tip of the British Isles, across the Channel and through Western France to reach Monte Carlo over the Massif Central and the Alpes Maritimes. There were no snow-ploughs or road-cleaning efforts in those days, and indeed the roads, away from the main thoroughfares, were nothing like the tarred highways that we happily accept today.

Victor Bruce saw the whole thing as a challenge. He should have been classified ahead on points when the cars reached Monaco the first time, since he had successfully attempted one of the longest itineraries, but the organisers had decided that the mountain trial should provide the result. This trial looped twice over the Col de Braus, today still much the same and beloved of car magazines wishing to test and photograph cars on a series of hairpin bends that appears to be never-ending. But at Monte time, it is frequently covered with snow and so it was in 1926. Many of the competitors did not start the test owing to the *conditions rigoreuses* that prevailed. No so Victor Bruce, who took the AC round and won by just 7.78 points from M. Bussienne in a Sizaire-Naudin tourer. This was not the only success gained by the Bruce family on the Monte Carlo Rally, for Bruce's wife was the winner of the first Coupe des Dames to be awarded on the Monte Carlo when she competed on the 1927 rally in another AC, this one a four-seater with a saloon body.

As times got leaner in the 1930s, rallying got more serious and one was able to see the gradual arrival of what we would recognise today as works teams. Some, mainly the German teams like Hanomag, Adler, DKW and Daimler-Benz, were there for political reasons; others like Frazer Nash, Hotchkiss, Ford, Bugatti, Riley, Talbot and Triumph were just keen to prove their cars in competition and sell more than they had the year before. They were a long way from employing superstar rally drivers at millionaire salaries, but there was a definite trend for successful rally drivers to secure employment with factories – or even end up owning them.

One such was HJ Aldington, who started competing in trials and races with a Frazer Nash in the 1920s and finished up owning the AFN company. He took

LEFT A family portrait of Donald Healey, home from his wins in the Monte Carlo and Alpine Rallies and enjoying a break with his wife, three sons and pet dog at his home in Cornwall.

RIGHT Try as he might, Erik Carlsson was not able to repeat his European victories for Saab in East Africa. Here he surveys the post-rally situation in 1962 at Nairobi racecourse with Pat Moss and Ann Riley, who also drove a Saab on that event.

over in 1929 as managing director and was later joined by his brother WH Aldington, who was a superb publicist. HJ had always been an advocate of competition as a sales device and right through the 1930s took every opportunity to enter events himself and encourage others to do so with cars produced by his company. The culmination of his efforts were the successes that his cars gained, with himself at the wheel of one of them, during the Alpine Trials of 1932 to 1934.

The success of Donald Healey in the 1931 Alpine Trial had created a fair amount of publicity for this continental event in Britain, and Aldington decided that Frazer Nash should be there winning. He entered the 1932 event with two cars, one for himself and the other for AG Gripper, an experienced driver who had done previous Alpine Trials in Rileys. They both came through with flying colours and were awarded Coupes des Glaciers for unpenalised performances as individuals. The following year, four Frazer Nashes were entered and three of them, including Aldington, formed the Frazer Nash team which went for the team prize, in those days called a Coupe des Alpes. He again had an unpenalised run, but sadly one of his team mates, TAW Thorpe, had an argument with a roadside marker on the timed ascent of the Stelvio Pass and lost 92 points. This cost the Frazer Nash team the coveted team Coupe and they had to be content with finishing second to the Riley team. Aldington could have asked Thorpe to

retire, thus transferring Aldington to the class of individual competitors where he would have been awarded a Coupe des Glaciers, but this was a little too 'professional' for that age. It was a shame that his drive did not get greater recognition since he was one of only three drivers to be unpenalised and the others were driving a 1750cc Alfa Romeo and a 2300cc Bugatti, both of which were supercharged.

For the 1934 Alpine Trial organised by the Germans, who for some inexplicable reason had decided to run a much easier event, there were a total of six Frazer Nashes running of which three were in a team but Aldington had elected to run as an individual. Yet again, he had an unpenalised run – as did one of the other individual cars – but he also had the disappointment of seeing the team finish second, this time to BMW. The disappointment was not so great, however, since after the Alpine was finished he drove to the BMW factory and formulated a deal for importing their cars to Britain.

This entrepreneurial sense was never far below the surface in rally drivers of the period and it would be hard to find either a manufacturer who had not been involved in some kind of competition, or a successful driver who did not try his hand at car manufacture. Donald Healey was one of the most successful rally drivers of the 1930s and his career illustrates this very well indeed.

Healey was born in Cornwall in 1898, and when he had finished school he was sent to be an apprentice

with Sopwith Aviation, outside London. By being economical with the truth about his age, he entered the Royal Flying Corps and became a fighter pilot. He survived a bad crash in France and was sent back to England where he worked for the Aircraft Inspection Authority until the end of the war. In peacetime, he returned to Cornwall where he opened a garage business and started doing trials and other motoring competitions. He first came to notice in 1928 when he won the first long-distance trial in Britain. The following year he made an attempt at the Monte Carlo Rally and elected to start at Riga, capital of Latvia. Unfortunately, the snow was too severe for him to reach Riga so he put his car on a train to Berlin and started the rally from there. It was the kind of resourceful action that would have appealed to Victor Bruce. Even then, the 1929 rally was no piece of cake as conditions in Germany and eastern France were pretty atrocious with both snow and fog.

The following year, he finished seventh overall on the Monte Carlo with a Triumph, but then acquired a 4.5-litre Invicta and went for the first time to the Alpine Trial. There were only eight cars unpenalised at the finish and his was one of them. A Coupe des Glaciers at his first attempt! The trusty Invicta was taken on the 1931 Monte Carlo Rally with the chosen starting point being Stavanger in Norway, which it managed to reach. Not only that, it went on to win the rally with Healey setting fastest time on the Mont des Mules hill climb at the finish to clinch the result. The same car and driver combination went on to win a Coupe des Glaciers on the Alpine in 1931 and 1932.

He used the big car to compete in the first two RAC Rallies of 1932 and 1933 where he finished fifth and second in class respectively, but by then he had left the garage business and was working for Triumph in Coventry as their technical manager.

In effect, this meant that he was in charge of design and development, and the latter fitted in nicely with his sport. He took one of his new babies, a supercharged Triumph Dolomite, on the Monte Carlo of 1935 and was involved in a very nasty accident with a train on a level crossing which nearly killed him. His most successful design work for Triumph resulted in the Gloria and the Vitesse that was developed from it. He gave the new car its debut on the 1936 Alpine and won his fourth Coupe des Glaciers with it. But gradually, he let others take on the onus of driving the cars that he made in competitions. The Triumph company collapsed in 1939 and he spent his second war working for the Humber-Hillman company, developing armoured fighting vehicles. But in his spare time he was designing his own car which, as soon as peace broke out, he launched together with his own company, the Donald Healey Motor Company Ltd. For close on ten years it produced saloons and sports cars before its production was taken over by Austin, who produced Austin-Healeys right to the end of the 1960s. And those cars had an uncanny knack of winning Coupes des Alpes and other rallies that some think could only have been programmed into them by their creator.

When rallying emerged in the early 1950s from the post-war chaos of bombed cities and petrol ration-

ing, for a time it looked as if nothing had changed. The cars – for the most part – were pre-war designs, and the drivers were much the same bunch. But as the decade progressed and the works teams emerged and evolved, the professional driver arrived on the scene. Before this, a works driver might have been provided with a car, and might have had his entry fee paid together with a contribution towards hotel bills and petrol, but there was no suggestion that he might live off the proceeds as the top racing drivers were able to do.

It is difficult to point a finger and identify a particular person as the first works driver, because men like Walter Schock worked for Mercedes just as Donald Healey worked for Triumph. But when the completion of a full route reconnaissance became common practice and the works teams started to compete in more than just two or three events a year, it became impossible to fit in the demands of a rally season with

that of a conventional job. For many like Erik Carlsson, the answer was to work for Saab as a test driver – and do a lot of rallies in the course of testing. But there was always the need to prove one's ability first. Carlsson started, as did so many rally drivers of his era, on motorcycles. When he transferred to cars, he tried his hand at Volvos, Volkswagens and even Austin A40s before becoming very successful with an early Saab 92. It was his startling performances with that tiny car which earned him the sobriquet of 'Erik on the roof' – and the factory drive. He went on to achieve a hat-trick of wins on the RAC Rally and two magnificent wins on the Monte Carlo in 1962 and 1963. Better than anyone, Erik Carlsson personifies the transitional period between the serious amateur and the professional in rallying. His talent was so big that even today, some 25 years after his retirement, his ability and car control are the envy of many up-and-coming drivers.

LEFT Germany may not have produced a great quantity of rally drivers, but they certainly have produced some great ones and Walter Rohrl ranks highest amongst them. He is seen here in his Opel days, contemplating a tyre choice on the Brazilian Rally.

FAR LEFT Simo Lampinen and Arne Hertz on their way to winning the Scottish Rally for Saab in 1969. By virtue of having no front bumper, the car ran in the prototype category!

Carlsson was also the herald of a Scandinavian domination of rally driving that started in the early 1960s and is only just being challenged effectively today. His contemporaries in the Saab team such as Ove Andersson, Carl-Magnus Skogh, Ake Andersson and Carl Orrenius all came into Europe and set new standards of driving for others to emulate before moving on to other cars and other teams.

Ove Andersson, in particular, has had a very mixed and successful career. He moved from Saab to the Lancia team at its formative period and had a string of good results for them in 1966 and 1967. He then moved to Ford and, after winning several times with the Lotus Cortina MkII, gave the Escort Twin Cam its international debut on the Flowers Rally where he finished third overall. But it was with Alpine Renault that his greatest moments came. He won the Monte Carlo for them in 1971 and went on to add outright wins on the Acropolis, the Austrian Alpine and the San Remo all in the same year. Later still, he was to drive for Peugeot and won the Safari for them against the stiffest opposition in 1975. He had by this time established a relationship with the Toyota factory which led to him rallying their 1600 Celica and eventually founding Team Toyota Europe/Andersson Motorsport. This is the team that is currently running

Toyota's massive challenge for the World Championship and which has already given the Japanese manufacturer a Safari hat-trick and the first Spanish World Rally Champion Driver in the person of Carlos Sainz.

The French were the great rally competitors of the 1960s. It could have had something to do with so many of the important rallies taking place in France (Monte Carlo, Corsica, Geneva, Coupe des Alpes, Tour de France, Critérium Alpin, Rallye des Antibes, Critérium Neige et Glace, Mont Blanc, Critérium des Cevennes etc.) but it was also due to the interest of the French manufacturers in home-grown talent.

The Citroen team of René Cotton, himself an ex-rally driver, had the services of René Trautmann, Ido Marang, Paul Coltelloni, Jean-Claude Ogier, Bob Neyret and Lucien Bianchi. Little wonder that his ID 19s and DS 21s won most of the big rallies at one time or another and were a source of amazement to the drivers from outside France who saw how well those big cars could go, especially on rough roads. René Cotton died in 1971 and was succeeded as Citroen competition manager by his wife Marlene. Before that, Trautmann, whose first profession was that of photographer, went to Lancia where he proved equally at home with the ugly Flavia Zagato on rallies like the Coupe des Alpes or the Lyon–

LEFT After being one of the rally world's most successful drivers, Ove Andersson now runs its most potent team, Toyota Team Europe. His faith in the Japanese marque goes back over 15 years to when he started driving Celicas in Europe and South Africa.

TOP RIGHT Experience on the race track may be useful for a rally driver, but not everyone can benefit from such exalted tuition. Pat Moss is about to be shown the way round Brands Hatch in 1957 by none other than John Cooper, who later was to lend his name to a breed of Minis in which Pat won many rallies.

Charbonnières, both of which he won for the Italian marque. Jean-Claude Ogier stayed faithful to Citroen and retired when they stopped rallying the DS 21 in the 1970s. Neyret took up long distance events and distinguished himself with the short chassis prototype DS 21 in Morocco and on marathons like the London–Sydney and London–Mexico. Bianchi, a Belgian amidst the French, so nearly won the 1968 London–Sydney with Jean-Claude Ogier but they hit a non-competing car head on while in the lead just hours from the finish. A dashing but always polite professional, Bianchi was dead just a few weeks later as the result of a crash while testing an Alfa Romeo 33 on a circuit.

Sadly, France's most respected rally driver of that decade was also killed testing an Alfa Romeo 33 on a race track. That was Jean Rolland who had started his rally career back in the 1950s by co-driving his friend Gabriel Augias in a Peugeot 203. Indeed, many French drivers of that period started their career that way and graduated to the steering wheel from the map. Augias and Rolland won their class on the 1960 Monte Carlo and that same year the young Rolland took the Peugeot on the Coupe des Alpes with Augias guiding him. An offer followed from the French Alfa Romeo importer and he was soon involved in driving first Giulias, then the GTZ Tubolare, and ultimately the GTA. The partnership of Jean Rolland, Gabriel Augias and an Alfa Romeo came almost to symbolise the Coupe des Alpes and it has always been consid-

ered a great shame that he was never able to claim a Coupe d'Or for three consecutive unpenalised runs because a rare mechanical failure let him down in 1965. He did, however, win a Coupe d'Argent based on his ordinary Coupes gained in 1963, 1964 and 1966.

The fortunes of Alpine Renault rested with drivers such as Gérard Larrousse, Jean-François Piot, Jean Vinatier, Jean-Pierre Hanrioud, Jean-Claude Andruet and Mauro Bianchi, brother of Lucien. The three who were in the team during 1967 and 1968 – Larrousse, Andruet and Piot – became known as the Three Musketeers, and three more different personalities it would be hard to find.

Gérard Larrousse started rallying in 1961 with a Simca Aronde borrowed from his mother. He enjoyed success beyond expectation with his humble mount and was able to move up to a Renault Dauphine 1093 for the 1962 and 1963 seasons. Continuing success with that car led to the offer of a works Renault from François Landon. Larrousse was always the master of tarmac roads and his ability to get the very best performance out of quite low-powered machinery was exceptional. For example, on the 1963 Critérium des Cevennes, his Renault R8 Gordini did better times on some of the tests than Rolland's Alfa Romeo, Pierre Orsini's Alpine Renault and the Porsche GTS of Robert Buchet. Finally, an offer came from Jean Rédélé at Alpine Renault and a fabulous season in 1967 saw Larrousse win eight rallies.

Always the quiet, reflective type, Larrousse never seemed to have luck on his side in the big rallies. He was leading the Coupe des Alpes that year when, almost within sight of the finish, a connecting rod bolt broke. And on the ensuing Monte Carlo Rally, again after a finely judged drive, he was in the lead only to go off the road on the Col de la Couillole where some bored spectators had thrown snow on an otherwise dry road behind a blind corner. The following year, he moved to Porsche and did some rallies for them – finishing second once again on the Monte Carlo – before discovering prototype racing. Today, he runs his own Formula One race team.

If Larrousse was taciturn to the point where, when he was rallying with the equally quiet Maurice Gelin, he was referred to as '*un solitaire à côté d'un autre solitaire*', then Jean-Claude Andruet was the complete opposite. A lawyer by profession, he too started in Renaults and won the national novice's title in 1965. By 1967 he was in the Alpine Renault team and proving his worth with wins on seven French rallies and outright victory on the Tour de Corse a year later. His style was always one of great brio whether on tarmac or gravel roads, and when he made an error it was usually a large one. His moods swung visibly between the ecstatic and the miserable, but somehow everyone was always pleased to see Jean-Claude and listen to his tales of the rally. His win on the 1973 Monte Carlo for Alpine was one of the most popular with everyone in the sport. He went on to drive for several other teams and won the Tour de Corse for Lancia with a Stratos in 1974, bringing his total number of victories on that rally to three.

The third Musketeer was Jean-François Piot, who is best described as a popular eccentric with a great talent allied to an unshakeable personal conviction that he knew best. A Renault salesman in Paris, he started rallying to help further his sales and, like the other two, ended up in a Renault R8 Gordini. He finished seventh overall on the 1967 Monte Carlo and then went to Sweden where the locals laughed at the gangly youth and his French car. They stopped laughing when he finished 11th overall. He went on to show a natural ability on bad surfaces by winning first the San Remo and then the Three Cities Rally, results which put him second overall in the European Championship of that year. A good season in 1968 with the Alpine A110 saw him poached by Ford and he finished fourth for them on the Monte Carlo in 1969. He returned to Renault in 1973 and started driving Renault 12s and 17s in long distance rallies which became his forte. Sadly, he had never believed in wearing seat belts and on a rally in North Africa driving a Land Rover 110, he was thrown out and killed.

Two of the most remarkable French rally drivers were Jean Vinatier and Jean-Pierre Nicolas. Like so many of their countrymen, their careers centred on Renault and then Alpine. Vinatier started driving in 1951 – with a 2CV Citroen – and spent years doing all kinds of rallies as co-driver in any cars that came

ABOVE One of the original Alpine Renault 'musketeers' was Gerard Larrousse. When he moved to Porsche, he was introduced to sports car racing and ultimately to the world of Formula One where he currently manages his own team.

TOP One of the most talented – and enigmatic – of French rally drivers was the late Jean-François Piot. He won few of the major rallies, but always seemed to be able to produce a virtuoso performance in adverse conditions and was equally at home with front or rear-wheel drive.

RIGHT Four-time winner of the Monte Carlo Rally, Sandro Munari. His first win was in 1972 with a Lancia Fulvia, but his hat-trick came (1975–77) with the fabulous Lancia Stratos.

along. It was not until he won the Tour de Corse in 1964 with a Renault R8 Gordini that anyone seemed to take any notice of him. His most famous victories were an endorsement of how he could weigh up an entire rally and drive to win it. He won the Coupe des Alpes with an Alpine A110 in 1968 and 1969 and both times had an unpenalised run. Regrettably, the rally was not held in 1970, but in its final resurrection in 1971 he was again unpenalised and they awarded him the highly coveted Coupe d'Or for three consecutive Coupes, the missing year notwithstanding. Only two other such awards were made in the history of the event.

The affectionate soubriquet of 'Jumbo' was applied early in his career to Jean-Pierre Nicolas, and success in rallying did not seem to diminish him. His career started in 1963 with Jean-Pierre as co-driver to his father, an ex-works driver for Renault, as they competed in a Dauphine 1093, but he soon progressed to a Renault R8 Gordini of his own and then to the Alpine team. He won numerous rallies for them between 1968 and 1975, but the season which

best demonstrated his all-round ability was 1978. He did the Monte Carlo with the Almeras Team in a private Porsche 911 Carrera and won it in the face of the combined might of Fiat, Lancia, Opel and Renault. On the Safari and Bandama rallies, he drove a works Peugeot 504 Coupé V6, hitherto not as successful in those long distance events as the 504 saloon, and won both of them. His association with Peugeot continues today with a management role in their highly successful one-make championships.

Considering the image of feminine fragility so often promoted by the French, it came as something of a surprise to the rally world in the early 1980s to find a French lady winning World Championship rallies and coming second overall in the World Rally Drivers Championship of 1982. Michele Mouton is petite and dark and, like Pat Moss before her, was quite capable of challenging the men on equal terms. She started rallying in the South of France with a Renault Alpine A110 in the early 1970s and gradually widened her scope to compete in foreign events counting for the European Championship. She was

LEFT Miki Biasion has good cause to look happy – he has just won the Safari in 1988, the first Italian driver to claim that honour. He won it again the following year.

European Ladies Champion five times, once in the A110 and four times in a Fiat Abarth 131. She regularly finished in the top ten on the Monte Carlo Rally and won the Tour de France.

But her major breakthrough came when she was invited to join the new Audi team in 1981. She promptly won the San Remo for them and the following year added Portugal, Acropolis and Brazil to her tally. Perhaps the results which really astounded the establishment were her second place overall on the Lombard RAC Rally of 1982 and third on the Safari of 1983. When the Group B era ushered in the Sport Quattro, she found the cars less pleasant to drive, and for her last competitive season she drove for Peugeot in the German Rally Championship, winning six events outright and becoming German Rally champion. Her main preoccupation now, apart from her family, is the organisation of an annual rally event called the Race of Champions which brings together in one competition all past and present rally champions for a televised contest.

When Italian teams rose to prominence in the 1960s and 1970s, it was mainly on success gained with imported drivers. But the involvement of Lancia, Fiat and Alfa Romeo created enormous enthusiasm for rallying in Italy. From being quite low-key, their rallies increased in status and their drivers started to create international reputations for themselves. Leo Cella drove for the nascent Lancia team in the mid-1960s and won the Rally of the Flowers (later to be the San Remo Rally) for them twice in the new Fulvia. He tried his hand quite successfully at the RAC Rally and the Swedish Rally but his principal skill lay on tarmac where his neat style and full use of the road nearly won him the Tour de Corse in 1966. He moved to racing and was killed in an accident with an Alfa Romeo, so it was left to his inheritor, Sandro Munari, to win that particular event for Lancia in 1967.

Munari was the great Italian star of that period. His amazing win with the little Fulvia in Corsica, where he failed by the slender margin of a single minute to be the first man ever to finish unpenalised, was just the start of things. His career had a set-back when on the Monte Carlo of 1968 his Lancia was hit by a non-competing car in Yugoslavia. His inspirational co-driver Luciano Lombardini was killed and Munari suffered injuries that kept him out of a rally car for a year. He bounced back in 1969 with a win in the Italian championship and in 1970 surprised everyone by leading the Safari at almost half-distance in a Lancia Fulvia. But it was his win on the Monte Carlo Rally of 1972 with the Fulvia that confirmed his talent. Thanks to that success, Lancia launched its Stratos programme of which Munari was the number one driver. He won many events with it including three consecutive wins on the Monte Carlo (1975, 1976 and 1977), one in Corsica (1976) and one in San Remo (1974). When Lancia was absorbed into Fiat in the late 1970s, Munari never seemed happy with the Fiat Abarth 131 and he decided to stop rallying, apart from continuing to make a few trips to the Safari which he never contrived to win.

The classic product of Italy's healthy rally scene is double world champion Massino 'Miki' Biasion. All his early rallying was done in Opels, starting in the year that Munari retired. Biasion is quite a serious fellow and does not conform to the normal idea of a fizzy, expostulative character expected of an Italian driver. It is perhaps indicative of his stable temperament that he has always rallied with the same co-driver, Tiziano Siviero, except on one occasion when Siviero was ill. Biasion's career with Lancia started with an attack on the European Championship with a Rallye 037 in 1983, which was entirely successful. The following year, promoted to the main team, he finished sixth in the World Championship for Drivers.

In the year of the Group B cars, 1986, he won his first World Championship event, the Rally of Argentina, but it was the advent of the current Group A four-wheel drive machinery that saw him come into his own. Wins in Monte Carlo, Argentina and San Remo saw him finish second in the World Championship of 1987, which was just a prelude to his grand slams of the next two years. Outstanding among his achievements was a double victory on the Safari Rally (1988 and 1989) which he became the first Italian driver to win. And on his first visit to the Lombard RAC Rally in 1990, he finished third overall and threatens to be the first Italian driver to win that rally as well. He continues today to be a leading driver for the Lancia team at the age of only 34.

The Swedes were the leaders of the Scandinavian invasion in rallying. This commenced with the activities of Erik Carlsson, Carl Orrenius, Tom Trana, Gunnar Andersson, Bengt Soderstrom and Ove Andersson in the 1960s. Subsequently, Sweden has provided many notable drivers but two in particular stand out, if for no better reason than both having been World Rally Champions. Stig Blomqvist is a durable winner whose successful career stretches from his first Saab win on the Swedish Rally in 1971 through a World Championship for Audi in 1984 up until today when he has just started a contract with Nissan for another attack on the World Championship. Indeed, Blomqvist is one of the most amazingly versatile drivers with equal abilities, it would seem, in a front-wheel drive Saab, a rear-engined Lancia Stratos and the four-wheel drive Audi Quattro.

Equally versatile and successful is Bjorn Waldegaard, who started out as co-driver to a friend, Lars Helmer. Lars was rallying a Volkswagen Beetle and the two of them did several rallies together in the early 1960s before they somehow discovered that Waldegaard was the quicker of the two. Good results followed and soon support was on its way from Scania-Vabis, the Swedish VW importers. A couple of amazing demonstrations of speed on rallies like the RAC and Scania-Vabis were persuaded to move up

RIGHT In rallying, a working breakfast means just that. Stig Blomqvist deals with his Swedish meatballs while catching up on other people's stage times from team manager Torsten Aman.

into Porsches. Waldegaard won the Swedish Rally three times for Porsche (1968 to 1970) and the Monte Carlo twice (1969 and 1970). When Scania-Vabis and the Porsche factory stopped, he went on to accept drives from BMW, VW Austria, Citroen, Opel and Fiat before having a couple of years with Lancia, for whom he won the Swedish and then the San Remo twice in a Stratos. It was that last win which caused him to fall out with Lancia management and he transferred straight to Ford, for whom he was World Champion in 1979. While still with Ford, he drove some rallies with Mercedes and got more experience of the endurance rallies. He moved to Toyota in 1981, joining Ove Andersson's new team just as it started to field competitive cars. He is still driving for them and has won the Safari three times for Toyota.

It would not be fair to leave the Swedes without mentioning Harry Kallstrom, who was one of the quietest and most humorous rally drivers of his generation. Like Waldegaard, he also started in Volkswagens, using his own car which doubled as a driving school car during the week. By 1963 he had progressed to a VW 1500 S in which he astounded the rally world by finishing second overall on the RAC Rally at his first attempt. He then had a couple of seasons with a Cooper S which culminated in a repeat of the 1963 result on the 1966 RAC Rally. A season with a dealer-supported Renault R8 Gordini saw him competing in some of the major European rallies, which brought him to the attention of the expanding Lancia team. He stayed with them, always driving Fulvias, for six years during which time he won the RAC Rally twice (1969 and 1970) and took the European Championship in 1969. When the Stratos programme matured he moved to Datsun, for whom he so nearly won the Safari in 1973, losing only on a tie-decider with Shekhar Mehta. Since the beginning of the 1980s, Kallstrom has retired to northern Sweden, still driving, but this time in trucks.

Debatably, the most influential invasion from the Nordic countries has been that from Finland. It has certainly been the most numerous and has brought a clutch of World Rally Champions and superstars into the sport of rallying.

TOP RIGHT The 'professor' in his laboratory . . . Rauno Aaltonen was one of the first 'Flying Finns' and created a reputation for knowing a great deal about how to make a rally car work. His most recent attempt to win the Safari was with an Opel Kadett GSi in 1987.

RIGHT During his long and successful career, Bjorn Waldegaard has driven 11 different makes of car from Volkswagens to Ferraris, but his World Championship came for Ford in 1979.

LEFT Even superstars need to have their lights adjusted. Markku Alen gives his all on a rally and here he was concerned that nothing should keep him from winning the 1986 San Remo with the Lancia Delta S4.

It started in a small way with the original Flying Finn, Rauno Aaltonen, co-driving with Eugen Bohringer and using his expertise on gravel roads to help the Mercedes win in Poland and finish fourth on the Liège–Sofia–Liège. An invitation to drive for BMC on the Monte Carlo in a Mini Cooper nearly ended his life when he inverted the car and was only saved from the ensuing inferno by the prompt action of his co-driver Geoff Mabbs. The year of his first full contract with BMC was 1963 and it saw him come within an ace of winning the Liège for them in a Healey 3000. He set matters right on that event in 1964 and went on to become European Rally Champion in a Cooper S in 1965. His attention to detail both in the car and in his approach to the rallies became legendary and he was nicknamed 'the Professor'. When BMC stopped rallying in 1967 he had just won the Monte Carlo for them by 13 seconds from Ove Andersson in a Lancia. With no difficulty, Aaltonen arranged a season with Lancia and went on to drive for BMW, Datsun and Ford. As the man who first took a Mini to compete in the Safari, he loved that event and returned time and time again in a wide variety of cars to try and win it. Sad to say, despite 25 years of trying, that win still eludes him, though he was declared the winner briefly in 1981 before his appeal relating to a cancelled section was overturned and he had to be content with second place.

In the wake of Aaltonen came a flood of Finns, if

LEFT Timo Makinen was always prepared to discuss his driving techniques with other rallymen – in this case Gunnar Palm, co-driver to Bengt Soderstrom – but few drivers could summon the sheer nerve to implement them on the descent from a snow-covered Alp.

RIGHT A seventh win the 1000 Lakes Rally for Hannu Mikkola (*centre*) in 1983, after a rally-long battle with Stig Blomqvist (*right*) and Markku Alen.

that is the correct collective noun for a formidable bunch of rally drivers. Timo Makinen joined BMC in the same year as Aaltonen and his first experiences were also with an Austin Healey 3000. Makinen's drives in that car saw him become acknowledged as the man who could drive it faster than anyone else no matter what the conditions. He finished second to Aaltonen on the 1965 RAC Rally in a particularly snowy year, but he had already demonstrated that he was equally at home in the front-wheel drive Cooper S by winning the Monte Carlo Rally of that same year in the most atrocious weather conditions. He also proved on that occasion, as on many others during his career, that he was adept at repairing the car by changing a set of points on a tight road section. He went on to 'win' the Monte Carlo of 1966 only to be disqualified in the lighting scandal and completed his hat-trick of 1000 Lakes victories in 1967 with a Cooper S. When British Leyland closed their doors in 1969, Timo migrated to Ford and took a hat-trick of wins on the RAC Rally between 1973 and 1975 as well as winning the 1000 Lakes for them in 1973.

Also a three-time winner of his home event, the 1000 Lakes Rally, was Simo Lampinen whose career started with Saab in the early 1960s, but he changed to Lancia in 1970 after some freelance drives with the DAF team. His wins were nearly all with front-wheel drive cars with which he felt very much at home, but after winning the Rallye du Maroc in 1972 with a

Lancia Fulvia, he diversified and was successful with such cars as the Lancia Stratos, Fiat Abarth 131 and the Peugeot 504.

Following hard on the heels of these three pioneers was Hannu Mikkola who came to the attention of the world outside Finland by his performances at the wheel of a Volvo 142S. He was offered a drive on the 1968 Monte Carlo Rally by the Datsun team, and when he actually finished in the unwieldy Fairlady he was promptly approached by Lancia and Ford simultaneously. After a couple of drives for the Italian team, the Ford deal won through and he proceeded to give them three straight wins on the 1000 Lakes. He also won the World Cup for them in 1970 and became a history maker when he and Gunnar Palm won the East African Safari in 1972, as they were the first overseas drivers to win that rally. He left Ford to drive for Fiat, Toyota and Mercedes before returning to drive for Ford in 1979 and 1980. But his golden years were with Audi, who employed him to drive their startling new Quattro. He helped them to win the Manufacturer's Championship in 1982 and won the Driver's title for himself in 1983. With blond good looks and a quiet personality, Mikkola was a different kind of champion to the more extrovert Finns that had preceded him.

When it comes to charisma, however, the Finn who really has the superstar approach is Markku Alen. Like Mikkola, he started in big Volvos and went

first to Ford, but was very quickly snapped up by the Fiat/Lancia combine with whom he spent 15 years driving all that they had to offer. During that time, he and his regular co-driver Ilkka Kivimaki notched up 19 World Championship victories and helped both Fiat and Lancia to a total of ten World Championships, but Markku has never managed to win the Driver's title. He did have it in his grasp for ten days at the end of 1986, but then the results of the San Remo were annulled and his crown passed to Juha Kankkunen. It is Kankkunen who today leads the efforts of the Finns to stay in the vanguard of world rally drivers. He came into rallying in 1979 and after signing for Toyota in 1983, he shook the establishment by winning the Safari at his first attempt. Since then he has won two World Driver's Championships driving for Peugeot in 1986 and for Lancia in 1987.

But it is impossible to leave the Finns without mentioning one who is sadly no longer with us. In 1968, Pauli Toivonen became the second Finn to put his name on the European Rally title driving a factory Porsche 911 T. Twelve years later, his son Henri astounded everyone by winning the RAC in a Sunbeam Lotus at the tender age of 24. He went on to drive for Lancia after three seasons of hectic European events with first Opel and then Porsche. With an instantly likeable personality and loved by the *aficionados* for his visually alarming style of driving, Henri won the RAC Rally on the debut of the four-wheel-

drive Delta S4 and went on to win the Monte Carlo in 1986. But before his talent could see its full flowering, he and his American co-driver Sergio Cresto were killed in an horrific accident while leading the Tour de Corse.

The tale of the Finns is never ending and there are still two more World Champions from that small country to be mentioned. The first is Timo Salonen who, despite the fact that he has been in top-class rallying since 1976, seems only now to be hitting his best form. Like so many others, he spent a couple of years with Fiat before signing for a long spell with Datsun, achieving some remarkable results with their 160J. When Peugeot came to choose their team for the 1985 season, Salonen was not their first choice but he showed them his gratitude by winning the Driver's Championship and helping them to two consecutive Manufacturer's Championships. When Peugeot stopped competing in World Championship rallies, Salonen moved to Mazda where he always seemed to be able to extract the best from a car that was noticeably slower than its rivals. For the 1991 season, he transferred to Mitsubishi.

Then there is the truly amazing Ari Vatanen, whose reputation for speed is blemished by the occasional accident but whose personality is so charming that he can be forgiven almost anything. His World Championship came in 1981 as a consequence of driving for Ford, with whom he had a long and successful association. After a period at Opel for whom he won the Safari, he joined Peugeot and was the driver responsible for their early wins with the 205 T16. An accident in Argentina in 1985 nearly killed him, and his physical and mental recovery from that was both long and difficult. It was not until 1987 that Vatanen emerged once again at the wheel of a Peugeot to win the Paris–Dakar. Rallye-Raids have become his forte but drives with Ford and Mitsubishi have shown that he has lost none of his speed on European events which he continues to do alongside his long distance commitment to Citroen.

Germany has always had a greater preoccupation with racing than with rallying, but that has not prevented there being German rally drivers of the very highest quality. Walter Schock collected European laurels twice for Mercedes, in 1956 and 1960, but did not endear himself to the sporting community by withdrawing from the RAC Rally of 1960 when his only rival for the championship, René Trautmann, crashed his Citroen. The man who was to replace him as a Mercedes works driver was Eugen Bohringer, who started rallying when he was 37 years old. His first major event was the Monte Carlo Rally of 1960 where he finished second behind Schock, and in 1962 he won the European Championship for Mercedes. But it was his wins for that marque on the Marathon de la Route (Liège–Sofia–Liège) in 1962 and 1963, and his fantastic drive to second place on the very snowy Monte Carlo Rally of 1965 in a Porsche 904 GTS, that made his unique reputation.

Twelve years after Bohringer's European Championship win, that title went to another German driver, Walter Röhrl. Tall and ascetic where Bohringer was short and stocky, Röhrl's approach to rally driving has been very different from the exuberance of the Scandinavians, but no less effective for it. Starting with some sensational drives for Ford Germany in a Capri 2600, he secured a drive with the Opel tuner, Irmscher, and won the European Championship for them in 1974. By 1978 he had joined the Italians, and drove Fiat Abarth 131s and a Lancia Stratos on his way to securing the World Championship for Drivers in 1980. He drove for Opel, Lancia and Audi in rapid succession, winning his second World Championship in 1982 with an Ascona 400. A truly remarkable feature of his list of results is that he has won the Monte Carlo Rally four times, equalling the record of Sandro Munari, but also effectively surpassing it since his four wins came in four very different cars: Fiat Abarth 131, Opel Ascona 400, Audi Quattro and Lancia Rallye 037. Now officially retired, Röhrl's last season of competitive driving was spent helping Audi win the 1990 German touring car championship as partner to Hans Stuck at the wheel of an Audi 200 V8.

Over the years, British drivers have been at or near the head of the action on rallies all over the world, but major championship success always seems to elude

RIGHT The Matador cometh . . . World Champion in 1990, Carlos Sainz began the following season by winning the Monte Carlo Rally for the first time.
BELOW Is it Finns first and rivals second? Timo Salonen (right) and Henri Toivonen exchange banter at the *parc fermé* in Monaco during the 1986 rally.

ABOVE An unequalled record of success in rallying belongs to John Buffum who, thanks to his dedicated pursuit of 11 North American rally championship titles and his European programmes, has won well over 100 international rallies during his career.

them. Paddy Hopkirk, who for so many years was one of a trio of BMC brigands that took European rallying by storm with the Mini Coopers, won the Monte Carlo (1964), Austrian Alpine (1964), Acropolis (1967) and Coupe des Alpes (1967) but was never in the hunt to dislodge the Scandinavian hordes. Vic Elford, whose Monte win with a works Porsche in 1968 inspired great hope, won the GT category of the European Championship in 1967 with a similar car but eventually went over to motor racing. During that period, the most consistent British rally driver was Pat Moss, who was rarely content to be chasing the Ladies Award and preferred to be going for outright victory. She made the switch from show jumping horses to wrestling with rally cars in the late 1950s when she put in some excellent drives in cars like Morris Minors. But it was once she got her hands on the Austin Healey 3000, originally the 100/6, that her talent was given its true chance. Her performance in winning the Marathon de la Route (Liège-Rome-Liège) in 1960 would be enough on its own to establish her in the rally drivers' Hall of Fame. Over the years, she racked up results in Mini Coopers, Saabs, Ford Cortinas and Lancias that were the envy of many male drivers and she showed that she was equally good at long distance events like the Safari as she was in European sprint rallies. Today, married to Erik Carlsson, she has once again concentrated her efforts on the world of horses, though the principal rider is now Susy, their daughter.

It was Roger Clark who came nearest to fulfilling British hopes of major worldwide success when he took the new Ford Escort Twin Cam to victories in the Tulip and Acropolis rallies of 1968. Like some of the French rally stars, Clark had used a Renault Dauphine at the start of his career and then moved via a Mini Cooper to a Ford Cortina GT. It was in the Cortina that he made a habit of winning just about everything in the British Isles with the sole exception of the RAC Rally. Unfortunately, his success with the Escort came at a time when drivers like Timo Makinen and Hannu Mikkola were also riding high at Ford, so the lad from Leicestershire had to take a back seat when it came to World Championship events. However, in typically irreverent fashion, Clark won the RAC Rally in 1972 for Ford, the first Briton to have done so since Gerry Burgess won with a Ford Zephyr in 1959. That was enough to keep him rallying with Ford but even a second win in the RAC Rally in 1976 did not see him elevated to the A-team. He remains the only British rally driver to have won a World Championship Rally and is now grooming his son Matthew to have a crack at the title.

Any look at the rally drivers of the world would not be complete without a pair of gentlemen who are two of the best ambassadors that the sport could have. Rallying is not as big a sport in the USA and Canada as it is in Europe, but the rallies that are held in North America are fought out with all the vigour of World Championship rallies, as the rally circus used to discover in the years when the Press On Regardless, the Criterium de Quebec and the Rideau Lakes were WRC qualifiers. The man who dominated North American rallying for some 15 years was John Buffum. He discovered rallying while serving with the armed forces in Germany and his first major event was the 1969 Monte Carlo where he finished 12th in a Porsche 911. On returning to the US and his home in Vermont, Buffum took to rallying first his trusty Porsche and then a Ford Escort RS. It was during this period that he earned the sobriquet of 'Stuff'em'. He went on to win an amazing total of 106 championship rallies which included European rallies such as Cyprus (1984) and Sachs Winter (1983). He was the SCCA US Rally Champion 11 times and the North American Rally Champion nine times. After he stopped driving the Escort in 1976, he drove a Triumph TR7 for four years before migrating to

LEFT 'Thanks, pal' . . . One of the more formidable combinations in 1960s rallies was that of Paddy Hopkirk, Henry Liddon and a white and red Cooper S, seen here after their Monte win of 1964.

Audi and various species of Quattro. Indeed, he came several times to Europe and Africa to help the Audi team and drove a three-seater Quattro as a chase car on rallies like the Ivory Coast. Though he was serious about his rallying, John Buffum managed to appear somewhat laid-back about it all. He was always ready with a word of advice or even practical assistance so that he was known and welcomed just about everywhere.

The other gentleman is Shekhar Mehta who hails from Kenya via Uganda and India. As an East African resident, it was only natural that his early experiences should be on the Safari and it was there that he quickly graduated from an old BMW into competitive Datsuns. He won the event for the first time in 1973 driving a 240Z, and used this win to persuade Datsun to give him some drives outside Africa. Lancia adopted him for the 1974 Safari and he became one of the few drivers ever to get a Fulvia to the finish. Again, he persuaded Lancia to let him gain experience in Europe and took one of their Beta Coupés to fourth place on the San Remo, This wider experience was to stand him in good stead when he rejoined Datsun in 1975, as he went on to win four Safaris in a row for them between 1979 and 1982. This brought his total of Safari wins to five which, not surprisingly, has not yet been beaten

Mehta did much of the ground work for Peugeot's attack on the Safari in 1985 and narrowly escaped from a development car that caught fire while testing. Peugeot did not win the rally either year that they entered it, but Mehta had the satisfaction of finishing eighth in 1986 with a 205 T16, and the work that he had done for the Safari enabled Peugeot quickly to switch their attention to Rallye-Raids when Group B ended in December 1986. It was while competing for Peugeot on one of these events, the Rallye des Pharaohs, in October 1987 that Mehta rolled his car while leading and severely damaged his back. Since then, he has not indulged in any serious driving, but his interest in rallying has not dimmed one iota and he has taken on an interest in helping to run the Safari. His infectious laugh and good humour look like being a part of the international rally scene for many years to come.

Finally, one comes to the current World Rally Champion – Carlos Sainz. It would appear to be true that, thankfully for those who have to work in the sport, World Rally Champions are created with a pleasant nature and a sunny temperament. Certainly Carlos Sainz seems to have sprung from that mould – and sprung is the right word as it has taken him just six full seasons to become World Rally Champion. He started rallying when he was 18, but for a while it seemed as though racing might captivate him. He won the Spanish national racing series for Renault R5s in 1983 and came to Brands Hatch to compete in the Formula Ford Festival. He finished fourth in his first heat having never driven a single-seater before and the experience was such that he thought to seek a budget for a full Formula Three season. However, Renault Spain had other ideas and proposed that he should do a programme of rallies with an R5 Turbo. He won his regional championship for them in 1984 and went on to be runner-up in the Spanish Championships of 1985 and 1986. For 1987, he transferred his allegiance once again to a Ford but this time it was a Sierra Cosworth with which he won the Spanish Championship outright both that year and the next.

Wisely, he was taking the opportunity at the same time to do major rallies outside Spain such as the RAC, Corsica and the 1000 Lakes. This meant that at the end of 1988 he was much sought after; he chose to go to Toyota as they had, in his opinion, the best car and were offering him a full programme. Once he got used to the full potential of the Celica GT4, results were not long in coming and only a mechanical problem denied him a win on the Lombard RAC Rally of 1989. His 1990 season was a dream, as he went from winning his first World Championship rally on the Acropolis to a win in New Zealand and then an amazing defeat of the Finns on their home rally, the 1000 Lakes. The final touch for his championship year was to win the Lombard RAC Rally outright, and he started 1991 with wins on the Monte Carlo and Portuguese rallies.

It is interesting that the world of racing nearly caught Carlos Sainz. If asked to what he attributes his phenomenal success as a rally driver, he will modestly praise the team and the car that he drives. But he brings to the modern rally car the qualities that are needed to extract from it the top levels of performance. His approach is 100 percent professional, from the question of keeping himself completely fit to understanding just how the various suspensions, transmissions and tyres will affect the way that the car performs. Above all, his driving style does not produce the extrovert over-committed slides that characterised the rally winners of the previous couple of decades. That is not the way to be fast with modern machinery and Sainz uses an excellent memory for roads coupled with the pace note skills of his co-driver, Luis Moya, to produce strings of fastest times which look effortless to the spectator. He did his first Safari in 1990 when he finished a commendable fourth overall. It will be interesting to see how he progresses in rallies like the Safari that, despite practice, still require a higher degree of improvisation than the European type of event.

The signs are that he will follow in the footsteps of Miki Biasion and add the Safari to his laurels before many seasons have passed. Rallying is full of challenges, every one a little different from the last – not unlike the drivers that compete in them.

CHAPTER 4

MORITURI TE SALUTANT

ORGANISERS AND REGULATIONS

It must have been in the mid-1930s that competitors in motor rallies first started looking at the event regulations with a view to defeating rather than obeying them. In rallying, there has always been an element of the competitor versus the organiser instead of competitor versus competitor. This is probably thanks to the fact that, on a rally, the competitor is tackling the route with no other rally car in sight, or at least very rarely. In racing, he would only have to look a few feet either way to find out what his rivals were doing.

The attitude of some rally organisers has helped to foster this attitude, especially in those events where the challenge set by the organiser in his choice of roads, schedules and methods of marking was seen to be the main adversary. If one takes an Alpine Trial, the top prize of a Coupe des Glaciers was given to someone who completed the route without penalty. This was not affected in any way by the performances of other competitors. Consequently, the rally driver tended to see himself as being in competition with the route and schedule – and with the rally organiser. The same could almost be said of the Marathon de la Route, where the indefatigable M. Garot let it be known that, as far as he was concerned, his ideal rally had but one finisher who was, of course, the winner.

In most modern rallies, this is not the case. The adoption of special stages and the rapid communication of their results to the competitors has meant that, more than ever before, they are involved in a straight fight with one another. The disappearance of the classic road rallies like the Coupe des Alpes and the Marathon de la Route has all but eliminated the situation where the driver feels that his main challenge comes from the event. There have been exceptions to this such as the amazing scenes that followed the finish of the 1966 Monte Carlo Rally, when the organisers did everything in their power to exclude the Cooper S that had won since they believed that it must somehow be illegal. They ended up throwing out all three Cooper S's plus a Lotus Cortina and a Hillman Imp for having non-standard headlamp bulbs and dipping systems.

In the case of the new endurance events, the Rallye-Raids such as Paris–Dakar or Paris–Moscow–Peking, the event can be seen as a challenge to get to the finish issued by the organiser to the entrant, but the way that such events are structured, with generous amounts of service time and a relaxed schedule away from the meat of each day's run, mean that there is every possibility of doing so. It is not the object of the organisers to try to reduce the field to a very small number of runners, although they do occasionally miscalculate, as happened in 1988 when 251 of the entries in the Paris–Dakar went over the maximum lateness time at the end of the first African stage. The only major event to retain the old style of pressure all the way is the Safari, and there are signs that even there a change has been wrought on the 1991 event with longer rest halts and the route split

up into more digestible pieces. We should look, then, at the preparations made by the competitor and the organiser for a modern rally and see where, if at all, they come into conflict.

For the competitor, all the initial decisions are about compatibility and suitability. It is possible to contemplate going off and tackling the Monte Carlo Rally in your mother's shopping car, but there are many things which could, and probably would, stand in the way. The Monte Carlo is an international rally which is part of the FIA (*Fédération Internationale de l'Automobile*) World Championship. In order to be able to drive in it, the crew need to be in possession of international competition licences which are valid for rallying. These are issued on behalf of FISA (*Fédération Internationale du Sport Automobile*) by the national automobile club and each of those may have slightly different qualification requirements for the international licence. Normally, it means that the prospective competitor has to complete successfully on a certain number of national rallies, thus demonstrating his competence at a lower level, before they issue him with a full international licence. All members of the crew will need the same type of licence, and if the entry is being made by a person who is not going to be one of the crew or, say, by a company that is sponsoring the entry, then they will need to purchase an entrant's licence. This is quite important because when the entrant's licence is taken out in the

PREVIOUS PAGE Let no one say that rallies do not visit areas with stunning scenery. Central Greece has more than its fair share, and these rally spectators have more than Stig Blomqvist's driving style to appreciate.

LEFT Security and control of servicing can be major problems for organisers whose route passes through remote areas. On the 1969 Safari, this Peugeot is passing through major habitation.

BELOW As well as spectator safety, the rally organiser has to think of reducing danger to the rally crews from 'natural hazards'. The straw bales would probably not have cushioned Bjorn Waldegaard's BMW 2002 TTi very much had he not taken the jump correctly.

LEFT The modern rally car is sufficiently noisy – especially now that four-wheel drive has tripled transmission noise – that intercoms are needed even for normal conversation between special stages.

sponsor's name, then that name appears in the programme, entry lists, and in the final results. The purchase of the entrant's licence often includes a permit which allows the car to be decorated with sponsors' names and logos within certain limits. For instance, most countries ban 'offensive material' while France bans advertising alcohol and Germany does the same for tobacco products.

The next thing to decide is whether the car is suitable, and indeed whether it would be acceptable to the rally organisers. The subject of homologation will be discussed in the next chapter, but in essence all cars that compete in rallies have to possess a valid homologation form endorsed by FISA. This is the car's 'licence' and means that a specific model does belong to one of the categories of car that are admitted to the rally. These categories are listed in the regulations for the rally along with all the other information that is specific to the event. The homologation form is compiled by the manufacturer of the car and they normally complete them only for cars which they consider to be suitable for competition. More important still is the fact that the homologation is only valid for five years after the production of that model ceases. Consequently, if mother's shopping car is a Ford Escort Mk I, there will be no possibility of an entry for the Monte Carlo Rally.

For a works team, these steps in the process of entering a rally would be much more straightforward, as they would have a team of fully licensed drivers at their disposal and a workshop of suitable cars. From time to time, however, they would be faced with the task of choosing a new rally car because a manufacturer always likes to be rallying a current model. In the same way, their driver line-up would change occasionally, either when someone left them for a better offer from another team, or when they felt the need to strengthen their team by acquiring new talent. The most frequent cause of drivers moving

ABOVE Striped tape and plenty of information help to guide spectators to safe areas. The one thing that the tape fails to protect them from is the dust, which gets everywhere.

LEFT Scandinavian winter rallies have few problems with security either for closing the roads or in terms of large gatherings of spectators. In fact, the best way to spectate is by travelling with a ski-doo or on skis cross-country.

between teams is when one manufacturer comes up with a new and more competitive rally car and there is a general migration towards it. But generally speaking, loyalties seem to last longer in rallying than in motor racing and many drivers spend the majority of their careers with one team.

Once the entrant is sure that he has an eligible crew and an acceptable car, he can go ahead and make the entry. This will involve getting the entry form from the organisers and filling it in with all the required details of the car and the crew. For an international event taking place outside the entrant's country of origin, the form will next have to go to the governing body in his own country for endorsement by them before being sent on to the organising club. Normally, the entry fee has to be paid at the same time, unless there is some form of dispensation for foreign competitors. Then there is a wait until the closing date for entries is past, at which time the organiser will send out letters of acceptance to those crews whose entries have been accepted. Some rallies are oversubscribed and the surplus entrants are asked if they would like to go on a stand-by list in case accepted entries fall out before the rally starts. Once a letter of acceptance is received, a contract exists between the entrant and organiser and, short of the event being cancelled, it will be honoured.

Next comes the matter of preparing the car for the rally. It is necessary to make a careful study of the specific regulations for the event issued by the organisers, and if the rally is using international categories the considerably more formidable Appendix J of the FIA's Sporting Code must also be scrutinised. This lists all the compulsory modifications that must be carried out, as well as detailing the limits of any tuning or other preparation that the entrant may have in mind. This latter exercise must be done with the homologation form alongside the regulations as there are many cross-references between them. In the case of national events where international categories may not be respected, reference may have to be made to national regulations published separately from Appendix J.

The mandatory items that will have to be fitted to the car are normally those concerned with safety: a roll cage to protect the crew, fire extinguishers, master switches for the electrical system that also shut down the engine, seat belts, protection for fuel and brake pipes, laminated windscreen, safety fuel tank, and towing eyes on the front and rear of the car. Without those, the scrutineers who examine the car before the rally will not allow it to start. At the same time, they will want to see the crash helmet and fireproof overalls that are going to be used by the crew. There are also checks during the event that this personal equipment is being used on the special stages. John Buffum and Doug Shepherd were summarily thrown out of sixth place overall on the 1978 Criterium du Quebec when it was reported that they had completed a special stage without wearing crash helmets. They had taken them off to change a punctured wheel on their Triumph TR7 V8 during a special stage and, in their hurry to waste no more time, had overlooked the matter of replacing them.

Then there is the question of how much other preparation is going to be carried out on the car. If it has been entered in international Group N, this means that very little can be done by way of modifica-tion from standard. The engine, gearbox and axle can be stripped and the assembly checked, but no machining can be done to the parts except to certain components that can be modified within the limits spelled out on the homologation form. The suspension units can be changed for different settings and a certain amount of welding may be done to strengthen the bodyshell, but all the standard trim must be retained. The seats can be swopped for competiton seats but the rest of the internal trim has to be left alone, except where the roll cage and other accessories need to be fitted. All this means that the rules have to be read quite carefully, especially as the event regulations may allow some waivers. For instance, bigger petrol tanks are sometimes allowed so that the car is able to cover longer distances on rallies where petrol stations are infrequent.

For 'rough' events, some form of comprehensive underbody protection will be necessary to protect vulnerable items such as the engine sump, the gearbox casing, the drive train and any pipes that may run under the car. The generic term for these protectors is 'sump guard'. The early ones were usually made from steel and were there purely to protect the engine sump. As the design of these guards became more complex and their duties increased, they started to be made of aluminium alloy or from cast magnesium alloy. In this form, they were used as a kind of sledge under the front of the car so that

should it come up against stones, packed snow or ice, the effect would be to lift the car up and over the obstacle rather than hitting it head on. These days, such protection is manufactured from a variety of plastics, with the ultra-light and ultra-strong kevlar-carbonfibre a frequent choice of works teams. Complete underskins for rally cars now only weigh a few kilograms but can provide all the protection offered by the sump guards of a decade ago which weighed over 40 kilograms.

If the car is entered in international Group A, which is invariably the case with works teams, then much wider modifications are allowed, and items such as suspension components and brakes may be freely homologated for a particular model by its manufacturer. Since the factory team will have developed and homologated these parts for the model that they are entering themselves in competition, it is wise for the private entrant to choose that model for his own entry as, hopefully, all the special parts will be available through the factory's competition department. Most manufacturers, quick to see the commercial potential of such sales and wishing to encourage private owners to use their cars for rallying, have departments allied to their works team which sell these parts. They have staff who are able to offer advice to private entrants on what would be the appropriate suspension or gear ratio to use for a specific event.

The possibilities which exist for improving a car under the Group A regulations are quite considerable. The engine tuning is able to double the horsepower of the standard unit, while six and sometimes seven-speed gearboxes are available to transmit that power to the wheels. It is not surprising, then, that a fully prepared Group A car can cost up to four times the new value of the standard car on which it is based. Certainly, the amount of detail work done by a works team on the preparation of its cars cannot be equalled by private entrants, which is why so many of them stick to Group N. A reliable Group N car can often be sufficiently competitive to chase the factory cars into the top ten on all but the biggest rallies.

There is another golden rule to follow here and that is to keep things simple during the preparation of the car and not go overboard in the changes that are carried out. Too many private entrants seek to outdo works teams by making radical changes to the suspension and seeking their own solutions to problems. While such independence is to be admired, in reality a private entrant cannot match the development budgets of modern works teams who carry out extensive testing to come up with spring rates and damper settings that actually work. Rather than try to outdo them in such areas, the private entrant is better advised to attend to the detail preparation of his car in relation to the strength of the bodyshell, the effectiveness and reliability of the fuel and electrical

RIGHT It is essential to wear clothing appropriate to the event, although modern safety rules tend to enforce the use of flameproof overalls. This was not the case in 1932 when this Ford V8 and its four-man crew went topless to Monaco.

LEFT When competing in a stark prototype like the Ligier JS2, considerable thought must be given to the equipment taken in the car, as there will be very little room to stow it safely.

RIGHT The Italian spectators in Tuscany always give the competitors some worries. This is Juha Kankkunen in 1986, trying to keep his Peugeot between the stone wall and the human wall.

systems, and the elimination of unnecessary weight within the limits prescribed by the regulations.

Group N or Group A, standard or super-tuned, there are plenty of things which need to be done to make the car fit for a rally. The co-driver will need some type of odometer fitted with which to navigate from the instructions provided by the organisers or from his own route notes. He will also need a map light with which to read those instructions at night. If more than one spare wheel is being carried then it needs to be firmly fixed in place, but not so that it

cannot be reached quickly. Some form of special jack will need to be carried because the normal jack provided with a standard car is not designed to work when the car is on loose or uneven surfaces. It sometimes happens that the punctured tyre has come off the rim, so the jack needs to be able to lift the car a much greater distance than is normal in order to be able to fit the spare wheel. To achieve this, separate jacking points are needed. These should be fitted above the lowest point of the bodyshell and allied to a mechanical jack with almost infinite lifting powers.

The Bilstein 'monkey-up-a-stick' jack is popular with rallymen for just those reasons. Finally, the electrical system of the car may need rewiring to take the extra current needed for spot and fog lamps, and its fuses may be replaced by circuit breakers that can be re-set, thus obviating the need to find spare fuses in the dark or when you are in a hurry.

The preparation of the rally car also extends to the question of the service vehicles that will tend it during the rally, since they need to carry spare parts that are appropriate to its preparation. It is no good carry-

ing replacements that do not fit or have the wrong internals. Ford Motor Company used to run an advertisement in conjunction with Shell which stated that 'the man who loads the service vans is as important as the rally driver.' The actual message of the advertisement was that he was the one who put the Shell oil and lubricants in the van, but the more general point is also correct. For a works team, the provision of service to their rally cars has now reached staggering proportions, but lesser mortals can get by with far more modest support if the planning is done correctly. The essentials are petrol and tyres; the rest is luxury and insurance against follies by the crew or fragility of the car.

With the entry on the rally made, and the car preparation in hand, it would be easy to think that there was nothing left but to turn up on the day of the start. A true amateur might decide to do just that because he lacks the finance to do a complete reconnaissance, but certainly the factory teams take their independent survey of the route extremely seriously and make a major part of their expenditure in that area. It is a big help to know where one is going when the pressure is on during an event. A drive round the entire route of a rally prior to taking part certainly guarantees not getting lost and will maximise the enjoyment from the investment of entering the rally.

Fortunately, on a modern rally, the organiser does not leave it to chance that you might be able to find the correct route from a list of village names or road numbers given at the back of his regulations. That is what used to happen on the majority of European events as little as 15 years ago. Indeed, it was rumoured that the organisers of the Marathon de la Route only ever did one recce of their Liège–Sofia–Liège and that, ever after, they just placed the controls at the same locations and left the rally crews to find their way between them. The effect of this was that teams would go and find the shortest way between the control locations, with the result that very often cars would be using different routes on the day of the rally. This system had its swansong on the 1974 Austrian Alpine where the route was not adequately defined in several places despite the organisers issuing a printed map and a road book. In a botched attempt to try and make only one route available – that chosen by his cars – the Alpine Renault team manager blocked one of the alternative routes which had been selected by the BMW and Fiat teams. At the end of the rally, protests flew about and it took a tribunal of FISA to come up with a set of results – six months after the rally had finished.

Fortunately, a system of setting out the route of a rally without recourse to road numbers, maps or village names was already being used by one major rally. It was called a Tulip road book, after the rally that was using it. What would happen was that the Tulip organiser, Piet Nortier, would take a trip round his route and as he went he would sketch each junction, together with any sign-posts, and note down the

ABOVE It is always difficult to judge whether it is better to stop and change a punctured tyre or to continue prudently. Presumably Ronald Holzer's Lancia Delta did not have two spare wheels.

LEFT Too many helicopters flying around a rally can lead to all kinds of trouble, but there is no doubt that the film shot from them can bring the sport to a much wider audience.

mileage from the start of the section. This became a popular way of accurately defining the route of any rally and ensured that there was only one official route that did not depend on exploration by the competitors. It also meant that if someone did take an alternative route that turned out to be shorter, then he was clearly off route and could be excluded if caught. Today, it is rare to find any international

rally that does not provide such a road book to its competitors.

The idea of such a road book with schematic drawings did not start with the Tulip Rally, as an examination of the 'road chart' issued by the Royal Scottish Automobile Club on the occasion of the Prince Henry Cup of 1911 shows quite clearly. This event, jointly run by the Royal Automobile Club and the Imperial

superb little drawings of churches. It was a road book of which a modern organiser could have been proud.

But being supplied with such a comprehensive document does not remove the desirability of going round the route beforehand. Doing so enables the crew to be familiar with the tricky bits of navigation and to add any personal notes that might be of help on the rally. Although there is no encouragement given to people to speed around the rally route before the event takes place, the prudent crew tend to drive each section at a steady pace and take a note of the elapsed time. This gives them some idea as to which sections may be difficult to achieve in the time allowed when it comes to the rally.

Even more beneficial is to drive over the special stages and make pace notes of them. Pace notes came into being in the early 1960s with the Mercedes and BMC teams. They were foreshadowed by the use of a system for grading the severity of bends used by Stirling Moss and Denis Jenkinson to win the 1955 Mille Miglia road race for Mercedes. In the next few years, various works teams were to adopt some kind of system for identifying the sharp corners on a special stage or test. Their systems varied from blobs of paint on walls to measuring the distance of the bend from the start of the test. The idea to take this further and to use shorthand notes to improve on the accuracy of a driver's memory when dealing with hundreds of kilometres of mountain roads was a natural extension of rally reconnaissance. The difference was that, instead of noting down that a road over a particular mountain was 'very fast and open going up, but with hairpin bends starting from kilometre 7, summit at kilometre 12 then narrow and twisty on the way down, slippery under the trees before the finish

Automobile Club of Germany, was held to commemorate the Coronation of King George V and went from Edinburgh to Windermere. Each competitor had a bi-lingual road chart which showed sketches of the road junctions alongside their mileage from both the start of the section and from the previous junction. There were bridges, bad bends and level-crossings marked, as well as the names of pubs and

LEFT An extreme example of being dressed to meet the conditions . . . The crews of the open Lancia F&M Specials on the 1969 Tour de Corse wore wet suits. Timo Makinen adjusts Paul Easter's seatbelt while Luca Montezemulo looks on.

at kilometre 22', every single bend and piece of straight road linking the bends would be individually noted and read back to the driver during the rally. A 22km test would be covered by some eight to ten pages of hieroglyphics which gave the direction and severity of every bend as well as any additional information such as the condition of the road surface.

Pace notes confer an enormous advantage over someone who is driving the road blind, so anyone doing a rally would be foolish indeed not to make the most of an opportunity to use them. If finances forbid a reconnaissance, then it is often possible to copy a set of pace notes from another driver or, in those cases when they are available, to use those supplied by the organiser. There are a few different systems of

notation in use and it may take a while to get used to somebody's else's pace notes, but whatever they are it is possible to be quicker and safer with them than without. A piece of advice is to read right through them before the rally starts so that there is nothing in them that you do not understand and have not checked with the man that wrote them. During a pace note swap in the BMC team, the co-driver read 'long flat right and how!', which the driver took to be an exhortation to stay flat out through the whole corner. After the accident, it was revealed that the full sentence should have been 'long flat right and house, turn right.' Incidents like this led to less pace note swapping, especially when Timo Makinen was discovered to have the habit of dropping into the mid-

RIGHT On a rallye-raid like Paris–Dakar, it makes sense to carry survival gear as well as more normal equipment. The rule should be to take only what can save time or a life.

dle of his notes helpful items such as 'long straight, dog, hairpin left'. As the dog would undoubtedly have finished his transaction between the recce and the rally, Makinen's notes were not always considered reliable by his team mates.

With the recce complete, it is then up to the crew to sit down and work out where they will place whatever service they have, and what tyres they will need to use for the various special stages. In a works team, this is done by several people who have a formidable task to co-ordinate what amounts to a small army of men and equipment. For a private entrant with just one rally car and one service van, the logistics are much simpler. Hard decisions may have to be made, since they cannot expect to see the van after every special stage and they will have to make some compromise between desirability and practicability in planning the schedule for their service crew. It is worth bearing in mind that the service personnel are as much engaged in a rally-type event as the cars that they are there to look after. They have a route to follow and a time schedule to which they must keep, so in bad weather or difficult traffic conditions their task may be every bit as demanding as that of the rally crew. Certainly, rally mechanics see themselves as an elite, capable of servicing and repairing cars in unbelievably short times as well as being able to get through to their rendezvous no matter what impediments are put in their way. It is part of the attraction of rallying that it offers participatory supporting roles of this kind.

A final check on the car before the rally should culminate in a road test, which is preferably done at night so that, in addition to checking out all the other systems, the lights can be set to the driver's preference. It is essential that this test is a realistic one and that the car should be driven at something like rally speeds, provided a road can be found where this can be done in safety. It is surprising how many things come loose or fail to work in the way expected when a car is being thrown around and this is not always appreciated when it is stationary. A case in point occurred before the 1965 RAC Rally when Simo Lampinen went to the factory to try his Triumph 2000, a feature of which was overdrive on the top two gears. The overdrive switch was fitted to the steering column, which in normal driving was quite acceptable, but for the rally he wanted it on the gear lever. There was a certain degree of cultural resistance to the idea until he took the electrician concerned out for a drive. While negotiating a roundabout on the Coventry by-pass in a four-wheel drift at maximum engine revs, Lampinen demonstrated the loss of control that occurred when trying to change gear and operate the overdrive switch at the same time. The electrician, once he had fully recovered from the fright, had no problem in agreeing to carry out the modification.

Much simpler things can need attention which are only discovered at the last moment. These can include light reflecting into the driver's eyes, or the pocket devised to hold the rally paperwork showering it all over the floor on hairpin bends. Also, fussy drivers are likely to complain about cans of de-mist spray rolling around under the brake pedal. Perhaps the most important thing if pace notes are being used is to ensure that the intercom system works, and works well. There are plenty of good ones on the market, but they are only as good as the last battery that is put in them.

Normally, the formalities of the rally will require that the crew produce their licences – both competition and normal driving licence – plus any visa from their national organisation if they are competing abroad, and a copy of the car insurance that is valid for its use in the rally. At or about the same time, the

car will be subjected to a technical examination. This scrutineering has two facets: one is to check all the mandatory safety equipment and to veryify that the car looks fit to do the rally, while the other is to see that it conforms to the homologation form, a copy of which must be provided by the entrant. Of course, at this point, no one asks to have the engine taken apart to check the bore and stroke, but that might well be done at the finish, especially if the car has done well on the rally.

Some rallies place seals on the engine and the bodyshell so that it is possible to tell whether either of these components have been changed during the rally. The principal fraud that they wish to prevent is one where an identical-looking car is substituted during the majority of the event for the one that is presented at pre- and post-event scrutineering. There are stories that circulate still of how teams on Monte Carlo Rallies used to produce new cars out of furniture vans but no one was ever caught doing it. The suspicion is that such events were about as believable as finding little green men in your garden, but, just in case, the seals are placed on the car and its engine prior to the event and checked during it and again at the end. All that remains for the crew is to do the rally. For its organisers, the problems are just beginning.

To successfully organise a major intenational rally, the work has to be arranged like the painting of the Forth Bridge: as soon as one event is over, the planning of the next one starts. For this reason, most World Championship and other major rallies have at least one full-time executive who provides that continuity. Lesser events may have to make do with a part-time administrator, but the work is there to be done nevertheless.

Except when the rally is a completely new event, in which case it is unlikely to be of any great size and certainly not an international rally, there will be an established format which has evolved over previous years. There may need to be changes to that format, but at least the organiser can normally build on what has gone before. His three main preoccupations are the route, the sponsor and the start-finish location. Contrary to expectation, this last item is not always decided first, as an examination of the British WRC qualifier, the Lombard RAC Rally, will reveal. This has the habit of moving its start-finish venue from one city to another while still using the same forest areas around Britain for its special stages. The Monte Carlo is stuck with its tradition of many starting points and a single finish in Monaco, while the San Remo Rally really doesn't have too many options unless it decides to change its name.

LEFT Spectator safety is an increasing concern for rally organisers, who do not want to find themselves the subject of regulations which they might not be able to enforce. The main hazard on gravel special stages are the stones thrown up by the rally cars.

RIGHT Big crowds do not always spell danger, but it helps if there is somewhere for them to stand away from the road, where they can see the action clearly.

In laying out the route, the organiser has to take into consideration a whole range of criteria. The special stages have to represent a certain proportion of the route and they have to comprise the right kind of challenge for the rally crews, otherwise there would not be a rally worth doing. There has to be some thought given to the types of stages and the surfaces that they comprise. It would be thoughtless and potentially dangerous to have gravel roads alternating with tarmac ones as cars would then inevitably be tackling stages on inappropriate tyres. This is no problem for rallies like the 1000 Lakes or the RAC Rally, where the vast majority of stages are on gravel roads, but rallies like San Remo or the Acropolis which have stages on both types of surface are normally considerate enough to group them together so that tyre and suspension changes have to be made as few times as possible.

Consideration has also to be taken of the liaison sections between those stages, to ensure that there are adequate places for the competitors to service before and after each stage. It is also necessary to arrange separate access routes for the spectators that will not involve them using the same roads as the competitors approaching and leaving the stage. These problems are often almost insuperable without the help of the police who, in addition to closing the actual road on which the stage takes place, will often close access roads to prevent them being blocked by the parking of spectators' cars. A classic example is the famous special stage over the Col de Turini on the Monte Carlo Rally which is used three times during the last night of that event. The test is closed to normal traffic some eight hours before the rally is due, to prevent spectators driving onto the test and parking their cars on the side of the road. Official cars and the cars driven by the ice-note crews from the various teams are still allowed through, but that is all.

On modern rallies, the sheer quantity of spectators is amazing and the organisers have to think how they are going to provide parking, access and safety measures for thousands of people. Since the fatal accident to spectators on the Portuguese Rally of 1986, there has been a great deal more thought put into these questions and although it is not always possible to fully marshal every bend on a rally with 600 kilometres of special stages, every rally now makes sure that plenty of advice is given to spectators on where it is unsafe to stand and watch. In addition, spectator control cars pass through the stage just prior to the arrival of rally cars and their crews take the responsiblity to move spectators from dangerous places or stop the stage from being started if the crowd is out of control. Most rallies now have a few shorter stages near the beginning of the event which are designated as spectator stages. A fee is charged for entrance and spectators will find grandstands, roped off areas and facilities more normally associated with permanent race circuits. These stages are not well liked by the drivers as they tend to be artificial in nature with water splashes and jumps that have been constructed for the occasion, but they do mean that tens of thousands of people can see the rally cars performing in a safe, controlled environment.

It is the enthusiasts, who like to go to the 'real' stages where normally there is no entrance fee and a certain spirit of adventure is needed to get there at all, towards whom all the public relations work on safety is directed. The sheer numbers of such folk that do go and watch rallies in remote places where the special stages are located takes some believing. Statistics from a recent Lombard RAC Rally indicate that something like 750 000 people entered the 30 or so stages during the last three days of the rally, while the figure on the 1000 Lakes of 250 000 is even more impressive considering that the total population of Finland is barely five million. On remote mountain roads or forests it is hard for an organiser to ensure the security of the onlookers, but they do their best with the measures at their disposal. It is a requirement of FISA that they have a doctor and ambulance at the start of every stage, and that service is there as much for the spectators as it is for the competitors.

All these things need to be paid for – and though the acquisition of a sponsor might be thought of as a purely modern exercise, in reality all rallies have needed a backer to generate the funds required to run the event. Entry fees alone have rarely been sufficient to do that. Events were often associated with newspapers who could give publicity which, in its turn, would encourage municipal authorities and private companies to add their backing. It is as well to remember that events like the Coupe des Alpes foundered as much for lack of money to pay the costs of road closures as they did from the social consequences of their event. When special stages on the public highway need to be closed, policemen are needed to enforce the closing orders, and there is no reason why they should give their services for nothing. The situation is not eased even if private roads are used for special stages, since the owner will demand payment to cover their repair. The RAC Rally, which uses Forestry Commission roads for the bulk of its special stages, has to pay over £65 000 each year for the use of their roads during the rally.

Thus sponsors are a major preoccupation for a rally organiser and that is true even for an event such as the Monte Carlo Rally which can call upon the considerable resources of the Principality of Monaco. Its main sponsorship in recent years has come from the commercial radio station in Monte Carlo and from the French daily sporting newspaper *L'Equipe*. The Portuguese Rally started life as the Rallye TAP with the national airline as its sponsor, but now takes its sup-

RIGHT Publicity and sponsorship are vital for holding major rallies. The Acropolis Rally is fortunate indeed to have such a striking backdrop for its start ramp and, since 1979, the support of Olympic Airways to bring journalists and competitors from abroad.

BOTTOM LEFT The summit of the Col du Turini is a famous place for spectating on the Monte Carlo Rally.

BELOW Fast sections, as here in Dalby Forest, Yorkshire, can prove spectacular, but make it difficult for the organisers to set a realistic target time for the special stage.

LEFT As Bo Lungfeldt takes his Ford Falcon Futura Sprint to fastest time on the Monaco circuit test in 1964, it is clear that it is the media that take the risks while the spectators opt for safety.

port from the Port Wine Institute and the Portuguese Tourist Board. The Olympus Rally, which was the USA's WCR qualifier between 1986 and 1988, originally had Toyota sponsorship but this did not suit the other motor manufacturers and FISA eventually banned such direct trade sponsorship, effectively kicking the Olympus into touch. Other rallies are more fortunate and none more so than the RAC Rally who have had a firm relationship with the finance company, Lombard North Central, since 1974.

What the sponsor does for the rally in terms of promotion and marketing is as important as the cash contribution to help it pay its way. The importance of television cannot be ignored and neither can the fact that rallying is infinitely more difficult and expensive to televise than, say, snooker or even horse racing. Thus every inducement to film the event and get that footage shown on television is important to the fortunes of the sponsor and the event.

Once the organiser can feel that he has the structure of his event and his budget sorted out, he needs to approach the authorities for the various permissions that he will need to run the rally. From those in charge of the roads, whether they be public or private bodies, he will have to get road closure agreements and, in the case of private property, may have to come to some commercial arrangement concerning the admission of spectators and the display of advertising on the site. These arrangements may bring more revenue to the event, but they certainly extend the rally organiser's responsibilities far beyond what was expected of him 20 years ago. In addition, he will have to get clearance for his entire route from the national automobile club and the police. In England

and Wales, this function is governed by statute and the Rally Authorisation Department set up by the RACMSA on behalf of the government handles all aspects of the approval of the route. Sometimes it may be necessary to modify it to avoid a local carnival, or major road works or some other temporary hazard that would cause problems on the day.

In the case of the rally being an international event, it must be entered on the FIA international calendar the year before it is to be organised, and an international permit has to be sought from FISA through the national club of the country where it is being held. At the same time, indemnity insurance has to be arranged to guarantee that if there is a major accident then the organisers are insured against any successful claims. In the same way, every entrant in the rally has to carry insurance in case he too is involved in a third party claim.

Approval of the organiser's regulations by both the national and the international authorities is followed by their distribution. The entries then start coming in and will continue to do so right up to the closing date for entries. The reason for having a cut-off point in this way is to enable a proper programme to be printed and for the organiser to properly 'seed' the entry that he has received. Only 20 or so years ago, there was very little attempt made to place the cars and crews in any kind of order according to merit or potential performance. The result was often that the difficulties of overtaking slower competitors in dust, snow or mud played a large part in penalising competitors. The East African Safari always had a ballot by which the entries were drawn from a hat, but this was only the democratisation of a bad system. Even on the Monte Carlo Rally there were problems, since the itineraries from the various starting cities converged on a single town from where all competitors tackled a combined route down to Monaco with the special stages as part of it. Knowing which starting point would arrive – and thus leave – from the converging point first could mean the difference between doing the first test in freezing conditions at night, or in the morning sun on a wet road.

It is nice to be able to say that the RAC Rally was one of the first rallies to introduce the idea of setting the known fastest drivers and cars off first, thus reducing considerably the necessity for them to squeeze past slower cars on narrow forest tracks. Another step forward was taken at the 1967 San Remo Rally when, thanks to a timely protest by the drivers and the presence of snow over many of the narrow special stages, the organisers agreed to let the quicker cars and drivers start first. Other events gradually started to do something about such matters, since each of them had some kind of problem with baulking or bad visibility while overtaking. It can be quite a surprise to someone who has not tried overtaking on snow just how big a blanket of ice crystals can be raised by a car with studded tyres going at speed.

Finally, in June 1971 the CSI introduced the idea of having a proper list of seeded drivers who had to be given early starting numbers on all international rallies. By the time the World Rally Championship came along in 1973, this had developed into 'A' and 'B' Priority rally drivers with properly established criteria for choosing them. This has now made it much easier for organisers to put their entries in an order which will put all the top drivers at the front of the field and which will hopefully result in a minimum of pushing and shoving once the event starts There is still the problem of trying to do the same for the rest of the non-seeded entry, which may represent some 80 per cent of it. This is a painstaking task that has to be done on the basis of the information supplied by each entrant about his previous results and take into account the performance of the car in which he has entered the rally.

Almost the last task for the rally organiser is to assemble the officials, timekeepers and marshals that he will need to run his event. This is truly a formidable task, as upward of 10 000 people may be needed to run a major event effectively. The largest number of these are involved in the running of the special stages, and in many countries each stage is delegated

RIGHT Sometimes it pays not to be first car on the road. Running at number 51, this Volkswagen can find more grip than the early cars.

to one particuiar motor club. They elect a stage commander and he runs it like an individual event. He will need timekeepers at the arrival control, the stage start and the finish. There will need to be a telephone link between the flying finish line where the time is taken and the stop line where the time is recorded on the competitor's card. He will need marshals at every junction on the stage, a radio network under a communications officer so as to be able to speak to each marshal's post. At each post, the passage of each car is noted so that, if one goes missing, the search can be narrowed to a reasonable distance.

At the start of the stage, there will be a doctor and an ambulance with a full crew. On some events with long or particularly mountainous stages – the Tour de Corse is an example – there will often be a medical helicopter on call as well. It was aerial intervention of this kind that saved the lives of Ari Vatanen and Terry Harryman when they had a very serious accident in the Argentina Rally in 1985. If medical aid is needed at an accident, news of which would have been passed back to the start by radio, then either the rally can be stopped and the ambulance sent in or a variation of the racing idea can be put into operation whereby the ambulance goes in bearing yellow flags and any rally car catching it must stay behind until it stops at the accident site.

Away from the stages, there need to be marshals running ordinary time controls, service areas, *parc fermés* and passage controls, where the time cards have to be collected and their contents relayed back to the results team at rally headquarters. Also being fed back from a separate network of information crews will be information and stories concerning the rally crews. Stage times and rally gossip are processed by the relevant teams back in rally HQ and emerge as official results and press releases often just minutes after the top cars have cleared a stage. Gone are the days when the competitors, press and public were kept in ignorance of what was going on until the rally was over. Fans huddled over improvised fires in the snow banks overlooking the summit of the Col de Turini on the last night of the Monte Carlo Rally are provided with up-to-the-minute reports and stage times from Radio Monte Carlo and know as much about the position of the rally cars passing in front of them as the spectators at a motor race.

Back in the early 1970s, the Austrian *Alpenfahrt* astonished the rally reporters attending the event by arranging to have the Austrian Army use its mobile radio-telex facilities at the end of every special stage so that a print-out of times could be available in the press room within minutes of each car finishing. That was pretty advanced for its time and it is not practical to have such equipment available on all rallies. Thus what happens is that the organisers arrange to have passage controls at convenient places, normally after a group of stages, where the time cards are collected

TOP LEFT Plenty of marshals and good communication between them is the recipe for keeping control of modern rallies. If a car goes missing, the stage commander can know within minutes in which section it has stopped.
LEFT To come out of the darkness into an arena of TV floodlights and popping flash guns is a hazard against which no rules and regulations can protect the rally driver. Here Per Eklund runs the gauntlet on the 1987 Lombard RAC Rally.
RIGHT Most modern rally timing is done with digital watches and handwritten times, but in the 1960s it was the Longines printing clock that reigned supreme and it was the co-driver's responsibility to press the button at the right time.

LEFT Dust can be unpleasant for the crew of a rally car which is generating it, but when one rally car is catching another, it can be positively dangerous. In circumstances like these, overtaking has to be a matter of co-operation between the competitors.

RIGHT The provision of prizes and their presentation is a major preoccupation for a rally organiser. Pat Moss and Ann Wisdom have just picked up their spoils after the Marathon de la Route in the Casino of Charbonnieres.

from each competitor and the times telephoned or faxed in to rally HQ and the waiting results team. Sometimes there may be a computer terminal at the passage control into which the times are fed by an operator, but more often this is done at one central point. In this way, results are available to the competitors and to the media as soon as possible and errors are kept to a minimum.

Not all rallies in the 1970s were as good as the Austrian in keeping their competitors informed of the current positions and this sometimes had quite serious consequences. On the 1972 Acropolis Rally, Simo Lampinen and Bo Reinicke in a Lancia Fulvia thought they were leading comfortably with just one difficult road section to got. They took it easy on the basis of the last results issued by the organisers only to find that they had been pipped at the post by the Fiat 124 Spyder of Hakan Lindberg and Helmuth Eisendle. The rally was lost by a margin of 29 seconds.

On an 'itinerant' rally like the Paris-Dakar or the Australian Safari, it may be possible to get away with a smaller total number of workers, but when one considers that there may be up to a thousand of them on such an event and that their jobs are done once a day for ten days or so, then the number of man-days begins to approach that of a rally like the RAC or the Monte Carlo. Many of these officials and marshals give their time for free and indeed some of them even cover their own expenses, but their enthusiasm matches that of the competitors and they get an equal satisfaction out of being on the rally.

As the rally approaches its finish, the organisers have to ensure that the staging of the arrival of the winning competitors is done in suitable fashion. This usually means a city centre arrival ramp, music, lights, ladies and champagne – a formula that changes little from Darwin to Dakar or from Middlesbrough to

Monte Carlo. The only thing which can throw a blight over such celebrations is if the winning car is found to be in some way outside the regulations for the rally or if some previously overlooked transgression by the winner is brought to light by another competitor. The organisers have usually taken the opportunity to have the cars superficially inspected by the scrutineers both before and during the rally, but it is only at the end that they may really investigate and have parts stripped for inspection. The Monte Carlo Rally did have a reputation for such dramas and the rally of 1966 was infamous in that respect, as we have seen, with technical examination of the winning Cooper S's and Lotus Cortinas taking place well into the next day before they were excluded for an infringement of lighting regulations with their single filament headlights. Similarly, a protest from another competitor has to be formally heard by the Stewards, and resolution of such questions, especially those that require further investigation and testimony, can take a very long time

Generally, most people involved in the sport are now of the opinion that, fascinating though such affairs may be to the non-motoring press and to the legal profession, they are to be avoided at all costs, since they prevent anyone from taking commercial benefit from having won the rally. Thus the regulations are framed so that they are difficult to break without it being evident, while the penalties for such misdemeanours by works teams have been elevated to the point where they are scrupulous in their attempt to avoid them.

With the rally over, it only remains for the competitor to return home, hopefully clutching the spoils of this event to plan his attack on another, and for the organiser to immediately start work on his event for the following year.

CHAPTER 5

THE WORKS TEAM

If you had to define in a single sentence what are the aims of a works team's preparation for a rally, it would have to go something like this: they are trying to develop the fastest and most reliable car for the conditions that pertain on that rally while striving to eliminate failure due to misfortune of any kind, whether it be a mechanical failure or a failure to achieve the tasks set by the rally. That last subject, the elimination of failure, is the one on which perhaps more time and effort is spent than most people outside the sport would realise, since rallying is teeming with possibilities for bad luck, error and misjudgment.

The phenomenon of the works team has been with rallying right from the early days. Many of those competitors in the Paris–Rouen Trial were in effect factory cars entered to prove their worth and promote sales. When the Prinz Heinrich Fahrt was in its heyday before the First World War, it was very much a head-to-head conflict between factory teams such as Mercedes, Opel and Daimler to the point, in fact, where their professionalism was a reason for killing off the event. Then there were the works-supported Rolls-Royce cars in the early Austrian Alpenfahrts. In its successor, the Alpine Trial, held between the two World Wars, the level of factory interest was such that in 1932, *The Autocar* wrote that 'in the Alpine Trial there were very few genuinely privately owned production cars . . .'

However, it was not until the 1950s that the works teams emerged as identifiable entities. The reason for this was that most rallies at that time raised their complete ban on organised servicing. It had become clear to the majority of people involved in the sport that it was simply impossible adequately to patrol a route of several thousand kilometres in order to ensure that no one broke servicing regulations. Indeed, to enforce such a ban 100 per cent it would also have been necessary to marshal every little turning or byway that led off from the official route. There was a widespread practice of siting assistance vehicles where at least they could not be seen by other competitors passing along the official route. There is a classic story from the Alpine Trial of a team manager who knew that another team were indulging in illegal, off-route service and sent out a photographer to procure evidence. In due course, he walked up to his opposite number and showed him the incriminating pictures only to have them trumped, as it were, by a set showing his own cars also *in flagrante delicto*. It was agreed by common consent to destroy both sets of photographs.

Throughout the history of rallying, there has been a constant battle of wits between the organisers of

PREVIOUS PAGE Accessibility is an important consideration for fast servicing. If something serious occurs then body panels and closures can be removed and, if necessary, replaced.

LEFT As the works teams evolved in the 1960s, more manufacturers provided dedicated facilities in which to prepare their rally cars. In 1964 Ford transferred their motor sport department to Boreham in Essex, where the workshop and stores were devoted 100% to rallying.

RIGHT The Cooper S was a complicated little car, so the BMC works team avoided adding complications in its preparation for rallying, and concentrated on making everything that could be changed as serviceable as possible.

the events and the professional competitors on this business of assistance or repairs for competing vehicles. On the early East African Safaris a whole range of components on the cars were marked with special paints before the start, and these were then checked during the rally and at the finish to be certain that nothing had been changed. The Safari organisers were very fair about it, and if, for instance, they found that the competitor had changed a front suspension unit, the penalty was only a certain number of marks and not exclusion. But not all organisers could be bothered to go to such trouble, and eventually even the Safari dropped the idea. In modern rallies, seals or identifying marks are normally only put on the engine block and on the chassis.

The major works teams that emerged during the latter part of the 1950s were Mercedes, Volvo, Saab, BMC, Ford and Citroën. They could be distinguished not so much by the fact that the entries were made in the factory name – René Cotton's Citroën team nearly always made theirs in the name of *Écurie Paris Île de France* – but by a common livery, a registration mark local to the competition department, a driver known to be retained by the team, and the fact that whenever they stopped for service it was at the vans or estate cars belonging to the factory. Many of the works team liveries – and this was long before the

arrival of major sponsors – became extremely well known and were frequently copied. One example was the BMC habit of using red cars with white roofs, which provoked a whole rash of private cars with similar toppings, but since it was not a standard shade they could never quite get the same red that the factory used.

The works teams have always tried to have their cars performing at their very best. This has meant doing as much development as possible in relation to the rally that they were about to enter, so as to ensure that their cars were as good as they could possibly make them. In the early days, this normally meant making sure that the engine developed peak power and ran smoothly throughout its range. With rallies like the Austrian *Alpenfahrt*, it was clear that gearing was very important and nearly everyone who went to that event came back the following year with lower gearing to tackle its formidable hills. Once those two items had been dealt with, it then became apparent that brakes and suspension required attention to ensure that the car's overall performance could match that of its engine.

As we saw in Chapter 2, all these areas have benefited from various inventions and technological developments over the years. While it is difficult to say that any particular item was invented to respond to a problem encountered solely in rallying, it is certainly true that in order to make their cars more competitive and reliable in rallying, the factories have forced the emergence of practical solutions from patented theory. The universal joints that transmitted the ever-increasing power of the Mini Coopers between 1962 and 1967 are a case in point. The hardening and machining processes involved in manufacturing those items were transformed out of all recognition by the need to keep the BMC Cooper S's at the forefront of the rallying world.

The changes and development that can be carried out in the way of preparation even by a factory team must have their limits. At the dawn of the sport, the technical rules were fairly rudimentary, but they gradually evolved so as to set limits on what the entrant could do to his car while still classing it as the same type and model. Generally speaking, up until the 1950s there was not too much time spent setting out detailed technical rules to control the preparation of the cars. It was sufficient for an entrant to state that he was entering such-and-such a model and make a full declaration on the entry form as to the type of engine, gearbox etc., and the organisers were satisfied. For example, the cars entered on the Alpine Trials between the two World Wars were required to be production touring or sports cars of which no fewer than 50 similar vehicles had to exist. The entrant was reasonably free to change minor things such as engine ancillaries, and even the bodywork could be varied provided that it conformed to what were described rather vaguely as the 'international rules'.

With the advent of chassis-less or monocoque construction, such freedoms were not to be so easily granted. Generally, the greater technical sophistication of the second half of the century and the mass production of cars where several models shared the same bodyshell but were powered by different engines meant that previously clear lines of demarcation were now blurred. It was all too easy to swap engines and other components in the fashion of the American Hot Rodders. It was decided by the international controlling body, at that time the CSI, to introduce what is known as the International Homologation Form.

This is a form filled in by the car manufacturer in which he states the model and type of car that he seeks to homologate, and then lists the answers to questions about its engine (capacity, bore, stroke etc), the fuel and ignition systems, the gearbox, the suspension and the accommodation provided for passengers. He is also required to attach to the form photographs of the car's general appearance and other specific areas such as the under-bonnet layout. The form is then checked against samples of the product by representatives of the manufacturer's National Automobile Club, and if it meets with their approval it is registered in Paris. Copies can then be supplied to all those competitors who are going to enter the car in competitions and to the technical

commissioners of the events themselves.

The original homologation forms were quite simple affairs, perhaps just two single sheets of paper with some pretty fundamental information about the vehicle. Today, they have grown until even the simplest form contains fourteen sheets, while supplementary information, added as the production car develops and new competition parts evolve, can eventually take up another hundred or so sheets. Knowing where to look for the correct dimension of a brake or an inlet valve is something left to experts who are familiar with that particular form, and each modern works team employs its own homologation expert.

The very earliest homologation forms did not depend for their validity on the car manufacturer making any specific statement about the number of models that had been produced to this specification, but this was soon introduced when it was realised that they could easily produce a form which related to a one-off rally special and not to the general pro-

RIGHT If the rally is dirty, then it will be a dirty job to work on it. Hot brake-discs and muddy overalls are all part of the job for a rally mechanic out on an event.

duction run. While this was unfair to the smaller manufacturer, whose annual production was in terms of hundreds rather than thousands, an attempt was made to cater for them in that much smaller production numbers were required for qualification in the GT classes, which were just the type of car likely to be produced by a smaller factory.

Allied to these 'car passports' were international rules and regulations guiding what could or could not be done to the standard car by the person preparing it for the event. This meant the end of such exotic modifications as were seen on some of the Monte Carlo entries during the 1930s, for instance, when a few of the cars looked as if they were auditioning for parts in the post-war film starring Tony Curtis called 'Monte Carlo or Bust'. Some of the ingenious devices fitted to the cars in that film – skis as supplements for the front wheels, for example – were indeed devised, if not actually used, for cars on Monte Carlo Rallies of that era.

The regulations that were created in 1957 eventu-

ally became the famous Appendix J to the Sporting Code of the FIA, which today is the bible for all who participate in motor sport with production-based vehicles. The regulations of Appendix J define the areas that one may work upon to improve performance, whether it be in the engine, the transmission, the chassis, the bodywork or the suspension. Together with the homologation form, they present the engineer employed by the works team with defined limits as to what he may and may not do to make the car better able to survive and to win the rally in which it is to be entered. At the same time, Appendix J also lists out all the safety requirements for competition cars relating to items such as roll cages, fuel tanks, fire extinguishers, brake systems, safety belts and circuit breakers.

The first step for a works team is to ensure that the homologation form is correctly filled in, and that where tolerances are allowed they are claimed in such a way as to benefit the engineer working on the car. Before the FIA and its sporting wing, FISA, insti-

LEFT The works teams run by the Saab factory were the smallest but also the most effective. With annual resources of less than the budget for a single car on a 1990 World Championship rally, they conquered Monte Carlo, the RAC and countless other rallies; but though Erik Carlsson and Gunnar Palm often led the Safari, they never won it.

BELOW Ford's win on the 1964 Safari Rally with the Cortina GT heralded a very successful next 15 years. The four-wheel drive revolution then left them behind, but they bounced back with the Sierra Cosworth in 1990.

tuted a system of more rigorous checks during the 1980s, there were examples of what are commonly known as homologation specials. These differed in how they were to be regarded as 'special', but they all had in common the fact that a certain amount of wool was being pulled over someone's eyes. In short, there were grave doubts that the model existed either in the numbers attested to by the manufacturer or in the specification defined on the homologation form. A few examples will illustrate the general point.

During 1975, Chrysler UK homologated an 1800cc version of their popular Avenger which was fitted with twin Weber carburettors. The production of 5000 cars on which this homologation was based had taken place in Chrysler's associated factory in Brazil, and though doubtless the roads of Rio de Janeiro were clogged with them, the only examples to be found in Europe were in the British-based Chrysler rally team. Fortunately, the Brazilian block Avengers never left the UK to seriously challenge the European teams or their homologation would certainly have been questioned. There were also some doubters when Lancia homologated their sensational Stratos in October 1974 as they were supposed to have 400 production models. People just could not believe it to have been possible, but they were counted and that was that. It did later transpire that quite a large percentage of the production cars were at the moment of inspection unfinished, but the inspectors were prepared to accept the principle of intent to produce and count them as complete cars.

Some people did get caught stretching credibility to its limits. There was a rapid version of the BMW 5-series homologated during 1976 called the 530iUS which, as its name suggests, was fitted with a three-litre fuel injected engine and destined for the American market. The only problem was that when FISA instituted a casual check with their colleagues in the USA who went browsing in several North American BMW dealerships, not one single example of the model could be found, let alone the 5000 of them that were required by the homologation regulations to have been built. BMW suffered the indignity of having their homologation withdrawn and being fined. But this is not a unique example and other manufacturers were guilty at that time of claiming engines and induction systems for their cars which frankly existed only on their homologation forms and on their racing cars. The only difference was that, when confronted with their subterfuge, BMW came clean.

The phrase 'homologation special' is now used quite loosely to mean any car whose production run is undertaken principally with competition in mind, though many examples of the car may be sold for ordinary road use. Such was the case with some of the cars homologated in the latter years of Group 4, which came to an end in December 1981 when it was replaced by Group B. Examples of those special production Group 4 cars were the Opel Ascona 400 – it took its designation from the number of cars that had to be produced for recognition in Group 4 – and the Fiat Abarth 131, both World Championship rally winners.

Another example of a Group 4 car was that homologated by Vauxhall and called the Chevette HS 2300. So many people took the HS to stand for 'homologation special' that it was bound to have a difficult time of things. However, it passed its homologation inspection with flying colours and made its World Championship debut on the Swedish Rally in 1978. But then Vauxhall's two works entries were thrown out of the Portuguese Rally before it had even started when it was discovered that the cylinder head on the team cars was a Lotus-designed variant that was significantly different to that on the production car. The catch here was that the homologation form failed to ask the question that would differentiate between the two cylinder heads, and it was only by an inspection of a standard car and the rally car that the difference could be discerned. The new question was rapidly added to the homologation form by FISA! Indeed, the original form has greatly increased in size over the years as a result of new data being required to resolve problems of this nature.

The Group B cars that replaced the Group 4 cars were very much in the tradition of homologation specials, since only 200 of them had to be produced in order to obtain recognition by FISA. Opel produced the Manta 400 and Toyota did a special production run of their Celica Turbo, while Lancia homologated the Rallye 037, but these were the last two-wheel-drive cars to head effective works challenges for the World Rally Championship. The reason for that is quite simple: Audi had brought the four-wheel-drive revolution to rallying in 1981.

The arrival of four-wheel-drive Group B homologation specials subsequently became a flood, with Lancia producing the Delta S4, Peugeot the 205 Turbo 16, Audi the Sport Quattro E2, Austin Rover the Metro 6R4, Citroën the BX 4TC and Ford the RS 200. Prototype Group B cars were also seen from Mitsubishi with a Starion 4WD and Opel with a Kadett 400, but the highly controversial cancellation by FISA of Group B eligibility for World Championship rallies in 1986 put all these cars on the shelf. Many have found a home in rallycross and similar off-road motor sport. Peugeot turned their technology towards producing the ultimate in Rallye-Raid machines. Certainly the investment made by the car companies in Group B has not been wasted. They have all had some competition success from the actual cars, while embracing four-wheel-drive technology in general has enabled many of those manufacturers to make volume production cars with permanent four-wheel drive.

So the situation today is that to have his car homologated for rallying, a manufacturer must produce 5000 identical models. Since these will by necessity be of a complex and high-performance

LEFT Even a simple tyre change can be fraught with problems when the rally regulations say that the car must be off the public road. Schmidt Motorsport mechanics show ingenuity while looking after Marc Duez and his Metro 6R4 on the Ypres Rally in 1986.

BELOW LEFT Rally mechanics must resign themselves to the fact that the immaculate car that took them weeks to prepare can be reduced to a very sorry state by a rally driver in a matter of seconds. And he will expect them to repair it so that he can carry on!

LEFT Where the useable life of components is short, they have to be changed before they break. The TWR mechanics had a complete rear-axle change on a Group A Rover down to a fine art.

BELOW Windscreens are a popular service item especially when, as in the case of Hannu Mikkola's Audi on the 1984 New Zealand Rally, the car has been on its roof.

specification, each manufacturer first has to decide whether he can sell the 4900 or so cars that he will not himself require for competition purposes. Fortunately, with such a big worldwide market for cars, a significant number of manufacturers have seen fit to produce such cars in the requisite numbers and have found that they can sell them as flagships of their range. Perhaps the best example of this is the trio of Sierras that have emerged from Ford – the Sierra Cosworth, the Sapphire Cosworth and the Sierra Cosworth 4WD. So successful have these models been both in terms of competition and road use that Ford are also bringing out an Escort Cosworth 4WD to advance their rally fortunes yet further. In similar fashion, the Japanese manufacturers have gone overboard in the post-Group B production of four-wheel-drive machines. Toyota has always been in the vanguard of the action, but Mitsubishi, Mazda, Subaru and now Nissan have all followed suit.

With a suitable car properly homologated, the manufacturer then needs to decide on what basis he will organise the works team that will enter it in rallies on his behalf. Most of the original works teams that grew up in the 1950s and 1960s were based completely within the mother factory. They were seen as off-shoots of the engineering, testing and development departments and indeed, in less sophisticated times, the idea of competition and development did go hand in hand. Nowadays, the engineering of a new car is handled by vast teams of engineers who may be working at different locations or even in different countries. The parameters to which they work are those of vehicle legislation, manufacturing cost and customer preference. The necessity to make a modern rally car perform in the way that it does with

400bhp and four-wheel drive requires engineering that differs quite considerably from that needed in road cars. One discipline may have benefits and lessons for the other, but they are not the same.

To illustrate this, the easiest example to take is the bodyshell of the car. Twenty-five years ago, when the CSI was contemplating a regulation to allow the fitting of roll cages to protect the crew, their main concern was that these cages should not be allowed to strengthen the basic car. After all, the idea of rallying was to prove whether one production car was better than another; it was the fundamental test on which all the early races, rallies and trials were based. However, the preparation of cars for rallies had always involved strengthening the bits that were known to break. When such knowledge was incorporated in the production car, it was termed 'improving the breed', but if found on an actual rally car it could easily result in disqualification. There were many ways round it, and when homologation was in its infancy this was none too difficult. But even on rallies like the East African Safari, where they were proud of their reputation as a test of standard cars and took great trouble over the scrutineering before the start, there were ways to get round the problem. Joginder Singh, a triple winner of the event, would always take his rally car out to test it a few days before the rally and, purely by mischance, get involved in an accident that would require repair. If in repairing it, certain things had to be welded and extra metal used then that was just one of those things . . .

Over the years, it has become accepted that a bodyshell on a rally car may have a roll cage that is welded in as part of the structure and that the shell itself may be strengthened by the addition of mate-

LEFT Ford of America gave the Europeans a surprise with excellent performances from its Falcons and Mustangs in the 1960s, but these Lincoln Comets were not well suited to the East African Safari, and wholly inadequate testing was the key.

TOP RIGHT Rally car testing has to take into account what the driver may inflict on the car during the heat of competition. It is extremely difficult to reproduce punishment such as is about to be handed out to this Audi Quattro, but every attempt is made to test under rally conditions.

rial. Consequently, the first thing that is done today in the preparation of a works rally car is that the engineer looks at the design of the bodyshell and designs a cage to go in it in such a way that he achieves two objectives. The first is to stiffen and strengthen the shell so that springs and dampers of a very much higher rate may be fitted without the risk that the shell itself may become a torsional part of the suspension. The other is to counteract the original designer's brief which was to provide transverse weaknesses in the shell so that, in the case of a head-on accident with a road car, the engine and gearbox would be propelled downward and backwards and not into the passenger compartment. This otherwise desirable effect has to be eliminated on a rally car, otherwise when it hits a large pothole at 120mph on the East African Safari, the crew could find themselves sitting on top of the engine.

Strength and rigidity are what are needed in a rally car bodyshell. The first quality will make it last and the second will make it handle well once the right combination of springs, dampers and roll bars are fitted. It is difficult to make people understand that although a car with nice soft suspension will give a comfortable ride over a rough road at a reasonable speed, if you want to go fast then you need a hard suspension allied to the greatest amount of wheel movement that can be built into it. In the early 1970s, Peugeot took it on themselves to start rallying their 504 saloon after

numerous successes had been obtained by their Kenyan importers in the East African Safari. They hired top drivers like Hannu Mikkola and Timo Makinen to try out their cars, and the first tests were held in Morocco on the unbelievably bad road from Irhem to the Tata oasis. For mile after mile, this is no more than a river bed and certainly not the place where one would normally reckon to achieve high speeds. To start with, the Peugeot engineers had set up the test car with soft suspension and plenty of ground clearance. The Finns brought it to a halt in 20 kilometres or so with the strut inserts poked up through the bonnet. They told the engineers that much higher-rate springs and dampers were required. These had to be fetched from France, but when they came the same test car was eventually making regular trips along the 110km route at rally speeds without any problem. Except one, which was that the bodyshell was not quite strong enough and had bent sufficiently to prevent the doors opening and closing, so that the drivers and engineers took to entering and leaving the car through the windows.

Having the rally team as a separate entity, capable of pursuing its own engineering ends, makes enormous sense. Some feedback is essential or the lessons learned in taking production based components to their ultimate performance level will not be of any help to mainstream engineering, nor to the designers trying to conceive the next production car.

RIGHT Agility and a good sense of balance enable several jobs to be done at the same time – the Toyota *corps de ballet* in action.

The rally engineers that work with the team need to possess all the normal qualifications plus those of diagnosis, analysis, diplomacy and insight. They will have to assess problems and suggest solutions, and then accompany the rally car out on test to check that the modification does add to the speed or reliability of the car. This is as true of the men that work on the engines and transmissions as it is of the suspension and chassis engineers. Seeing the car in action during testing in conditions similar to those of the rally will help an engine man to realise that a rally driver does not spend all his time with the engine at maximum revolutions. Indeed, he may be asking it to pull from much lower crankshaft speeds than the engineer ever imagined, which means that the next engine could have its camshafts, timing and fuelling adjusted to make the most of that fact.

A similar consideration applies to the drive train of the car. Since the adoption of four-wheel drive on rally cars, the engineers involved have been discovering that the way a rally car handles has a great deal to do with the way the transmission is set up. This was first apparent to a lesser extent with rear-wheel-drive cars when it was found that they steered more positively if the limited slip differential was designed to free up the instant the flow of power from the engine ceased. On a four-wheel-drive car, there are three differentials: front, rear and centre. All of them may be fitted with some kind of limiting slip device which can be chosen from a clutch type (ZF or Salisbury), a viscous coupling (FF Developments) or a gear type (Thorsen). Each type of limited slip device can be set up to react differently, while some cars deliberately choose not to run limited slip devices in the front or centre differentials. In addition, there is the torque splitting function that is part and parcel of the centre differential, and there can be various ratios other than the original 50:50 with which the Audi Quattro appeared. Then there is the question of the ratios of the three differentials, which together will decide what kind of overall gearing the rally car possesses. The result of all this is that there are a fearsome number of combinations facing the transmission engineer, and though not all of them can be tried in testing, enough will have to be run through to enable him to make a judgement on what will give the car its best combination of traction, braking and handling.

The two top rallying teams in the world at the moment are Toyota and Lancia. During the 1990 season they split the honours evenly between them, with Lancia capturing the World Manufacturer's crown and Toyota the Driver's with Carlos Sainz. Both are complete operations handling everything to do with their rally cars, including the engines. Certain components such as the bodyshell and integral roll cage may be contracted out to specialists like the German firm

of Matter, while special gearboxes for the Toyota come from Xtrac in England. But as far as possible, Lancia and Toyota keep control of the majority of their car preparation and engineering by carrying it out themselves. Other teams with less facilities concentrate on the engineering of suspension and brakes, which need to vary from event to event and are also subject to driver preference. They then contract out the preparation of the engines and transmissions, while keeping a core of mechanics to build the

cars from the sub-assemblies and parts supplied from outside.

Like rally engineers, rally mechanics have to be capable of doing everything that is expected of a normal employee plus having to handle the extra demands that rallying brings in its wake. That means they have to be able to build rally cars to high standards in the clinical surroundings of the rally workshop, and change a component against the clock while lying in a muddy puddle on the side of the road. Their feats are almost legendary and fall into two distinct categories. The first could be called the party trick. It is where, for instance, one component or sub-assembly has to be changed for another and it is a job which has been known about and prepared for in advance. In this category come the turbocharger, gearbox and axle changes which are done in minutes rather than hours thanks to careful thought and planning having been given to the problem at the time the rally car was prepared. For example, by the use of power tools and clean-break hydraulic couplings, the TWR mechanics during the 1985 season got a complete axle change on a Group A Rover down to about ten minutes. When they had first started, it had taken over half an hour and, in a normal garage, it would take almost three times as long again.

The second category comprises those actions which enable a car to finish when it should not really have continued running at all. The ability of mechanics to effect some kind of repair on a stricken car is called 'bush engineering'. A good example was Pentti Airikkala's Vauxhall Chevette, on a British forest rally in the 1970s, which had its rear axle casing break. By using a length of substantial chain, pulled into place with a winch and steel wire, the wayward part was persuaded to remain roughly in place so that the half-shaft could continue to drive the wheel, and Airikkala reached the finish.

The whole business of servicing on a major international rally is one which today requires a budget as big as the rest of the rally programme put together. In addition to the use of personnel who go out and look at the route of the rally exclusively from the point of view of service, and who then work out the movement of all the service vehicles, spare parts, wheels and tyres, and mechanics during the rally, there is often need to hire in more mechanics to supplement permanent staff. This is because in order to give adequate cover on a big rally like Monte Carlo, Corsica, Acropolis or Safari, where easy movement of service vehicles from one place to the next may be prevented either by the terrain or by road closure orders for the rally itself, extra service vans are needed. Finding enough good mechanics who also have a ready familiarity with the particular rally car that is being used is not easy. One solution is to use a helicopter which transports the best mechanics from service to service and can always keep them ahead of the rally. When helicopters were first used on the Safari it was thought that they were a flamboyant extravagance, but the teams gradually came to see how they could actually save money by using such devices.

Prior to the use of helicopters, the works teams had discovered the benefits of using radios to talk between the rally car and the service vehicles. The next development, since VHF radios were notoriously short of range, was to use a light aircraft circling above the rally to provide the link in the communications chain. The first instance of radios being used successfully in rally cars was on the Monte Carlo of 1967 when the son of the Philips importer in Switzerland, Patrick Lier, used one to keep his Hillman Imp in touch with its sole service car. Once accepted generally by the works teams, their use spread widely and the introduction of Citizens' Band radios from the USA helped to ensure wider availability of the technology. The Tower of Babel situation that resulted from everyone on a rally having their own radio network has led to rally organisers getting involved in the process of licensing radios, so that there is a fair distribution of frequencies between the entrants.

But all this technology and the use of aircraft and helicopters in addition to the 20 or so vans means that the rally planners for each works team have a very large task on their hands to get the logistics right. They have to do all the traditional work such as deciding where service is going to be done and finding a suitable garage or piece of hard standing if such is available, as well as working out a schedule so that each van, support car and possibly even motorhome can get to its various destinations with time in hand. On top of that, they have to establish a communica-

LEFT Jacks are wild when it comes to an axle change in the middle of a rally – Walter Rohrl's Opel Ascona in the process of changing axle ratio during the 1973 Austrian Alpine Rally.

RIGHT As the private 850 Mini of David Hiam crosses the border on the 1961 Marathon de la Route, in the background an estate car servicing for the works Citroen teams awaits the arrival of their cars.

tions network so that the rally cars can communicate with priority and have their information or requests passed on to the relevant people. In the 1960s, when Ford were building up their rally team which is still in operation today, the man doing the rally planning for Ford was Bill Barnett. He used to incorporate all his planning into a single bound volume, which was then issued to each rally car and service van. In it was every piece of information that anyone in the Ford team on that rally might need to know, including the basic service schedule, the rooms booked at hotels, the locations of all Ford dealers along the route, and even the home telephone numbers of Ford personnel who were not on the rally but who might be called upon to run the odd errand. The whole thing was known as 'Bill's Bible' and ran to some 60 pages. Today's manuals on service and communication produced by rally teams may eclipse it in size, but the principle remains the same.

Once the rally is under way, the value of having these jobs done correctly becomes apparent. A poor service schedule will result in the vans being late or, worse, not finding their service points at all. If the radio network is functioning correctly, the team manager can keep in contact with his rally cars and service vans so that he can be aware of their progress around the route. The acid test comes when something goes wrong with one of the rally cars and a change has to be made to the carefully laid plans. This is when the spatial perception of the planners is really put to work. First, it is necessary to introduce the concept of chase cars. These are cars carrying a basic minimum of tools and spares which have an experienced rally driver at the wheel accompanied by a mechanic capable of navigating. Each is

assigned to one rally car and they try to follow it up to the start of a special stage, loop round to meet it again as soon after the stage as is practicable, and then follow it into the next service point.

This is taking the business of 'eliminating failure due to misfortune' to its giddy heights, and chase cars are not over-popular with rally organisers unless they are responsibly handled. But it is always possible that the rally car will have its problem away from such aid. In that case, it may be necessary to get the assistance to the rally car and this is where the flexibility of the team's communications and service plan comes to the fore. If a rally car is stopped in a special stage, there may be a road which leads in to a point very close to where it is stopped. The chase car crew may be instructed to find it, and if they are successful then the mechanic may race on foot into the stage with tools and a spare part. Any diagnosis will have been done over the radio between the driver and engineers while the chase car is getting to the scene. If the rally car is still mobile but in need of extensive surgery, it may be a question of moving the main service van towards it on an intercept course so that the work may be carried out at a rendezvous.

All things are possible and it is the team which reacts to the problem quickest that may win the day. There is a quote from Des O'Dell, Peugeot team manager, which appears in the front of Andrew Cowan's book about winning the 1968 London to Sydney which says it all: 'Please remember . . . there is always a way. The problem is thinking about it in time.' The works team tries to do all its thinking before the rally even starts, but the nature of rallying is such that the unexpected will always crop up to test it and its members to the full.

CHAPTER 6

LONG DISTANCE INFORMATION . . . .

The earliest events were often as much a test of the endurance of the driver and his passenger as they were of the car. For instance, the pioneer manufacturer and driver Henri Levassor is best remembered for his solo drive from Paris to Bordeaux and back in just over two days. In fact, all those early events were run virtually non-stop so that, even with changes of driver, endurance was a very important aspect.

The evolution of rallying into a sport dependent on set average speeds between controls and the use of difficult roads and adverse weather conditions to provide a result, meant that sheer endurance was eclipsed by other factors. Competitors on Monte Carlo Rallies could, when their schedule permitted, sleep in the car or even check into a hotel, while other events became more compact or ran in convenient stages with night halts in between the competitive road sections.

But there has always been a place for events that put a high premium on the endurance of both car and crew. One of the earliest of these was the Peking to Paris, which captured the public imagination back in 1907. Adopted child of *Le Matin*, the Paris newspaper that first printed the details of the challenge, it attracted fewer entries than the organisers hoped, and just five of them actually shipped their vehicles to Peking and came under starter's orders in June. Sixty days later, the Itala of Prince Scipione Borghese and Luigi Barzini reached Paris, having completed one of the most amazing motoring feats of any age.

Their car had been dismantled and carried over obstacles. It had been pushed, pulled, shoved, towed and rocked to get it through territory where horsepower still came on four legs. They had slept in the car, in a tent beside it, and in castles and monasteries. They had been entertained by Grand Lamas, by the Automobile Club of Moscow, by the Irkutsk Cycle Club and by an Ekaterinburg mine owner high in the Urals. These were hardly the kind of things which people today would associate with endurance rallying, but the Rallye-Raids of the 1990s do have points of similarity, especially when it comes to sleeping in tents next to the cars.

This was not the style favoured by the members of the Royal Motor Union of Liège when they ran their first endurance event from Liège to Biarritz and back in 1927. Rumour has it that they wanted to fit the event into a weekend. Certainly, there was no time wasted and no pretence of staying a day or two to spend money in Biarritz. The subtitle of this event was *Le Marathon de la Route* and it stayed with all the events that they ran right up to the last one in 1969.

Evidently Biarritz was not far enough to extend them properly, as on that first event all six cars that finished were credited with zero penalties. This was despite their having covered 2300km in 68 hours at an average speed of 33kph, with a penalty for exceeding 40kph on any section. The aim had been to have but a single car finish without penalty, and for all the others to be late somewhere on the event. For 1928, the rally was extended to go to Madrid, which made it 3300km, and the average speed was bumped up to 38kph. This resulted in the ideal result – just one car with zero penalties, the Bugatti 49 of Maurice Minsart. The following year, the route was the same

PREVIOUS PAGE Helicopters are an essential tool of the organisers during a rally like Paris–Dakar. Strict control means that they have the only ones flying and can thus be sure that they have full control of any situation.

RIGHT Every means was used to get competing cars through to Paris from Peking. The Itala of Prince Borghese was lifted, towed, dismantled and sometimes even driven to overcome the primitive conditions that had to be faced.

but the result was not, since no fewer than nine cars finished with zero penalties. Something had to be done, and one can never accuse the Royal Motor Union of Liège of being scared to take the appropriate measures. For the 1930 event, the route stayed the same at 3300km but the number of controls was almost doubled and the average speed lifted to 50kph. This made the Liège–Madrid–Liège the toughest event in Europe, with 66 hours of non-stop motoring to be shared between the crew, who also had to do all the necessary navigating, refuelling and service within the time allowed. Several key features were introduced which became standard for later Marathons, such as the requirement for cars to wait at controls until their due time came up, starting two cars at a time from a time control, and giving a five-minute gap between such departures.

The Marathon de la Route went from strength to strength, taking its route to turning points at first Rome, from 1931 to 1960, and then Sofia, from 1961 to 1964. But its *modus operandi* was always to take the performance of one year and turn the screw for the next, to be sure that improvements in cars and crews would not allow its results to be cluttered by too many clean sheets. This philosophy of endurance, and demanding that the rally result be decided by road penalties incurred on open road sections, made the Liège a very different challenge to, for instance, the Alpine Cup where the main rewards were handed out for unpenalised runs and special tests were used to produce a final result.

And it was this philosophy, of course, which led to the Marathon de la Route's eventual demise, since it had continually to search for roads which had a minimum of other traffic using them. It was this that provoked the shift from Rome to Sofia in 1961, so that the rally could be taken away from the relatively crowded roads of the Alps and its most competitive sections relocated in Yugoslavia and Bulgaria. It managed to retain its classic sections in the Italian Dolomites right up to the end, so that names like Vivione, Gavia and Stelvio became rally-speak for the most difficult roads that one could imagine.

The Liège was an event that simply bred legends. The *Commissaire Général* who took over responsibility for it in 1935 was a quiet, bespectacled gentleman called Maurice Garot, but his ability to demand the maximum from cars and drivers during the event that he directed for almost 30 years would easily have qualified him for a place of honour in the Spanish Inquisition. Hard on the competitors he may have been, but he was always generous in his praise of those who rose to the challenge of his event.

Such a man was Johnny Claes who first won the Marathon in 1951 at the wheel of a Jaguar XK 120, partnered by Jacques Ickx, the Belgian journalist and father of Jacky Ickx. In the 1953 event Claes, in his Lancia Aurelia GT, took with him as co-driver a pre-war winner of the rally and a man who had done no fewer than 12 Marathons, Trasenster. Unfortunately, on the journey south Trasenster fell ill, and by the time the rally was in the Dolomites he was no longer capable of driving, or indeed doing very much at all. He was seen by a doctor first at Brescia and then at Turin before the start of the last night in the French Alps. Claes was in the middle of a titanic struggle for

RIGHT Evan Green was prepared for snow and ice on the early stages of the 1968 London to Sydney. His works BMC 1800 was also ready for close encounters with kangaroos, carrying what became known in the business as a 'roo bar'.

LEFT Although the Safari Rally has evolved into a solely Kenyan event, Mount Kilimanjaro in neighbouring Tanzania still provides a backdrop to one of its sections.

ABOVE Occasionally there is a defined road even in the desert, but the absence of open sand usually means more rocks and other similar hazards.

RIGHT Nothing is quite the same in the desert. The sand does not give very good support and jacks need to be specially designed to work at all.

the lead with Christillin/Fiorio in a similar Lancia and Olivier Gendebien in a Jaguar XK 120. As the rally progressed, his rivals kept expecting to see him retire from fatigue at the next control, but somehow he was always there. After Claes had been driving for 30 hours without relief, Trasenster recovered enough to be able to drive for about an hour, and then it was Claes again all the way to the finish. Apart from winning the event, Claes was on the receiving end of a rare tribute from Garot to the effect that 'in the history of motor sport, there was no exploit of endurance to rival it.'

In the year that Johnny Claes was receiving such praise, the Automobile Association of East Africa ran a motor rally at Easter under the title of the Coronation Safari. The event was held partly as a celebration of the accession of Queen Elizabeth II to the British throne, but it also took advantage of the fact that an extra holiday had been granted to the citizens of East Africa for the Coronation, which gave the competitors and officials the free time to run a full-scale rally. Like the Marathon de la Route, there was not even a whiff of a special stage and the whole thing was decided on road penalties pure and simple. Again, like the Marathon, the organisers couldn't be bothered to start people one by one, although the Safari did go a bit over the top on that first event by running a mass start from Nairobi. This was done by way of the 42 Nairobi starters following the Mayor to the end of the 30mph speed limit, whereupon he gracefully pulled over and they roared off to start the rally.

The cars were organised into classes by their price in Nairobi rather than by their capacity, which was the system that was almost universal in Europe. The reason for this was simple: they saw their event as the definitive test of which car was worth the money paid

for it in the showroom. They also saw the event as being a challenge to both car and crew, for the varied terrain and weather conditions occurring in East Africa could mean that the skill and ingenuity of the crew were as thoroughly tested as in the Peking to Paris. The various classes had differing average speeds to maintain, but nearly all proved to be impossible. The winner was Alan Dix in a Volkswagen 1200 which collected 17 minutes of penalty, despite a fairly major accident into a hidden ditch some five hours from the finish which bent the steering and put the co-driver completely through the windscreen. The fastest car was actually a Chevrolet driven by John Manussis and John Boyes, which suffered the indignity of having to be kept afloat with empty petrol cans when it went off into a river on the final wet night back to Nairobi from Tanzania.

That first Safari had average speeds ranging from 43mph to 52mph, and sections which required the drivers to go some 28 hours without stopping, except for replenishment to the car and to themselves. The higher speeds reflect the lack of Alps and Dolomites in East Africa as well as the more open nature of the roads and the lower traffic density. In fact, the biggest hazard was hitting wild animals, and one of the more memorable moments of Safari history was made in 1963 when Erik Carlsson and Gunnar Palm lost the lead after their Saab 96 had been in collision with an anteater. For some reason, the world has always remembered that collision better than the fact that subsequent conditions on the rally were so severe that they reduced the entry of 84 cars to just seven finishers.

Unlike the Marathon de la Route of M. Garot, the Safari organisers were not anxious to tie the knot too

RIGHT American influence showing up on the 1977 London to Sydney Rally. This one went via Singapore, in deference to the main sponsors.

BOTTOM LEFT Although they never received much attention outside Australia, the post-war marathon rallies were highly regarded. The vestiges of the building site can be seen on the front of this Morris Minor competing in the 1953 6500 mile Redex Trial.

RIGHT This cannot have gone down well with the gentlemen from Crewe, but this Rolls-Royce was entered on the 1970 World Cup Rally. It is seen here in pre-event testing.

tight; they have always been at pains to relax average speeds if necessary and introduce rest halts if suggested, but somehow the very nature of the event is to turn it into a matter of endurance for car and crew. If it is a dry year, then the drivers attack the sections with more verve and spend long periods standing while the mechanics repair the damage, while if it is wet, then the same time may be spent pushing and shoving to get the car through at all. In both cases, the average speed becomes unattainable. On the 1972 Safari, for example, the rally started at Dar-es-Salaam in Tanzania and headed to Nairobi for its first rest halt of some six or seven hours. But, so late were some of those who had struck trouble on those early sections that they checked in at Nairobi only to have a cup of coffee and be sent off on the loop to Uganda straightaway. Thus what often appear to be generous rest allowances on paper, dissolve into sleepless snacks

when cars are allowed to run many hours behind the scheduled time. In some ways, this is similar in effect to the shift of opening and closing times of controls on the Marathon de la Route.

For almost 20 years, only local drivers won the Safari. The first overseas drivers arrived in 1958, with two Monte Carlo winners in the persons of Ronnie Adams from Ireland and Per Malling from Norway. The following year, the European teams arrived in something like strength, with Ford entering Zephyrs and Rootes a team of Hillman Huskies for Peter Harper, Paddy Hopkirk and Peter Jopp. By the time it had progressed to full international recognition in 1962, over a third of the entries were from outside East Africa; but try as they could, the overseas drivers seemed destined to lead but not to win. It took until 1972 when Hannu Mikkola and Gunnar Palm romped home in their Ford Escort RS before this

ABOVE Mentors of the modern Paris–Dakar: on the right, Gilbert Sabine, father of Thierry, who inherited the organisation and the tradition, and on the left, Jean Todt, whose Peugeot team brought their enormous support to rally-raids when Group B rallying collapsed.

LEFT Vic Preston Junior had fun getting this pre-rally shot in the game park with his works Lancia Delta in 1988, but encountering a giraffe at night in the middle of a Kenyan road is likely to be a doubly fatal event.

BOTTOM LEFT Diamonds may be a girl's best friend, but the only rocks that a rally driver gets intimate with are much less appealing. Ari Vatanen and Bernard Giroux on the way to Vatanen's first Paris–Dakar win for Peugeot in 1987.

piece of history was finally undone. But it cannot be any coincidence that Mikkola and Palm had been the winners of the World Cup Rally two years earlier in 1970, and that also at the wheel of a works Ford Escort, albeit one with a less powerful single-cam engine.

The 1970 World Cup was the second event of a marathon tradition that had its roots with Peking to Paris but also owed much to the European rallying concept and to the East African Safari. The first of these marathon events – marathon with a small 'm' in deference to the Liège event – was the 1968 London to Sydney Rally. This sprang into being at the behest of two newspapers, the *Daily Express* in London and the *Daily Telegraph* in Sydney. In that respect, it was following in the tradition of many of the early motor sporting competitions, which had also been created by newspapers.

The London to Sydney seemed to come at just the right time to fill a gap that existed in contemporary rallying. The governing body of the time was the *Commission Sportive Internationale* of the FIA, which quite simply had not cottoned on to the fact that rallying had spread outside Europe and that it was a sport which deserved World Championship

status. In 1963, the RAC had taken the initiative and created what they called a World Cup for car manufacturers which was based on the results of five events. These were the Marathon de la Route, the Swedish Rally to the Midnight Sun, the Canadian Shell 4000, the East African Safari and, of course, the RAC Rally. It was won by Ford in its first year, but was soon to disappear since the Marathon de la Route became a circuit event in 1965, the Swedish Rally went to a winter rally in the same year, while the Shell 4000 disappeared entirely.

The CSI continued to run its European Rally Championship for Drivers which was started in 1953, and then in 1968, after some heavy lobbying by the car manufacturers, it finally introduced a European Rally Championship for Manufacturers. But this was hardly enough, since it did not recognise that rallying was no longer a purely European activity nor that the new markets for motor cars were also outside Europe. The lobbying continued and it eventually resulted in a full World Rally Championship emerging in 1973. Curiously, the manufacturers' lobby was so successful that the CSI completely forgot to include a drivers' championship as part of the new World series, and it took them until 1977, after a great deal of comment from journalists who believed that rally drivers were just as newsworthy as the cars they drove, to institute an FIA Cup for Drivers. A full World Rally Championship for Drivers did not appear until 1979.

In its way, the 1968 London to Sydney was a part of the lobbying carried out by car manufacturers. It was a major event, running over 25 days and four continents, which did not fit any of the CSI categories. It attracted a great deal of manufacturer support, indeed almost to the point where the entries on the 1968 RAC Rally and the 1969 Monte Carlo Rally suffered as a result of factory involvement on the London to Sydney. One of the moving forces behind the event was Tony Ambrose, ex-European Rally Champion co-driver, who was largely responsible for the route and the general concept of the event. It covered 7000 miles from London to Bombay with only one scheduled halt of six hours, though the long sections through Europe ensured that no one was going to reach Bombay without having had some sleep outside the rally car. A sea crossing to Perth was then followed by another 3400 miles across Australia to the finish in Sydney. Because main roads were being used rather than jungle tracks, the average speeds were quite high and often topped the 60mph mark. This was certainly true of the first difficult section of the rally in north-eastern Turkey where the 170 miles between Sivas and Erzincan had to be covered in 2hr 45min. But as with the Safari, the organisers had given generous allowances for maximum lateness so as to keep the majority of the runners in the rally.

There were, in fact, only 70 places on the ship to Australia, which could have been a problem as there had been 98 starters. As it happened, 72 reached Bombay and somehow room was found for the extra pair aboard the SS *Chusan*. In Australia the rate of attrition was higher, since the roads through the Australian outback and in the Australian Alps and Flinders Range were more testing than those of Turkey and Iran. And in best newspaper tradition, all the drama was reserved for the closing stages. It was here that Roger Clark and Ove Andersson broke their Lotus Cortina's axle and lost an hour replacing it, while Gilbert Staepelaere and Simo Lampinen smashed a gatepost with their Ford Taunus 20 MRS and lost almost three hours tying the bits together. But most dramatic of all was the demise of long-time leaders Lucien Bianchi and Jean-Claude Ogier in a Citroën DS 21, when they hit a private Mini just 110 miles from the final control and could not continue. Indeed, Bianchi was quite badly hurt and was taken to hospital with a broken ankle and minor cuts to the head. His hasty exit from the London to Sydney denied it a non-British victor and thus some of the status that it could have inherited from having the popular Belgian driver win in a French car. The victory of Andrew Cowan, Colin Malkin and Brian Coyle in the Hillman Hunter was well deserved, but did less to ram home the point to the Paris-based CSI.

In the euphoria following the success of the London to Sydney, there was talk of it becoming a regular event, perhaps once every four years. But the reality

ABOVE Ever courteous, the late Thierry Sabine shows the way to a charming pair of competitors in the 1985 Paris–Dakar. Navigation by compass and bearing is a real necessity in the desert.

of the situation was that it was quite an expensive little jaunt for the works teams, who were obliged to send service crews and spare parts to places of which they had previously never heard. It was certainly more expensive even than the Safari, and that event was liable to deplete severely even the largest of European manufacturers' budgets if done properly. As it happened, the rally world was still waiting for its World Championship when, two years later, along came the World Cup Rally.

This had a different organiser, the Australian promoter Wylton Dickson, and a different newspaper, the London *Daily Mirror*, behind it. But it was run on the principle of the London to Sydney, only turned round and directed at Mexico City to coincide with the razzmatazz leading up to the World Cup football competition of that year. Where the London to Sydney scored in novelty and number of continents, the London–Mexico went for distance and altitude records. Its total distance was some 16 000 miles, of which 4500 were completed in Europe on roads 'borrowed' from such rallies as the Marathon de la Route (Yugoslavia), Coupe des Alpes (France) and the TAP (Portugal). A ship then took the cars on from Lisbon to Rio de Janeiro while the drivers were permitted to fly. (Bob Neyret stole a march on them all by using the time to go and win the Moroccan Rally for Citroën while his other rally car was crossing to South America.) Once there, the rally set new benchmarks for timed stages by using some that stretched for over 500 miles, while the sections in the Andes that took the cars above 13 000 feet in altitude persuaded many crews to take oxygen cylinders in the rally cars.

Of course, there was rest for the crews, but the sheer length of the event and the long distances between suitable halts meant that it was much harder on the drivers than a normal rally. The works teams committed themselves fully to the London–Mexico, with Ford striving to outdo Triumph, Citroën and others in service organisation. Ford's efforts paid off with a win for Hannu Mikkola and Gunnar Palm in a Ford Escort fitted with a special single camshaft 1800cc engine rather than the Lotus-designed Twin Cam that they normally used for rallies. A version of this car was subsequently used for motor sport by Ford and sold as the Escort Mexico, spawning its own championship in Britain and providing cheap access to the sport for many young drivers.

The London–Mexico was a great media success, and though the cost of participating was high, the CSI could see at last that rallying existed in more places than just Europe. Indeed, some of the Ford works drivers were invited back to do the Rally of the Incas in Peru later that year, an event that brought the existence of South American rallying to everyone's notice. The decision to grant a World Rally Championship was now not far off, and that, together with the cost of doing marathons properly, meant that nothing quite like those two events has happened since.

That is not to say that nothing at all happened.

Wylton Dickson came back with two follow-ups to the London–Mexico, the first of which was a 10 800-mile trip from London to Munich, via a double crossing of the Sahara Desert, in 1974. It was quite an event in every sense of that word, for it was designed for the standard of entry that had been received on the two previous events and the works cars were just not there. What it lacked in manufacturers' entries, it made up for in over-optimistic private entries who might have made it through to the finish on the original London to Sydney but were to stand no chance once the desert sands were reached. Navigation where no roads existed proved too much for the majority of the crews and those that did reach Tamanrasset on the far side of the Sahara could count their lateness in days rather than in hours and minutes. Of the 70 cars that started, only five managed the whole route and a further 14 were classified as finishers having been given permission to miss the furthest section of the route. Interestingly, the winner was a private Citroën DS 23 crewed by three Australians, André Welinski, Ken Tubman and Jim Reddix, all of whom had a record of success in various round-Australia marathons.

Non-stop sections of over 60 hours' allotted time, with maybe half-a-dozen time controls within them, were nothing unusual in this kind of event and it was not such a surprise, therefore, to find a three-man crew winning. Wylton Dickson's next marathon was also won by a three-man crew, two of the original winners from the London to Sydney, Andrew Cowan and Colin Malkin, accompanied this time by Mike Broad in a Mercedes 280 SE. The date was 1977 and the name of the event was again London to Sydney, but this time it was sponsored by Singapore Airlines. It is no surprise, then, to learn that it went via that country, and that as a consequence the route covered a record 19 329 miles. It was an event magnificent in its concept, but it was clear from the entries that were received that 'normal' rallying was now properly structured and was receiving the majority of the car manufacturers' rally budgets.

There was a further marathon held in 1978 which took place in South America and covered about 18 000 miles. It visited nearly all the countries on that continent and consequently lasted almost five weeks. The Mercedes factory entered in a big way and the rally was really a battle between their six crews, who fought it out almost to a standstill. Victory finally went to the marathon expert Andrew Cowan, who was driving a 450 SLC co-piloted by Colin Malkin. One could be forgiven for saying that these latter marathons were not serious, but they were indeed tough events and the lack of serious consideration given to them was simply a result of their not attracting a representative entry from the rally world. Much later, in 1988, an attempt was made to hold another event round South America, but this encountered organisational difficulties right from the start. The only good news on this particular horizon is that it would seem that there is a distinct possibility of the 1968 London to Sydney being re-run in 1993 – on its 25th anniversary – with the eligible cars being those of the period. Several owners are already re-preparing their 1968 mounts in anticipation.

If Wylton Dickson did not exactly found a dynasty with his 1970s passion for marathon events, one seed that he sowed certainly took root, though it took two other men with a passion for adventure to nurture it into bearing fruit. The first of these was Jean-Claude Bertrand. In the late 1960s, he had been living in Abidjan for 15 years and was President of *Ecurie Ivoire*. He decided to run a Safari-type rally named after the largest of the Ivory Coast's rivers, the Bandama. This event was first held in 1968 and ten years later was admitted into the World Rally Championship.

Having witnessed the efforts of the UDT World Cup Rally to cross the Sahara successfully in 1974, Bertrand dreamt up the idea of having a rally from Abidjan to Monte Carlo across the Sahara Desert. His precise idea was that prospective competitors should come down in December to do his Bandama Rally, which traditionally took place over the Christmas holiday, and then they could do Abidjan–Monte Carlo. Following this, with a short space for repairs and relaxation, they could do the Monte Carlo Rally which started in the third week of January. Left to his own devices, one feels sure that Jean-Claude would eventually have linked up all the World Championship rallies in this way so that professional rally drivers would never need to visit home at all. Anyway, the Abidjan–Monte Carlo was held between 28 December 1974 and 10 January 1975, with a route which went through Upper Volta, Niger, Algeria and Morocco before coming up through Spain to France.

The element which made this type of event differ-ent in character from the normal kind of rally was the crossing of open spaces such as are provided by the Sahara Desert. In places, there is a clearly defined road, but mostly the navigation is by compass rather than by map or Tulip road book. With its vast open spaces, North America had seen several such events run during the 1960s and 1970s, of which perhaps the most famous was the Baha 1000. This started in southern California and ran non-stop for 1000 miles down the Baha peninsula into Mexico. It was attempted several times by European drivers such as Erik Carlsson in his Saab, but it did not prove to be a fruitful garden for their talents. Desert racing became popular in the late 1970s on the back of the Baha's success, but when control of the sport, as is so often the case in entrepreneurial America, slipped away from the National Automobile Club, it lost any hope of becoming an international force. But its machines, from the vast Ford Broncos of Bill Stroppe to the VW-based dune buggies, set an example that was to be picked up with the French events of the 1980s.

Jean-Claude Bertrand's idea of a link-up between the Bandama and Monte Carlo rallies never really became a reality, as the kind of vehicles which were necessary to cross the Sahara were not best suited to the Monte Carlo. Indeed, by the second such event, which was the Abidjan–Nice of 1976, it was being won by Range Rovers which at that time would not have been eligible for either the Bandama or the Monte Carlo. The Bandama was destined to go on and qualify for the World Championship, which made the question of vehicle eligibility even more problematic. But what Bertrand had found was that his Abidjan–Nice was quite popular in its own right, and to make it even more so, he had only to do one other thing and that was to start it in France. Thus he became the organiser of the Rallye 5/5 Echappement

LEFT Sadly, it is a frequent sight to see a vehicle burning during the Paris–Dakar. The high speeds generate a great deal of frictional heat in components, and thanks to the high fuel loads, any small conflagration that results can lead to total destruction.

TOP RIGHT It could be that Moses was in these reeds . . . Ari Vatanen making his debut with the Citroen ZX Grand Raid on the 1990 Rallye des Pharaohs.

Transafrica, which was held between 23 December 1979 and 13 January 1980 over a route which, like the old UDT World Cup, crossed the Sahara twice.

These events stirred a French passion for adventure in the desert driving almost anything with four wheels, and where there is a demand, someone will spring to fill it. Thierry Sabine, a flamboyant young man who had competed in at least one of Bertrand's events, reckoned that, through his contacts with transport companies operating in West Africa, he could put on an even better event. He did some planning and in 1979 the Paris–Dakar was born. Perhaps it was Sabine's amazing charisma – in later years he was to have a pre-event press conference in the *Théâtre Wagram* in Paris where he would ride onto the stage on a white horse, wearing full Tuareg costume – or maybe it was the detailed organisation which provided food and accommodation every night for journalists, competitors and organisers at successive remote locations in the desert, but the Paris–Dakar caught the imagination of both competitors and the media in double-quick time.

The Sabine philosophy was different to those of previous marathon organisers. He welcomed both works teams and private owners, but he wanted them to share a common experience. He did not want the factory entries to have everything their own way and took steps to limit their possibilities for servicing and communications. For instance, separate service cars were not permitted, but teams could enter trucks in the rally and they, carrying the spares, would turn up at the night's bivouac some hours after the rally cars. The mechanics, who could fly around in aeroplanes provided and controlled by the organisers, could then work on the cars all night as

there was no *parc fermé*. The same considerations, however, applied to private owners, who could rent space in other trucks entered on the rally, which would then bring their spares to the night halt just like those of the factory. He also widened the whole nature of the rally by accepting not just the trucks, which competed in their own division, but also motorcycles. These do not really come under the subject matter of this book, but it must be acknowledged that they played a major part in the successful evolution of the Paris–Dakar as a world-class event.

Very soon, the Paris–Dakar was big news in France and the word was spreading fast. A win in 1980 for Freddy Kottulinsky – with a Volkswagen Iltis 4WD off-road vehicle that was virtually a test bed for the new Audi Quattro – ensured that the Germans took notice, while the Range Rover victory the following year for René Metge brought it to the attention of the English-speaking world. Its format of long special stages which took up the majority of a day's driving, with just short liaison sections on to the next night halt, meant that it had a unique combination of speed and endurance that could not be matched by conventional special stage rallies. This was the inheritance of the Marathon de la Route and of the Safari, but with a rest for the drivers and time to catch up each day for the slower vehicles.

As there were no real restrictions on what could be done to a vehicle to make it suitable for the Paris–Dakar, the evolution of successful machines was swift and purposeful. The winning Range Rover in 1980 sported a few fibreglass copies of standard panels, and had lost most of its seats and internal trim in order to house such things as three 120-litre petrol tanks. Five years later, Patrick Zanirolli won with a

LEFT No problem about carrying unauthorised passengers on this occasion – the final leg of the Paris–Dakar is down the beach and everyone joins in the fun at the finish.

RIGHT In terms of what kind of vehicles are accepted on marathon events, the rule is that almost anything goes. Hubert Auriol drove this Volkswagen-based buggy on the 1988 Paris–Dakar.

others seriously injured. The organisers cannot remove the danger but they do at least have the best medical service on hand to tend to those who get hurt.

In many ways, it is thus ironic that Sabine was killed in his helicopter on the 1986 event and that Peugeot came with their works team to the event for the first time in 1987. A tree close to the spot where Sabine crashed was named in his honour, and the rally now has a control there whenever it uses the trackless waste of the Tenere Desert as part of its route. As far as is possible, the organisers of the Paris–Dakar, under the guidance of Gilbert Sabine, Thierry's father, try to carry on in the same tradition, keeping aerial assistance to a minimum and restricting the free use of radios for contact with the competing cars. One change that has been foisted on the rally by the relentless onset of professionalism is the need to reduce the amount of time in which cars can be worked on every night, by instigating *parc fermés* at certain spots. In an interview some three years after his son's death, Gilbert Sabine confided that he would be prepared to lose the works teams if it meant keeping all the private owners. When a rally has some 400 or so entrants every year, that point of view can be understood, though it is in fact the works teams that spend the majority of the money as well as creating the media attention that fuels the interest of all the other sponsors involved in the rally.

The success of the Paris–Dakar, progressing as it did from being regarded as an event for a particular species of lunatic in 1979 to major international recognition and a worldwide reputation by 1990, meant that other events were bound to be created in its image. The FIA recognised the new breed of event as Rallye-Raids and were soon authorising events not just in North Africa but also in Spain, Portugal, the Middle East, Greece, Singapore and Australia. For some time, there has been talk of the FIA running a worldwide Rallye-Raid Championship, but that has not yet come to pass. Many of the leading events such as the Rallye des Pharaohs in Egypt, the Baja Aragon in Spain and the Australian Safari have gone to great trouble to bring their event regulations into line with international thinking to ensure themselves a place alongside Paris–Dakar when the championship is created.

The Australian Safari is an endurance rally in the tradition of Paris–Dakar, and because it is able to run across areas that almost literally did not know of the

Mitsubishi Pajero that was a pure confection of kevlar-carbonfibre on a Pajero chassis with a much-modified engine and suspension. The Peugeots that dominated the event in the late 1980s were developed from the Group B 205 T16 that won two World Championships for Peugeot in 1985 and 1986. They were state-of-the-art 4WD desert racers, with 400bhp in a chassis which had an all-up weight of some 1300kg. They also benefited from extra long suspension movement and double dampers controlling each wheel.

Along with Peugeot's interest in the rally came an ever-increasing pressure on the lack of sophistication which the Paris–Dakar tried to retain. For example, on World Championship rallies in the 1980s it had become common practice for works teams to whisk mechanics ahead of the rally cars by helicopter so that the best men were always on hand. And if a car ran into a problem on a stage, then an intrepid pilot could put down close at hand to get the mechanics to the stricken car. Sabine was totally against this happening on his event. For one thing, the governments of some of the countries through which they passed would not be too happy about a multiplicity of such machines loose in desert areas, some of which were operational in a military sense. Thus the only helicopters allowed were Sabine's personal craft and the medical helicopters which flew after the competitors to rescue those hurt in accidents. The Paris–Dakar is above all a dangerous event and it is rare for a year to go by without at least one person being killed and

existence of man before four-wheel-drive vehicles were available, it comprises an adventure in the true sense of the word. It has had its precedents in Australia, for there have been any number of round-Australia trials sponsored by a variety of petrol and oil companies, but such events, tough and unremitting though they were, were for standard cars and stuck, wherever practicable, to what passed for roads. The Australian Safari plunged straight into the Paris–Dakar mould by contriving a challenge for off-road vehicles, cars and motorcycles.

This was first held in 1985 over a 6000km course and was won by Andrew Cowan and Fred Gocentas in a Mitsubishi Pajero. The same crew won again in the following year and indeed Mitsubishi have won all six of the events held up until 1990. In 1988, for the Australian bicentenary, the route was extended to 10 000km but for subsequent events it has gone back slightly to a more comfortable 8000km. The format of the event has settled on a start in Sydney and a finish in Darwin, with visits to several deserts and Alice Springs along the way. It runs over ten days, and during that time the organisation of the rally looks after everyone's needs in terms of accommodation and transport. The team managers, mechanics and media are transported from one night halt to the next in air-conditioned coaches. Servicing is prohibited except at the night halts, where the mechanics can labour away all night to try to have the vehicles on the starting line for the next morning. Only two mechanics per vehicle may be nominated and one team manager per team. Tyres, wheels and other spare parts are moved around by trucks, again supplied by the organisers, who also provide a tyre-fitting and welding service. All fuel is laid on by the organisers, though the competitor does have to pay for what he

uses! For any vehicle that cannot be repaired by its crew on the route, there is also a recovery service that sweeps along after the rally to pick up stragglers. And in the event of someone needing medical help, there are helicopters and ambulances constantly in attendance on the rally, able to reach the scene of an accident very quickly. If hospital treatment is required, the patient can be removed to the nearest Flying Doctor base.

The press get equally well looked after with their travel and accommodation arranged and telex, telephone, facsimile and radio laid on each night via a portable satellite link established by the Australian government's own specialist organisation, ITERRA. The organisers arrange for their own TV and video cameras to follow the event in helicopters and ground-based vehicles, to ensure that anyone who wants footage can have it. The entire rally – competitors, managers, mechanics, organisers, pressmen – all get to eat and sleep every night in 'Safari City', a transportable environment that provides all the comforts of home including showers and individual tents for those destined to get some rest.

The route is secret and is only handed out to the competitors when they start each morning, so that works teams and amateurs alike are saved the problems of trying to organise a reconnaissance of such a long and difficult route. This is the same consideration that has persuaded the Paris–Dakar to keep its route secret too, though they have the additional problems of traversing sensitive border areas and military zones. The 1991 Paris–Dakar tactfully avoided Chad as its civil war was reaching a climax just before the event was due to start. However, it did run into a problem in Mali where what appeared to be a renegade military outfit shot up a Team Citroën lorry and succeeded in killing the driver. No such problems worry the Australians, but they are concerned to the extent that protracted reconnaissances would vastly increase the cost of competing and could easily disturb their relationship with the people that live and operate in Australia's outback. While the Australian Safari is running, they have complete control over what goes on and would like to keep it that way.

So the situation is that the pure endurance event, where the car hardly stops and the drivers take it in turns to drive, has virtually gone out of existence. Even the organisers of events like the Paris–Moscow–Peking scheduled for late 1991 do not envisage that competitors will have to drive to schedules worthy of the old Marathon de la Route. Long distances will of course be covered but, as with the Paris–Dakar type of package, the organiser and his sponsor get little value if everything takes place at night and the drivers are too tired to talk to the press. Today, such events are big business and are run by companies set up specifically to handle the considerable logistics that are necessary to run them safely and profitably, but without losing that essential ingredient – adventure.

CHAPTER 7

HISTORIC RALLYING

THE MODERN NOSTALGIA

Until quite recently, rallying could hardly have been called a sentimental sport. It has always been concerned with novelty and innovation – the latest car, the latest tyre, the latest development to give the competitor an edge over his rival. For instance, no one would have thought of continuing to enter rallies in an Austin Healey 3000 when there were Porsches, Alpines and Lancias that could beat it; and they in their turn took up a position on the sidelines when the Ford Escort, the Lancia Stratos, the Opel Ascona 400 and the Audi Quattro came along.

But the upsurge of interest in rallying that occurred during the 1970s, and was sustained through the 1980s, also aroused interest in the cars of the previous decades. This was certainly true in northern Europe where the present-day rallyists had a strong feeling of nostalgia for the days when Mini Cooper S's, Austin Healeys, Saabs and Volvos ruled the rally scene. In the Latin countries of Europe, the revival of interest in competition with old cars centred originally on racing, and that trend can be seen most clearly in that one of the current European Historic Rally Trophy events is the Targa Florio, once a race but now a historic rally.

To try to find the launching point for the idea of rallies for historic cars is not very easy, despite the fact that they are a quite recent phenomenon. For some years in the 1970s, the Automobile Club of Monaco had run an event for historic cars which was loosely based on the pre-war rallies. It ran in May and took the old cars over a night section in the Alpes Maritimes before arriving in Monte Carlo. It was an event conducted purely for fun and there was no real element of competition except the teasing of your friends if you happened to be late or break down. The cars were chosen from the pre-war or immediately post-war periods, and the organisers made every attempt to get journalists invited to participate as co-drivers.

This event no longer survives but it must have helped to sow some seeds in various places around Europe. The question arose in Britain about whether there were enough old rally cars to run a retrospective RAC Rally on the 50th anniversary of its first edition. This was due to happen in 1982 and, with some aid from the long-term sponsors of their annual rally, the RACMSA ran the Lombard RAC Golden Fifty Rally in April of that year. They were pleasantly surprised at the number and variety of the entries, with any number of Cooper S's, Healey 3000s, old Jaguar MkIIs, Ford Zephyrs and Mercedes saloons and sports cars coming out of hibernation and making the event a real competition. With a format of races, driving tests, tarmac stages and hill climbs, it was not surprising that the Cooper S's dominated the event, with Paddy Hopkirk and Brian Culcheth taking the overall victory in a Cooper S borrowed from the Leyland Cars museum and re-prepared for this event.

At about the same time, there was a marked increase of interest in racing 'classic' saloon cars. Basically, these were cars that were more than ten years old, and they had to conform, in general terms, with the condition in which they had been raced when new. This interest, together with the success of the RAC Golden Fifty, saw the beginnings of a rush to both collect and compete in older cars. One man

PREVIOUS PAGE Sydney Allard was the only man ever to win the Monte Carlo Rally driving a car bearing his own name. His cars live on, such as this M-type seen here on the Pirelli Marathon.
LEFT The Welsh International Rally is known today as a forest stage event, but its antecedents go back to the 1930s when cars converged on Cardiff from several starting points in Britain. This gaggle of MGs were finishing the 1936 event.
RIGHT The growth of interest in historic rallying has brought about the restoration of many models that were almost forgotten. Gunnar Andersson drove this Volvo PV 544 on the 1964 Acropolis Rally.

who did more than his fair share of both creating enthusiasm and providing it with an outlet was Phillip Young. He undertook several expeditions to rallies such as the Himalayan Rally with cars ranging from a Morris Minor to an Austin Healey 3000. His conclusion was that major events were needed which would cater exclusively for historic rally cars. With the sponsorship of Pirelli, he created an event which he called the Classic Marathon and which awards Coupes for penalty-free performances on the road sections. Starting in London and finishing in Cortina d'Ampezzo, high in the Italian Dolomites, the Pirelli Classic Marathon has provided a focus for British interest in rallying historical cars during the latter part of the 1980s. There is also a well-supported club in Britain called the Historic Rally Car Register which helps to organise such events as well as assisting its members to find and restore old rally cars.

The mid-1980s saw the Italians taking a major interest in revivals of on-the-road events, and the first of these was the Mille Miglia. When it was originally held, it was classified as a motor race although its non-circuit format, use of time controls, staggered starting order and use of two-man crews made it more like a no-holds-barred motor rally. It had last been held in 1957, when an accident occurred at Guidizzolo, only 30 miles from the finish, in which the Ferrari of the Marquis Alfonso de Portago and Edmund Nelson crashed into the crowd, killing both the crew as well as ten spectators of whom five were children. The revival, launched in 1983, was designed

as a regularity event and by 1986 it was consistently attracting an entry of over 200 saloon and sports cars from the period of the 1950s and 1960s. Almost a quarter of these entries came from the USA and the vast majority were Ferraris of one kind or another. Such popularity was bound to create imitators and before long there were Historic events running under the name of San Remo and the Isle of Elba, both famous rallies in their own right. Old Alfa Romeos and Lancias which a few years earlier would have fetched a few pounds for scrap, unless they had some specific individual history, were suddenly very collectable.

FISA, as the governing body of motor sport, was quick to act and in 1981 published its Appendix K of the Sporting Code, relating to the classification of historic cars and their use in races and rallies. Initially, its interest had been roused by the return to the race track of many historic racing cars, but it had the foresight to write the regulations in such a way as to set down a basis for rallying as well.

For a new branch of the sport, historic rallying has in a very short time provided a great deal of diversity. This stems from the different requirements of the owners of the cars and what they are prepared to do with them. They range from the pure collector to the chap who enjoys rallying and sees historic cars and events as being a less expensive or perhaps even a more challenging way to enter the sport than by using a modern car. In between, there are all kinds of owners whose technical interest in the cars often

ABOVE All the fervour of the original event is created when the Mille Miglia returns to Brescia in northern Italy.

LEFT The MG marque covers the years with a wide range of sporting cars. This MG TF is seen among the Dolomites during the Pirelli Classic Marathon.

draws them into rallying, about which, to start with, they know very little. The consequence has been a great deal of experimentation in the events that have been organised, to try and produce just the right mix of competition and social activity to please one or more parts of this spectrum of owners. It has often happened, therefore, that people have entered an event and been hopelessly out of their depth, rather like the quiet American couple back at the end of the 1950s who entered the Coupe des Alpes in an open Mercedes thinking that it was a kind of sightseeing tour. There has also been the contrary experience where people have entered an event expecting a real test and discovered it to be almost entirely non-competitive. Gradually, the situation is settling down and individual events are developing recognisable identities.

The problem for a historic rally organiser is to know at which type of owner he should be aiming his event. For instance, the collector prizes his car for its intrinsic worth, which may be thanks to its rarity or because it won a particular rally or was driven by a famous driver. His joy comes largely from the pride of ownership and the restoration of the car to its origin-al condition. The kind of event that appeals to him is probably that which has practically no competitive motoring and could be best described, in the words of FISA, as a touring assembly. The lack of tests ensures that the car is not put at any serious risk, certainly not much greater than that involved in driving normally on the roads. The pleasures of motoring are mixed with social events and the opportunity to admire other cars and, in one's turn, be admired by others.

One step up from the purely social event is a rally run on similar lines but where a fair amount of route-finding and precise adherence to a time schedule is required. These rallies give an immense amount of pleasure to enthusiasts who take a lot of pride in their cars and yet welcome the chance to use them in a gentle competition. A typical example of this latter type of event is the annual Claret and Classics, which in 1990 was into its seventh year. The nice thing about such an event is the wide range of cars that it attracts for a week's run through Western France with the competitive part of the event based on regularity sections where cars have to maintain a set average speed, with secret controls and penalties for both early and late arrival.

Where there are no special stages or average speeds higher than 50kph, FISA is not too concerned about issuing permits for the rallies themselves and has passed this responsibility on to FIVA (*Fédération Internationale des Véhicules Anciens*). If, however, there are to be speed tests, races or special stages where the average speed is higher than 50kph, then FISA takes the responsibility. It ensures that the rally is run to the standards expected when the cars are going to be reaching high speeds, and that the car and crew are properly equipped to avoid the worst consequences of any accident. The requirements for the cars include the fitting of a basic minimum roll cage, fire extinguishers and seat belts, even if these may not have been part of the car's equipment at the time it was originally rallied.

There is a large contingent of historic rally car owners who want to extend them beyond the confines of a rally format dependent on a 50kph average. For these, there are full special stage events, which in every respect are like a modern rally but cater for the historic car classes defined by Appendix K. For these drivers, it is the thrill and challenge of handling a 30-year-old car on narrow tyres that is the main attraction, rather than the intrinsic value of the cars themselves. It is no surprise, therefore, that it is this branch of historic rallying where modern technology abounds in the form of suspension components and brakes which would be shunned by the rigorous collector. It is also where the use of modern crash helmets and fire-proof overalls sometimes give a rather non-authentic touch to the sight of classic machinery being driven to the limit, but are sensible precautions in a sport that is by no means free of danger.

Somewhere in between the two extremes are yet another category of historic rally car enthusiasts who, having got a car from the past, want to relive the exploits of the rallymen of the same era. It is this middle ground who flock to the Pirelli Classic Marathon, with its echoes of past events and plenty of opportunity to drive over the classic roads used by Alpine Trials and the Liège–Rome–Liège. Style is everything on such events. The onlooker will not see any fire-proof overalls or full-face crash helmets being used, nor will there be any electronic navigation aids. The participants are not allowed any form of organised service and, unlike the original Alpine Trial where Pickfords used to arrange the daily transfer of luggage for competitors, they are encouraged to carry everything they need with them.

The revival of the Mille Miglia in Italy falls into the same category whereby a positive attempt is made to re-create the style of the event but without closing the roads and racing as fast as it is possible to go. However, the combination of using the cars in the same condition, safety-wise, as when they were originally used in competition, and the fact that even a 50kph average speed can become difficult to maintain if there is a lot of traffic and the weather turns nasty, turned sour on the organisers when in the 1990 event there were several accidents. In the worst of these, American Bill Schanbacher, driving an OSCA, crashed and was killed. There were other incidents as well which caused the event to be terminated before the finish, and those still competing were conveyed to Brescia in convoy by the Italian police.

Not all historic rallies have encountered such problems and the vast majority of them provide the competitor with what he desires without causing injury or disruption. The signs are that the future lies either with basically non-competitive events or with those featuring special stages. In any event, by the end of the 1980s the sport had grown to the point where FISA felt able to run its own European Historic Rally Trophy. This comprises eight events of which, currently, three are in Italy with others in Germany, Belgium, Czechoslovakia, Austria and France. These rallies cater principally for special stage competitors, although entries are also accepted from those who merely want to drive the same route as the others, at a lower speed. The latter group do not, quite evidently, compete for the Historic Rally Trophy. FISA have been particularly insistent that these top-of-the-market historic rallies are organised exclusively for historic cars. There are some rallies, and the Manx Trophy is a good example, where an historic event is run as part of a normal modern rally, using many of the same special stages and making use of the marshals and safety equipment provided for the main event. In the case of the Manx, it is a top coefficient qualifier in the FIA European Rally Championship, but if it wants to run an event for the Historic Trophy, then it will have to run a separate event on a different date.

This is what has already happened with events like the Targa Florio which, under that name, has two rally dates in the calendar, one in May as a European Championship event and one in October as a Historic Trophy event. It is interesting to see that the format of the historic rally comprises a hill-climb in Palermo on the first day and then three-and-a-half laps of the Little Madonie circuit on the second day, with the laps split into a multiplicity of special stages by having the start of each stage at the exit of one village and the arrival of the stage at the entry to the next village. The success of historic rallies in general, and the European Trophy in particular, is certain to lead to other countries vying to run events qualifying for that series. It is not even beyond the realms of possibility that there will soon be historic rallies in countries outside Europe.

The main categories into which FISA has divided all historic cars are Veteran, Vintage, Classic and Historic. Veteran encompasses cars built between 1905 and 1918, Vintage cars have to have been built between 1919 and 1930. Classic covers those built between 1931 and 1940, and Historic takes in the years from 1941 until 1965. Since roll cages and other safety criteria were not generally introduced until 1966 and later, it is only in events that demand no higher average speed than 50kph that these cars are allowed to run in exactly the same state of preparation as when they were first used in competition. The one exception to this is the provision of seat belts, which are often made compulsory by the transport legislation of the country in which the rally is taking

RIGHT Paddy Hopkirk and Jack Scott drove this works Sunbeam Rapier on the 1962 Monte Carlo Rally. The Rapier is now a very collectable performer in historic events.

place, not to mention that in which the car is registered. Thus no ugly roll cage may disfigure the styling of the car, which is especially important if it is an open sports car, and its occupants may protect their heads with cloth caps or fabric helmets should they wish.

For the administrators of the sport, the decisions that they face in relation to historic rallying are indeed difficult. They do not want to see all the old rallies of yesteryear brought out of the cupboard, dusted off and re-run in just the way that they were, since the attitude of the public toward them will be no less tolerant now than it was when they were last held. Indeed, it may be even worse and they are not likely to be mollified just because the cars are 25 years old.

Using the current manufacturing breakpoint of 31 December 1965, after which cars are loosely classified as 'post-historic', there must be a limit to the number of cars available for historic rallying. Admittedly, there are quite a few cars still being built up around old chassis plates either from new parts or from those stripped from un-roadworthy cars, but even this market will eventually die out. Thus the potential for expansion in the sport is limited, unless, of course, the goal-posts are moved and FISA starts to roll that historic date foward to keep it a steady 25 years behind the current date. The signs are that this will not happen and that historic rallying, at least for the time being, will remain as a fixed window on the past.

There are many reasons why this would be beneficial. The year 1966 was when the first really major rule-change relating to the eligibility of cars came into force in international rallying. It was the introduction of Groups 1, 2 and 3 which led to a new breed of rally cars epitomised by the Alpine Renault A110, the Lancia Fulvia HF Coupé, the Ford Escort Twin Cam and the Porsche 911 T. They were not alone of course, but the choice of the end of 1965 as the cut-off date for manufacture means that the really successful versions of those cars cannot compete in historic rallies. The Alpine A110 is limited to a 1300cc engine, as is the Lancia, while the Porsche can only have a carburettor version of its two-litre engine. And the Ford Escort is not eligible at all since it, like the Saab 96 V4, was not manufactured until after the magic date. The Lotus Cortina is eligible though, as well as all the variants of the Mini Cooper and Cooper S. The same goes for the Alfa Romeo Giulietta and its variants plus the GTA and the GTZ.

The curious thing is that although this technical window on the past should re-create the classic conflicts of the great rallies of the 1950s and 1960s, the events so far held have tended to favour cars that were not very competitive when they were new. If

LEFT The MGB has proved to be one of the most popular historic rally cars. Its performance, plus the fact that parts are easily available, means that it is one of the more practical propositions.

BELOW It is a shame that the sign appears to welcome only Maseratis. Perhaps the Alfa Romeo is lost – or its supporters are in the next street.

LEFT Not all the historic rally cars are sports cars. This Wolseley took part in the RAC's Golden 50 Rally in 1982.

LEFT If it were not for the modern suit and tie, it would almost have been possible to credit this Darracq with being a competitor on the original Paris–Vienna. However, the car was not built until 1913 and this particular Paris–Vienna took place in 1965. It was won by Monsieur Chamboredon in his immaculate Darracq.

RIGHT The joy of being let loose again in a factory Cooper S is clear from this shot of Paddy Hopkirk on the 1982 RAC Golden 50 Rally.

one looks through the results of the major rallies during that epoch, it is a tale of Volvo PV 544s, Saab 96 two-strokes, Mercedes 230 SE and SLs, Ford Zephyrs, Citroen ID 19s, Renault Dauphine 1093s, Porsche 356 Carreras and S 90s, Triumph TR3s, Sunbeam Rapiers, DKWs, Peugeot 203s and Austin Healey 100/6s. The fact is that Paul Howcroft, European Historic Rally Champion for two years in succession (1987 and 1988), drove a Lotus Elan which in its day was never regularly used in rallies nor was it successful when it was used. And Jaguar E-types and MGBs have also been making their mark now, when they had not done so in the past.

The cause for this latter-day success of sports cars lies largely with the rallies themselves. In one sense, they are a little too straightforward when compared with their ancestors. It was common practice to run post-war rallies on a class improvement basis so that the only people with whom a driver was competing were the others in his class. If he could get a sufficiently large lead over them, then he was likely to win the rally outright. It was precisely this marking system that led to Geoff Mabbs winning the Tulip Rally in 1961 with a Triumph Herald Coupé. When it was seen that his amount of class improvement could be dramatically swollen by getting Tiny Lewis in the sister car to drop back, Triumph did not hesitate to do so. The Tulip then altered their system so that not only was there a question of improvement within the class, but the competitor also had to show a clear improvement upon the classes above and below him so that there could be no fix. However, this then worked peculiarly to the benefit of Rosemary Smith, who won the Tulip Rally in 1965 with a Hillman Imp. At a time control, high in the Jura at Champagnole, the runners in the class above that of the Imp had

been heavily penalised by a blocked road and thus what was a commendable performance became a winning one.

This class improvement system was often allied to some kind of formula designed to handicap the more powerful GT cars. In many of the French rallies this was done by allowing different times between time controls and different target times for special stages. Thus a big GT car might have 31 minutes to cover the 33km from Quatre Chemins to Sigale on the Coupe des Alpes while the smallest Touring car, a BMW 700 for instance, would have 36 minutes.

It was seen that what was needed in the modern rallies for historic cars was a retrogression of ideas on how the rallies should be marked, and this is gradually taking place. It was significant that the 1990 FIA European Historic Rally Trophy was won by a Belgian driver, Jean-Pierre Maghalaes driving an Alfa Romeo Giulia GT.

The other major factor which influences the kind of cars that are likely to win historic rallies, and where it is really difficult to turn the clock back, is the state of the roads. In post-war Europe, there were plenty of gravel roads, handily placed in the nearest mountains, on which to run rallies. The rapidity with which these have disappeared under tarmac is a tribute to the all-pervading influence of the motor car, but it also explains why touring cars were so consistently successful as rally cars during the late 1950s and early 1960s. High ground clearance and large suspension movement were greater assets than sheer power. So far, historic rallies have shown a natural reluctance to run on the kind of gravel road available to modern rallies for the very good reason that their clients do not particularly want to damage the underside and suspension of their pride and joy. This is especially so

when plenty of fun can be obtained out of driving on perfectly respectable tarmac.

However, there is bound to be a movement soon to encourage the use of historic rally cars on gravel road special stages. It will be a sport far from the authenticity of car and event craved by the majority of historic rally car owners, but it will certainly be exciting to watch. Already, the 1000 Lakes Rally in Finland has inaugurated its Veteran Rally, which ran for the first time in 1990 and was won by Timo Makinen and Pekka Keskitalo in a Cooper S. The rally is actually divided into two different events: one tackles special stages on gravel roads just like the modern rally and requires that the cars have roll cages, while the other runs round the same route but tackles some special tests which are 'in the spirit of earlier 1000 Lakes Rallies'. The RAC Rally, which is today an uncompromising gravel-road special stage event, has two connections with historic rallying. At the same time as the RACMSA runs its modern international, it allows the HRCR to use one of its tarmac special stages to run a single venue event for historic cars. Then, at a completely different time of the year – actually the traditional date for post-war RAC Rallies, in March – it runs its own Historic RAC Rally which aims to re-create the RAC Rally before it became a special stage event. Special tests at tarmac venues such as hill-climbs are mixed in with regularity sections timed to the second in order to produce a winner. The only thing that is

missing is some of the high-speed night navigation and endurance that used to be a feature of the 1950s RAC Rallies. The first of these RAC Historic Rallies was run in March 1991 and here too Timo Makinen won driving a Cooper S, this time partnered by Paul Easter.

The situation is such that historic rallying looks set to provide a wide range of people with enjoyment while it is able to maintain its own wide-ranging appeal. It is evident that no less rigorous standards of safety must be applied to those branches of historic sport where cars and their drivers are being fully extended. The question of spectator safety must also be considered for those rallies, since the popularity of the sport in general is going to mean that the old-timers will ultimately attract higher levels of interest than they do today. This is especially the case when so many of the retired rally drivers, like Timo Makinen, are finding a second wind and coming out to show what they can still do. But in applying regulation to the more serious rallies, care must be taken not to over-legislate at the expense of the entrant who merely wishes to exercise his lovingly restored car in the company of others of a like mind. By the same token, the liberties that are extended to 'touring' rallies should not be used as a cover for the revival of open road rallying, otherwise the civil authorities in the host countries will put restrictions on all rallying without making any distinction as to when the cars participating were built.

CHAPTER 8

GETTING STARTED

When you are established and looking back, getting started always seems to have been so straightforward. Just think for a minute about learning to ride a bicycle. Cycling looks easy but it is difficult to initiate. The novice can get desperate trying to find someone who can tell him how to start, since to all those that have mastered the art, it feels extremely easy. What it comes down to is a question of having the confidence to get up and pedal without stopping to think about the problems of balance.

Setting out on a career in rallying is like riding that bicycle, and there is no doubt that a large helping of confidence will prove useful. But this should not be overdone. In the spring of 1961, a Parisian garage owner called Pierre Madelaine, who used to rally a Renault Dauphine, was scheduled to do the Rallye Val-de-Loire. At the last minute, his regular co-driver fell ill and he telephoned to his motor club to find a replacement. The competitions secretary recommended a young man of 22 who duly turned up *chez Madelaine*. His appearance was not very promising since he looked much younger, thin and pale with only his blue eyes giving any feeling of vivacity. His rally experience to date consisted of putting his brother's Citroen on its roof on a minor rally a year previously. His name was Jean-François Piot.

During the rally, it became very foggy and M. Madelaine prudently slowed down. His weedy companion promptly started to tell him that they were not going quickly enough and were in danger of being late. If he, Piot, were driving, he would be going much quicker. This went on for some time with the driver bottling up his feelings until it came to the point where he could take no more. Furious, he stopped the Dauphine and told Piot that if he was so good then he should drive. Not content with taking the wheel, our young expert started to tell the older man about his technique for driving in fog. This was to keep the throttle down at a constant setting and do everything with the steering wheel. By swinging the car gently from side to side, it was possible to pick up first the right-hand verge and then the left. With the car moving like that, he explained, the driver was always ready to take appropriate action to follow the line of the road.

All went well until they came to a fork in the road where, of course, the right and left-hand verges went their separate ways. Following his idea of staying halfway between them, Piot planted the Dauphine firmly amid some trees growing between the two roads. Despite this regrettable incident, he must otherwise have made a good impression on Madelaine since the older man asked him to do other rallies with him and even let him drive! Piot's results in that Dauphine were eventually to lead to works drives with Renault, Alpine and Ford, but not everyone might have been as understanding as his companion on that first foggy night.

Certainly, a great number of successful drivers have started out as co-drivers and nowhere was this more common than in France. Jean-Claude Ogier used to navigate for René Trautmann and Lucien Bianchi, while Henri Greder spent two years learning about rallying by reading maps and timekeeping for Roger de Lageneste. While he was still driving his own Renault 1093, Piot counted among his co-drivers Guy Chasseuil and Henri Pescarolo, who were later to become successful rally and race drivers in their own right. In Italy, Sandro Munari made his break into rallies as co-driver to Arnaldo Cavallari, while in England Vic Elford accompanied David Seigle-Morris before launching out on his own.

PREVIOUS PAGE The greatest rewards in rallying can come from experiencing the beauty of remote countryside at the same time as motor sport.

RIGHT Rallying can have its moments, and when a driver is learning, one hopes that there will not be too many like this. Marshals and spectators survey Barrie Lee's Escort after an excursion in Dodd Wood on the RAC Rally.

RIGHT The Renault R8 Gordini was the starting point for dozens of talented French drivers. Bob Wollek, now a top-class racing driver, started his career in one, and now drives 1000 bhp Porsches.

BELOW The choice of a first car should be governed by its cost and simplicity; otherwise, repair bills will put the novice out before he has had a chance to learn how to drive quickly. The Ford Escort in all its forms – this is a Mk II with Roger Clark winning the 1975 Scottish Rally – has provided just such an entry point for many young drivers.

While it is certainly useful – and considerably cheaper – to start out as a co-driver, it is not the modern way. With special stage events and pace notes, the rôles of driver and co-driver have become more specialised and there is now much less cross-over between them. The modern rally is so designed that it makes little demand on the driving skills of the co-driver. Consequently, getting started has different criteria depending on which job you fancy.

Basically, a co-driver needs little in the way of equipment in order to start rallying. At the true entry point, which in Britain is a closed-to-club rally, that might comprise nothing much more than a couple of maps, a pencil and membership of the organising motor club. A further requirement would be the acquaintance of a driver who was looking for someone to navigate for him on a rally, but experience shows that motor clubs are full of such philanthropists. The kind of navigation that is found on club events tends to be rather demanding, because with the performance of modern cars and the low average speeds permitted on public roads, the only way to test the crew is to give the navigator plenty of puzzles to slow them down. The simplest form of such events has no real road timing at all and is called a treasure hunt. Clues of varying complexity mixed in with navigational instructions enable the crew to assemble the answers to the questions posed, and the winner is the one with the most correct answers. Other events have time controls and the puzzles lie in how their locations and the route between them are described. These are the events where the aspiring co-driver can find out whether he can read a map and perform calculations on the move without suffering from car sickness. They also hone his skills at handling route and time cards and make him familiar with the way much larger events work. If he likes that kind of thing, then progression to major events will be no

RIGHT Flying is not always the quickest way to drive – when the wheels are off the ground, it is impossible to accelerate. But how much a car should be jumped can only be discovered by experience.

BELOW For the novice, unlike Ari Vatanen, driving to the limit ought not to be tried so close to the edge of a large drop.

problem and invitations will follow from whatever success he enjoys in the lesser ones.

For the driver starting out in rallying, treasure hunts are not much use to him if he has any confidence whatsoever in his skill behind the wheel. It may even prove better to think of something not even remotely like rallying as a starting point. In most countries throughout the world, there is a marvellous sport for young people called karting, where they can get acquainted with competitive driving from the age of eight. It is no coincidence that many of the current top race and rally drivers started by racing a kart in one of the many classes that are available. There can be no substitute for getting nine years of driving experience behind you before you are allowed – in the UK at least – to drive a car on the public highway. In Scandinavia, young drivers can take to the ice on frozen lakes before they have licences to drive on the road, and there do seem to be quite a high proportion of them that have also driven motorcycles. Erik Carlsson was one and he always maintains that his motorcycling experience helped him to judge the

grip available on different road surfaces with greater certainty.

Whatever experience the nascent rally driver can obtain before he gets his licence for the road, there comes a point where he has to decide to enter a rally. For this step, he will need the right car. The days are gone when Gerard Larrousse could borrow his mother's Simca Aronde to do a rally at the weekend. These days, if the aim is to do a rally where there are special stages, the car and the crew need to have all the safety equipment required by the rules. This means roll cages and fire extinguishers for the car and fire-resistant overalls and crash helmets for the crew. They will also need to be licensed by their national sporting authority, which in the case of Britain is the RACMSA. This licence will be of restricted status when they start, but as they enter and finish events, it can be upgraded to first a national and finally an international rating.

The advice that is given to novices about the best kind of car with which to start rallying is legion. It goes almost without saying that both the car and its

preparation should be appropriate for the type of event that he is thinking of doing. If the country in which he lives has all-tarmac rallies, then it is best to have a car which suits those events; while if he lives in Scandinavia, it is gravel roads or ice-covered ones that need to be considered. One school of thought says that the best thing to do is to buy the most competitive car that your budget can afford, because raw performance will ensure worthwhile results. The drawback to this approach is that one accident may put the driver on the sidelines until such time as his funds have recovered, which will mean that he is not learning very much in the meantime. It would seem better to buy a car which is cheaper, by virtue of being less powerful and sophisticated, but still well prepared. He then needs to get into the habit of driving it flat out. Accidents will happen, but with money in reserve to repair the car, the young driver will be on the start line for the next event and, most important of all, he will be learning how to control a car near the limit of its capabilities – and near the limit of his own.

This question of car control is so fundamental to the question of success in rally driving that it cannot be overlooked. For more than 20 years, the international rally world looked and marvelled at the way the Scandinavians drove first on ice and snow, then on gravel, and finally on tarmac. They showed themselves capable of winning everywhere and only a handful of rally drivers from the rest of the world could match them. People pondered the reason for

this dominance but were unable to agree as to its roots. Now that Italians, Germans and Spaniards have come and ousted the Swedes and Finns from their seats among the gods, or at least asked them to move up the bench a bit, it is possible to be rational about such matters.

The plain fact was that the Scandinavian drivers came with a built-in advantage. They had access to snow-covered roads and the surface of frozen lakes for up to four months every year. Even in the summer, the majority of their secondary roads were surfaced with loose gravel and, apart from a short period around mid-summer, were unfrequented. To cap it all, from the latter part of the 1950s the Scandinavians had rallies with special stages where speed over a short distance was all-important. Before the 1970s, all rallies in France and Spain were on tarmac, with the occasional event on ice and snow; all the rallies in Britain were on tarmac with the exception of the internationals which used the gravel forest roads; and Italian rallies had to use the tiniest of tracks because their government had imposed a speed limit of 50kph on all parts of their rallies, including the special stages.

In all those countries, things changed and gravel roads became used more and more on rallies, while hundreds of lesser rallies sprang up beneath the big internationals to provide national drivers with the practice and experience that they needed. The Scandinavians had always had plenty of smaller rallies and single-stage events, summer and winter, and their

LEFT A full house Group A Lancia may seem to give the beginner a competitive starting point, but the cost needs to be carefully considered in proportion to the entire season's budget. A moment like this could lead to financial ruin.

RIGHT The choice of first events is also important. Sections such as this one on the Safari Rally can reduce a car to scrap in minutes, if the driver lacks experience of lesser rallies to know how to pace himself and the car.

winter events in particular enabled them to experience car control problems at quite high speeds without the risk of plunging off a mountain when they got it wrong. Gradually, the rest of Europe created an infrastructure of special stage events so that their young drivers could learn car control at first hand without having to encounter them for the first time when they did one of the major internationals.

The Scandinavian drivers are still at the top and there are far more of them around than population statistics alone should guarantee. But at least now they have been joined, and occasionally surpassed, by drivers from other countries. It will be interesting to see what will happen in the future. It seems to have been a trend in the past for Italy and France to supply the best cars and initially employ Scandinavians to drive them, but then to come up with World Champions of their own. Considering the enormous current involvement of the Japanese manufacturers in rallying, it will be a surprise if there is not a Japanese World Champion rally driver before the end of this decade.

Once the car is selected and prepared, licences obtained and a competent co-driver found, the next problem is to know which events to do. This may be decided to a certain extent by the budget, and even by the car itself, but either way it is essential to try and pick a good quality event. Too many newcomers to rallying are discouraged by doing an event where the special stages or even parts of the route are unnecessarily rough. The consequent damage to the car may swallow their budget for the rest of the season. It is always best to seek advice from established rally competitors in local or regional motor clubs, and to keep in mind that the whole object of these first rallies is to gain experience by finishing them.

The main problem about knowing how to drive rallies, when compared with racing, is that it is extremely difficult to get any idea of how other drivers are tackling specific corners or entire special stages. On a race track, a novice driver can try to follow the other cars through the corners and acquire a fair amount of knowledge on braking distances and the line to follow. In a rally, this never happens unless there is a situation where one car gets overtaken by another in the middle of a special stage. This is increasingly unlikely since the organisers do all they can to ensure that the experts are seeded in front of the novices. Apart from following the example of some of the continental drivers mentioned earlier and offering to co-drive for an expert, the inexperienced rally driver does not have too many chances to find out what is expected of him. In quite a few countries there are such things as single-venue stage events, where one stage is used many times and drivers get a chance to watch one another in action. And there are increasing numbers of rally driver schools where it is possible to gain some idea of the level of attack that is needed to produce a competitive time.

Otherwise, there is only the time recorded on the stage; and to find out how much faster to go in order to be a winner, a study is needed of times from drivers in similar cars. Very simple to say, but much harder to do. The evidence is that no one became a top-class rally driver by being too careful, and it has to be accepted that accidents will be part of the scene as the young rallyman learns to control his car. Going too fast is a virtue in the formative years, though it is less likely to be smiled upon once the status of works driver is reached. Given that accidents are part of the process of learning, it is sensible to start with a car

are now pace noted it is an unnecessary handicap not to realise that different techniques are needed to produce one's best performance on an event where the stages may be practised. In particular, the driver needs to get used to having someone else tell him what the road is going to do next rather than rely on his own senses and reactions. He needs to develop a focus of concentration that is entirely different from that in use on secret stages in order to be able to make the most of having practised the rally. This also extends to the manner in which he drives the car, which is likely to be less dramatic and more like the style that a racing driver might adopt.

This means, inevitably, that the best course of action for any young driver with aspirations to get to the top should be to start competing in international rallies outside his own country as soon as he can possibly afford it. It is sad to say, but winning national championships does not always lead to international stardom and it may also have an unpleasant side-effect in that the national champion has little experience on rallies of any type other than those which are

LEFT If all else fails, then make sure that you get the very best vantage point to watch the rest of the rally.

RIGHT An excellent example of steady progress towards the top is provided by David Llewellin, British Rally Champion in 1989 and 1990, who has driven Nissans, Audi Quattros, Metro 6R4s, Sierra Cosworths (here on the 1988 Lombard RAC Rally) and more recently a Toyota Celica GT4, before getting a full works drive for Nissan in 1991.

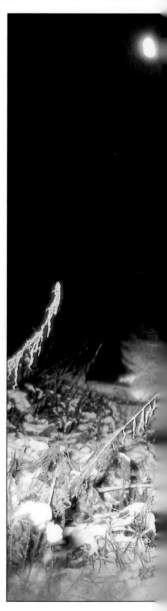

that can be cheaply repaired and to choose rallies that use special stages where an accident is not likely to result in catastrophe. Britain is fortunate in its use of forest roads, since these rarely have the kind of drops off the edge that can be found on a Monte Carlo Rally or in Corsica. In any case, the modern habit on British rallies is to provide caution boards and other warning devices at places which are truly deceptive and where major damage could result from an accident.

The one thing which Britain does lack is a large number of tarmac events. There are plenty of these in Ireland and there are a superb pair of rallies each year on the Isle of Man, one national and the other international, but it is necessary to go to France, Italy and Spain to find a broad range of tarmac events. Another consideration is the use of pace notes. These are just coming into use in Britain's forests with the Scottish Rally pioneering the way for the Lombard RAC and others to follow, while just a few of the Irish events allow the use of pace notes. Since the making of pace notes and learning how to drive on them are skills of equal importance to the rally driver as that of car control, it cannot be emphasised enough that any driver taking his progress in the sport seriously should not spend more than a couple of seasons driving blind rallies before moving onto practised events with pace notes. Driving blind is a skill that is still needed in rallying, but since the majority of international rallies

run in his own country. This is fine if, as in Spain, the national championship comprises rallies that use both gravel and tarmac roads, or, as in Finland, where summer and winter bring a contrast of gravel and snow. But it is not so convenient if all that is on offer at home is one type of rally or if pace notes are not generally accepted. It should not be overlooked in this context that the co-driver needs to develop his pace note skills in parallel with the driver, and no amount of map reading can prepare him for a virtuoso performance with pace notes.

When starting out, the rookie rally crew will probably not contemplate having any kind of service during the rally other than that which they can carry out themselves, and hopefully their first events will not demand much more than that. But very quickly they will find that the larger rallies are organised in such a way that it is much easier to have a service van with petrol, tyres and a few spares than it is to have to rely on ducking into garages for petrol and changing tyres from the boot of the rally car. It is not necessary to own a service van to have the use of one and it is

quite likely that if there is a firm responsible for preparing the rally car, they would be able to send one along crewed by mechanics who know something about the car. And they can carry some spare parts in the van on a sale-or-return basis.

Practising a rally and laying on service are just two ways in which the cost of the sport goes up, but both are enjoyable to the people that do them and there is no doubt that both activities can make the rally far more satisfying for the participants. There can be nothing more frustrating than to have paid to enter a rally, prepared the car, set aside the time to compete and laid out all the funds on hotels and travelling, only to have to retire with a broken throttle spring, or something equally minor, after the first special stage because there is no service car.

This one chapter cannot hope to be a complete compendium of advice for the budding rallyman, but one or two general thoughts and principles might be useful. The ability to drive a rally car at competitive speeds cannot be taught; it either exists in the person or it does not. What can be taught are the techniques

and the general approach to the driving that is necessary to be competitive. Someone starting in rallying who had never talked to another rally driver would have no idea of the possibilities of left-foot braking, of handbrake turns, of brake bias adjustment, or why to approach a sharp right-hand bend as if the car were turning left. These can be explained to him and he can go away and experiment to his heart's content, but they are just pieces of technique which will enable him to get out of tricky situations. They will not help him to go fast in the first place – they can just help him to go fast for longer.

As well as learning the techniques that have evolved as part of rally driving, the newcomer needs to pick up all he can about rally tactics. As an example, it is normally considered best to be first car onto a gravel special stage, since the surface is not cut up by the passage of other rally cars. But sometimes when the virgin surface is formed from loose gravel, which is familiarly called 'ball-bearings', there may be better grip available to someone who goes in at tenth car after the loose gravel has been swept away. Similarly, if there is fresh snow on the road, being first car does not make a lot of sense. On the 1971 Swedish Rally, when fresh snow had fallen just prior to the rally, Lars Nystrom, who started at number 50 in his BMW 2002 TIi, finished an amazing second overall. The explanation was that, unlike the top seeds, he had been running on what was almost a bare gravel surface after their studded tyres had swept the snow away for him.

This question of which moment to tackle a special stage is rarely open to choice. The running order on the Monte Carlo Rallies of the early 1960s was dependent upon the starting town, and good information on that subject could help enormously. However, the modern system of seeding and the use of neutralisation controls prior to each special stage mean that there is now little room for manoeuvre. It is still worth looking at the penalties listed in the regulations regarding early and late arrival at controls, because on a particularly dusty rally it may pay to take a minute of lateness at a time control prior to a stage in order to avoid worse losses by driving with visibility cut to a minimum by someone else's dust.

When it comes to equipment, common sense will normally serve to tell what is right and what is wrong in a rally car. A map light to read maps and pace notes at night is one thing, but a really good interior light is often overlooked so that when the search is on for a dropped fuse or time card, it is performed with an unwieldy torch and to the accompaniment of a great deal of cursing. It is all very well having a smart new electronic Halda fitted to the dashboard, but it is as well to check that the co-driver can reach the control buttons when he is firmly strapped in his seat. He certainly will not want to keep slackening them off every time he needs to press a button. Halda do provide a remote control switch for their electronic odometer,

ABOVE Erik Carlsson mastered the art of driving a small-engined car, the original Saab 92, by taking it to its limit everywhere. When he drove more powerful cars, driving just seemed easier.

LEFT To the newcomer, rallying can be very confusing. It is hard to find out what is going on at service points and in crowded controls, though few are quite as chaotic as this, the finish of the Paris–Dakar on the shores of the Atlantic Ocean.

but it is so much easier to think out the location of the device to avoid having to use one. It may also be an advantage to have the instrument mounted on a stiff pivot so that it may be turned towards the driver's seat on a rally where one man may be driving and navigating while the other sleeps. Careful thinking beforehand about minor items like these can make the business of competing far less of a trial for the crew.

The golden rule with equipment in rally cars is to take the minimum consistent with necessity. Some tools are always necessary, but on a rally like the Safari with longer spaces between service, a more comprehensive selection is a good idea. On a sprint special stage event, a pair of pliers, a screwdriver, some tape and a selection of tie-wraps may suffice. There is certainly no point in carrying weight that is not needed. This is particularly true of what comes

under the heading of 'personal equipment'. Some crews seem to take with them enough luggage for a fortnight's holiday in a hotel that possesses no laundry service. On the majority of rallies that take place in Europe this is simply not necessary, though a good case can be made for survival gear on the Arctic Rally, and for a tent and drinking water on the Moroccan Rally. It used to be that on the original Arctic Rally, a competitor was not allowed to start without possessing a large knife suitable for killing and disembowelling a reindeer, and a certificate that he had received adequate instruction from a Lapp hunter in how to carry out those operations skilfully. The reason was that it was not unheard of for a rally car to crash into a reindeer, mortally wounding it and at the same time disabling the car. The Laplanders were keen that the reindeer should be put out of its misery and that the rally driver, deprived of the use of his car's heater, should be able to open up the carcass and climb inside for warmth. Several drivers said that they did not mind killing the reindeer, but they preferred to carry a box of matches and burn the car in order to keep warm!

Wherever possible, anything which can be carried in the service van like drinks, food, clothes, spares and tools should be kept out of the rally car unless there is an overwhelming case for having it to hand. The ultimate professional team of Erik Carlsson and Gunnar Palm always had the minimum of things cluttering up their Saab 96. On looking in the back, the

only visible things were their rally jackets, neatly hung up with the crash helmets beside them. With increasing noise levels inside the modern rally car, intercoms have become *de rigueur*, with microphones fitted to the helmets and headsets used for normal conversation away from the special stages. Consequently, the rear of rally cars now tend to be a tangle of coiled wires with padded boxes to hold the helmets and hooks for the headsets. The trend for wide-backed seats with tall head-rests, together with the criss-crossing of tubes forming the roll cage, means that careful arrangement is necessary to ensure that helmets can be reached and replaced easily without cracking skulls or breaking intercom components.

While on the subject of cracking skulls, it is worth remembering that everything in the rally car should be treated as if it were in a spacecraft under weightless conditions. In short, everything should be fastened down so that, in the event that the car does have an accident, flying objects are not likely to injure the crew. It is quite normal to carry a tool bag, the wheelbrace and even the jack inside the car so that they are quickly to hand in the event of a puncture, but being struck on the head by a poorly-secured jack can turn a lesser accident into a more serious one. The restraint of less weighty objects can also be a good thing, since the driver is likely to be unimpressed if, when continuing after the accident, he is told that the time card/road book/pace notes have gone missing.

One word of advice must be about suitable apparel for the rally crew. Like the Boy Scouts, the motto is 'Be prepared'. If you do not know what the weather is likely to be on the rally, then ask someone who has done it before. If it is going to rain or be muddy, then the driver should consider having some rubber overshoes to slip on over his driving shoes when he gets out of the car. It is also a good idea to remove any rubber pads on the foot pedals, replacing them if necessary with serrated metal on which even a damp boot is unlikely to slip. If there is going to be snow, then consider having a pair of zip-up boots of a size that will fit over the driving shoes. Designer rally jackets can look very nice, but it is better to choose a jacket for its warmth and waterproof qualities if snow and rain are around. It is quite important not to bring too much water or snow into the car as it will quickly condense on the inside of the windows where, in really cold weather, it will freeze and defy the efforts of the heater to shift it. Another good idea is to have some kind of hat available to wear when the crash helmet is removed, otherwise the cold air swirling around a damp head may quickly bring on a cold, or worse.

If the rally is held in very hot weather, then the regulations for the event may permit the crew to wear single-layer fireproof overalls or even dispense with them altogether and adopt shorts and T-shirt. When wearing lighter gear, seat belts and even the seats

ABOVE Conditions for spectating on rallies may not always be ideal. It might well be wise to put a marker where you left the wellington boot and return for it later with a JCB.

LEFT It is not impossible for a private owner to win the Monte Carlo Rally as Jean-Pierre Nicolas showed on the 1978 event. However no one is pretending that it is easy.

ABOVE Professional confidence can make leaping into the unknown a spectacular but relatively safe affair as Timo Makinen demonstrates on the 1000 Lakes Rally. The problem for the beginner is finding a nice safe place to test his confidence.

RIGHT Confidence at an early stage is a good thing, but too much may lead to serious problems. One hopes that the damage suffered by this Fiat 128 on landing was not extensive, but at least it would have been cheap to repair.

themselves may chafe after a few hours, so foam padding should be employed. The most popular seat belt in rallying is Sabelt and they produce padded tubes to fit over the shoulder straps in the region of the collar bone. Even on a Safari it is possible to encounter rain and a light waterproof coat is a sensible investment, especially if it has a hood or sou'wester to go with it.

The final comments directed at the beginner concern the question of fatigue. It is unusual today to find a European rally that places any great demands on endurance, but they do occasionally require the rally crew to work what are known as unsocial hours. When a rally reaches the night halt at 8.00pm and departs at 6.00am the next day, this actually means that the crew check in at the control at 8.00pm then take half an hour finding the hotel, twenty minutes to get the room, an hour for dinner and rise at 5.00am the next day to get ready, grab a coffee and get back to the *parc fermé* in time to check out at 6.00am. This regime, if repeated over a few days, may start to erode the resilience of even the fittest person, and there comes a time when staying awake is a major problem.

The simplest answer to all the questions about how does one stay awake on a rally is that the wise man does not try to fight nature. The best remedy is sleep. Ten minutes sleep grabbed in the cockpit of a service van or rally car can revive the flagging spirit better than any amount of caffeine. If there is a paramount skill that a rallyman needs to acquire at an early stage, it is that of cat-napping.

CHAPTER 9

THEREBY HANGS A TALE

Rallying is a motorised adventure pursued by somewhat reckless people who would probably be in one kind of scrape or another even if they had stayed at home. With the expansion of their horizons achieved by the simple act of entering a rally, the possibilities for laughter, disaster and eccentricity multiply quicker than a Cray computing the odds on the Grand National. Thus rallying is rich in anecdote, and the only unhappy thing is that large amounts of it are unprintable.

What follows in this chapter is an attempt to show the variety of things that may occur to test the resourcefulness of the rallyman and how perfectly normal rally situations can easily turn into legend.

Perhaps the best example with which to begin is the occasion in 1967 when Timo Makinen was trying extremely hard to complete his hat-trick of 1000 Lakes victories in a BMC Cooper S. Equally keen to deny him were Simo Lampinen in a Saab V4 and a young Hannu Mikkola in a Volvo 122S. Less than four seconds separated Saab and Cooper when they came to the longest stage on the rally, Ouninpohja, full of the classic jumps for which the 1000 Lakes is rightly infamous. Makinen's engine was running hotter than it should have been, so he removed the bonnet-mounted lights and left the bonnet slightly open, restrained only by a leather strap. With only 10 of the 27 kilometres gone, the strap failed when the Cooper S landed heavily after a jump. The bonnet flew up and blocked all but a tiny strip of the driver's forward vision through the windscreen. A prudent person would have stopped and closed the bonnet, but not a Finn in full flight. Makinen was not going to cede one

second more than he could help to his rivals and kept going. By slackening his seat belts, he could crane his neck to see a little further round the obstacle and somehow managed to keep the little red missile on the track all the way to the end of the stage. His time was only ten seconds slower than Lampinen and represented an average speed of some 104kph/65mph. He went on to win the rally by eight seconds from the Saab driver, which means that had he stopped, it must have cost him the victory.

The ability to figure the odds in situations like that is what gives experienced rally drivers the edge when it comes to winning. Their most difficult choices come every Monte Carlo Rally when they arrive at the service point before the start of each special stage to be greeted by an enormous pile of tyres and the members of the ice note crew that have looked at the stage just before the police closed the road. In five minutes or less, they have to digest what the tyre specialists have to say, the information from the ice note crew, the evidence of their own senses and come up with a choice of tyre for the special stage so that the mechanics can fit them to the car. Very often the ice note crew, experienced rallymen themselves, will come up with a recommendation, though this can sometimes be less than helpful. One works driver was told by his ice note crew: 'I know exactly which studded tyres you want for this test, but they don't have them here.'

The possibility for error is enormous simply because the choice of tyres is large and the conditions on the stage can be very mixed. The only time the choice is easy is when the conditions are the

PREVIOUS PAGE A driver needs to have the greatest faith in his co-driver in order to sit in this position and operate the engine's throttle by hand. Juha Kankkunen and Juha Piironen got out of this stage on the 1000 Lakes Rally of 1990 and went on to finish fifth overall.

RIGHT Visibility impaired but speed scarcely reduced, Timo Makinen drives his Cooper S to victory in the 1967 1000 Lakes Rally. The offending bonnet strap and block can be seen clearly.

LEFT This choice of racing tyres was the correct one for Walter Röhrl during the 1985 Monte Carlo Rally, but a similar choice later in the event was to prove extremely costly.

same throughout. A most significant tyre choice, which in fact decided the result of the 1985 Monte Carlo Rally, was one made by Walter Röhrl. With four wins in that event already to his credit, he came to the start of the 27th stage with his Audi Sport Quattro comfortably in the lead from a charging Ari Vatanen driving a Peugeot 205 T16. His lead was largely due to an error on the part of Vatanen's co-driver, who two days previously had checked in at a time control four minutes early, thus bringing Vatanen eight minutes of penalisation. This deficit Vatanen was determined to catch back, and he was doing quite well with just eight tests remaining.

Whether he would have done it unaided will never be known since Röhrl effectively shot himself in the foot. The information on the stage was that there were eight kilometres up to the summit of the Col St Raphael which were one hundred percent snow and

ice, after which there were 22 kilometres of dry road descending in the valley on the other side. It is the worst possible choice to have to make and Röhrl plumped for racing tyres with a tread pattern but no studs. His gamble was that, with four-wheel drive, what time he might lose on the snow he would gain back, and more, on the tarmac which followed. Unfortunately, the 500-plus bhp of the Sport Quattro was not helpful when it came to controlling the grip going up the hill on the snow and Vatanen, who had chosen a winter tyre with studs, started two minutes behind Röhrl and overtook him long before the first eight kilometres were done. His advantage over Röhrl on the whole stage was in excess of two minutes, which meant that the estimate of the gain of the racing tyres on tarmac was not correct. Though there are those who say that, in sitting beside Ari for those 22 kilometres on tarmac with most unsuitable tyres,

Terry Harryman paid in full for his previous error. Vatanen went on to win the rally from Röhrl and set Peugeot on the road to their first World Championship.

Röhrl's choice was made in full knowledge of the conditions, but when the drivers arrived to their service points prior to the Moulinon–Antraigues stage on the 1972 rally, the situation was none too clear. In the manner of many classic Monte Carlo stages, this one climbs for some 17 kilometres to the Col de la Fayolle and then descends for another 20 to the village of Antraigues. The col is not particularly high and for years the stage had always been clear tarmac where racing tyres could be used. Indeed, this was the recommendation of every ice note crew who had been over the stage not more than an hour or so before. The dilemma came because it was raining in Le Moulinon.

It was not ordinary rain; it had a slightly solid quality to it and the drop in temperature made some drivers think that a little further up the hill there could be something much more interesting than cold rain falling. As it was, the tyre choices were immensely varied, with some competitors going on slick racers, others opting for racers with treads, and then there were those who chose winter tyres, again some with studs and some without. The plain fact was that this stage was one where racers had always been used and few service crews had many studded tyres available, so those who wanted them had to search in the

ABOVE Racing tyres on snow are a problem that the rally driver has to cope with if, as on the Turini, there is only a short distance with snow and the majority of the stage is tarmac. This is Stig Blomqvist on his way to third place on the 1983 Monte Carlo Rally.

back of trucks to see what they could find. That search proved immensely valuable since, within six kilometres or so of leaving the start of the stage, the cars were on pure, fresh snow. Those who had chosen racing tyres, like the Porsches of Bjorn Waldegaard and Gerard Larrousse and the Alpine A110 of Jean-Luc Thérier, had a terrible struggle to get through at all and were rewarded with penalties on both the stage and the subsequent road section. Timo Makinen, who chose winter tyres with 300 studs for his Ford Escort RS, said afterwards that he regretted not having ones with 600 studs.

The choice of tyres is not the only thing that can ruin a rally crew's performance, and the catalogue of mechanical mishaps is greater in rallying than almost any other branch of motor sport. One particular failure has led to a variety of ingenious solutions and that is throttle cable failure. It is typical of rallymen that, faced with an otherwise perfectly functioning car, they are prepared to adopt the most physically dangerous methods to be able to drive the car. One example was on a Geneva Rally in the 1960s when this problem came to Gunther Klass in a factory Porsche 911. Undaunted, his co-driver Rolf Wutherlich,

ABOVE With a little help from his friends, Ari Vatanen overcame this major handicap to progress after an accident with his Peugeot 205 T16 Grand Raid during the spectator stage that started the 1986 Paris–Dakar. He went on to win the rally.

the same man who had been in James Dean's Porsche at the time of his fatal crash, climbed onto the rear bumper, held open the bonnet with one hand and operated the throttle with the other. In that fashion, they were able to get out of the section and to the Porsche service. A more recent example was on the 1000 Lakes Rally of 1990 where Juha Kankkunen had to get out and sit on the windscreen of his Lancia Delta Integrale with his legs and arm under the bonnet while Juha Piironen steered the car out of the stage. In a 20km stage, they somehow only lost five minutes, which says a great deal for their speed of diagnosis, resolution and co-ordination.

Inevitably, someone raised the question as to whether Kankkunen had been breaking the rules in completing the stage with no seat belts. On close scrutiny, it turned out that the specific requirement was for seat belts to be worn by the crew while travelling inside the car on the special stage. Just as well for Arne Hertz in the 1983 Lombard RAC Rally, as he had to travel sitting on the right rear of Hannu Mikkola's Audi Quattro in order to keep the car level after the left front wheel had been torn off in an accident. Mikkola went from leading the rally to 26th, but

pulled back to finish second overall. A similar problem assailed Ari Vatanen with his Peugeot 205 T16 Grand Raid when he folded a front wheel underneath the car on the spectator stage outside Paris during the 1987 Paris–Dakar. To provide the necessary counterbalance to lift the collapsed corner off the ground and get the car out of the stage, he persuaded several hefty spectators, who were presumably Peugeot fans, to hang onto the rear using the roof rack to support themselves. The ploy was successful, though coming as it did at such an early stage, he did drop to 276th overall. But with such a long distance still to come in the desert, he was able to recover the lost time and went on the win the rally outright.

Redistribution of weight was behind the rearward location of Christian Geistdorfer's seat in the Fiat Abarth 131 of Walter Röhrl during the 1978 Lombard RAC Rally. Team engineer Giorgio Pianta had tested the car on several occasions with weights in the back and he was certain that moving the co-driver, while not increasing the all-up weight of the car, would give a significant increase in traction. The sight of the co-driver residing in the rear caused quite a stir, and for a while Röhrl was convinced that it worked. At least he finished sixth on the RAC, but when they tried the system again in practice for the 1979 Monte Carlo Rally, it didn't seem to work so well. Then on the stage from Pont des Miolans to St Auban, which ends with a series of uphill hairpins, Geistdorfer tried the car with two seats fitted in it. He started in the front and got in the back to go up the last part of the stage, but neither would say if they thought it was better or not. In any case, FISA quickly ruled that the co-driver had to sit in the front and that was the end of such experiments.

Of course there are events where having three people in the car is normal. The early marathons indulged in this form of crewing for the very simple reason that it was judged that, while a man might be permitted a few cat-naps while navigating, this was not desirable for the driver. Thus two drivers were taken who could share the work of two or more days non-stop driving. A three-man crew was also quite a normal sight on rallies like the Monte Carlo in the 1950s when private owners would often take a full complement in the car and share the duties between them. It could have some drawbacks, as Raymond Joss discovered on the 1963 Monte Carlo when he briefly put his Rover 3-litre off the road on the Chartreuse special stage. When he went off, he had a crew of three, two of whom got out to push, but when the car was freed, he set off with such dispatch that only one of them was able to regain the interior of the car. The other spent a pleasant night with the locals drinking mulled wine in the local bakery and watching the rally. Although the Rover reached Monte Carlo, it was promptly disqualified for not having the full crew aboard.

Naturally, it would also be a reason for disqualification if there were more people in the rally car than had started in it. One of the more controversial disqualifications was that of Tony Fall and Henry Liddon in the 1969 Portuguese TAP Rally. The incident in question happened with just a few yards of the rally still to be driven. The leading Lancia of Fall and Liddon had arrived to wait for the correct time outside the final control in Lisbon. Fall was greeted by his wife but such was the press of the crowd around the car that, when he was asked by the police to move

his car towards the control, Fall told his wife to 'hop in' while he moved the car the requisite ten metres. The disqualification was based on carrying an unauthorised passenger in the rally car! It was just as well that the antics of another Lancia driver, this time Simo Lampinen, on the 1000 Minutes Rally in Austria the following year did not come to official attention. Co-driver Mario Mannucci was temporarily lost at night in a forest between two villages when they came across a local man walking home. They asked for directions but eventually decided it was easier to take him along with them, which was no easy task in a small Fulvia Coupé. When they came within sight of the control they had been seeking, they reduced the crew to two and thanked their guide for his help.

Finding the way, especially on the older rallies where the route was not terribly well defined, was always a problem. It was particularly bad in the vicinity of large cities where an ordinary map was not much help in the network of roads. Occasionally, even the professionals were known to flag down a cab, stick the co-driver in it with a fistful of cash plus the address of the control, and then leave it to local knowledge. In France, most big rallies brought the Gendarmerie out in force and when a major event hit a big city, there was often a motorcycle escort arranged for each rally car as it arrived on the outskirts to whisk it into the control with minimum delay. At Reims on the 1964 Monte Carlo Rally, this was done to such effect that the competitors had only one complaint, which was that they could not keep up with the police as they sped through red lights with their sirens wailing. Just occasionally, the co-operative attitude of the French police could backfire. Rauno Aaltonen and Tony Ambrose were in the running for a Coupe d'Or on the Alpine Rally of 1965 when they arrived in the vicinity of Bonneville in the Haute Savoie. They had just finished one difficult section and were on a short liaison to the next one

across the valley of the Arve. As they arrived to a junction, where on recce they had turned right, there was a gendarme indicating that they should turn left. The dilemma was plain, for often the local police know a better way through a town than has been found by the crew, and on a traditional event like the Coupe des Alpes there was, of course, no detailed road book. But by following his direction, they were travelling in uncharted territory and could easily get lost, which is precisely what happened since the next junction had no gendarme. They found the way eventually but lost a minute at the time control and with it, their Coupe d'Or.

Rallying is a friendly sport even at professional level, but certain lines have to be drawn. A team manager would not look kindly upon one of his drivers who had stopped to pull a rival out of a ditch, especially if that car went on to beat one of his cars. Stopping to check that no-one is hurt is entirely another matter and it is only when a car has gone off so comprehensively that no sign of the accident can be seen by subsequent cars that there is any real problem. However, the question of stopping to tow a car out brought Anglo-Finnish relations to an all-time low on the 1985 Lombard RAC Rally. The rally leader, Markku Alen, slid off in Kielder Forest only to get his Lancia

LEFT People ride on the outside of rally cars for a wide variety of reasons. The mobile car wash on the 1966 Safari is using the weight of the co-driver to bounce it through the mud and water.

BELOW A bewildering choice of tyres can face a driver at a service point. In the left hand photo, Pirelli show what can be done by varying the racing and studded tyre theme for tarmac with varying amounts of ice. The right hand shot shows the variants on offer from Dunlop for snowy conditions, before the varying amounts of studs are fitted to them.

Delta S4 towed out a minute or so later by the Toyota of Juha Kankkunen in a gesture of Finnish solidarity. Had Alen stayed put for a while longer, then Englishman Tony Pond would have inherited the lead with his MG Metro 6R4. A contrary example came on the Safari Rally in 1972 when Ove Andersson was stranded between Dodoma and Arusha with no fuel after the Datsun service crew had failed to close the filler cap on his 180B some 300 kilometres earlier. Without help, he and his co-driver would have been out of the rally and forced to spend the night on the fringe of a game park with only lions for company. As it was, the Ford Escort of Timo Makinen stopped and donated a fuel bag with 20 litres of petrol which got the Datsun through to its next service point.

The servicing of rally cars has also generated a few stories. To start with tyres, their very supply has often been something of a saga. Prior to the Acropolis Rally of 1964, Dunlop's Oliver Speight hired a boat in Piraeus harbour and took a small raiding party out to a freighter which was refusing to release his supply of tyres for the rally. After a brief sparring match with the Captain, not all of which was verbal, the Dunlop men

returned with the tyres. The same firm was not so fortunate when in 1975 their truck carrying tyres to the Ford team on the San Remo Rally broke down in France, and the Italian customs would not let the replacement vehicle through the border as its paperwork was not correct. For an earlier San Remo in 1971, the Pirelli factory in Milan was besieged by its workers as part of a dispute, so helicopters had to be used to get the Lancia and Fiat tyres past the pickets. Aerial assistance was also the order of the day for the 1969 Spanish Rally, which was a crucial counter in the European Rally Championship for Harry Kallstrom and Gunnar Haggbom with a Lancia Fulvia. Team co-ordinator was Henry Liddon and his problem was that the cars were in Madrid and the tyres were in Italy with only 24 hours to go to the start of the event. Kallstrom got the car scrutineered and then, on the day of the start, he and the mechanics waited uneasily outside the Jarama Racing Circuit, scene of the first special stage, hoping that their tyres would arrive in time to start the rally. With less than an hour to go, a taxi came skidding round the corner and Henry Liddon emerged with two sets of racing tyres. Stuck

LEFT A Finnish rally driver has more experience of driving with studded tyres and is thus likely to opt for them when the choice is difficult. Ari Vatanen won the 1985 Monte Carlo Rally thanks to just such a decision.

RIGHT Sandro Munari's second place on the 1976 San Remo (*top*), four seconds behind Bjorn Waldegaard in another Lancia Stratos (*below*), should have been a win with Waldegaard second. But team orders given out before the last stage were misinterpreted by the Swedish driver.

in Barcelona airport, he had hired a Caravelle to fly the tyres onward to Madrid and had then rushed to Jarama with enough to do the first tests. His expense account must have made interesting reading, but the justification was that Kallstrom went on to win not only the Spanish Rally but the 1969 European Championship.

Harry Kallstrom won the RAC Rally that same year as part of his title chase and won it again in 1970, but that second win was almost as heart-stopping as his Spanish tyre saga. The rally was into its closing night, with Kallstrom established in the lead, when his engine lost its oil in the Welsh forest complex of Dovey and he arrived at Machynlleth with his main engine bearings run. The Lancia team knew where a replacement set was located and proceeded to strip them from the retired Fulvia of Simo Lampinen during the one-hour halt. At the restart, Kallstrom's car was driven straight to the garage and the second-hand bearings plus a new sump fitted. He left Machynlleth almost 40 minutes late and had to drive on the limit for several hours of road sections and special stages to get back on schedule. However, as

he arrived to the next main time control, still under pressure, he hit a bank at the side of the road while avoiding a small truck. The accident destroyed his front left-hand suspension and the car was incapable of being driven forward. Quick thinking on the part of the team manager Cesare Fiorio saw the car whisked through the control with the front end balanced on a trolley jack, while Gunnar Haggbom checked in with his time card. The repair was put in the hands of Lancia's most skilled mechanic, Gino Fraboni, and Kallstrom went on to win his second RAC Rally.

The ability of the Lancia team to react quickly and to innovate was one of the factors that gave them victories at a time when they did not have the quickest car. A perfect example was the tyre swap carried out by Lancia on the 1969 San Remo Rally. This event was held in March at that time, and it was quite usual to find snow on the tiny mountain roads behind the Italian Riviera. Special stages were run, without separate controls preceding them, in the middle of much longer road sections. The problem on this occasion was that the first tight road section,

LEFT From the time he left the BMC team with Rauno Aaltonen at the end of 1968, Henry Liddon took the chance to mix co-driving with team management so that he was better informed than anyone about what actually happened on rallies. For the 1971 Lombard RAC Rally, he drove with Timo Makinen in a Fiat Abarth 131.

RIGHT Contemplative genius of the workshop, the Lancia mechanic Gino Fraboni (*left*) was the fastest repair artist when it came to mending stricken Fulvias in the field.

from Pigna to Rezzo over the two cols of Langan and Teglia, was a mixture of gravel and tarmac in its first half and snow in the second half. The first would tear any studded winter tyres to pieces before the car had to tackle the snow-covered Passo di Teglia, which also incorporated a special stage. A poor performance on the Teglia would result in double penalty, first on the stage and then at the subsequent time control in Rezzo.

The Lancia team decided to change the front tyres just before the start of the snow and the special stage on the Teglia. They practised the job and got it down to just under a minute. Their cars started from Pigna with full-studded winter tyres on the rear of the front-wheel drive Fulvia and plain gravel tyres on the front. Not being in on the secret of what was about to happen, the other teams thought they were crazy and smiled. Their smiles faded when they saw the tyre changing under way and disappeared completely when the results were in. The three Fulvias of Rauno Aaltonen, Sandro Munari and Harry Kallstrom were over a minute quicker than any other car through the test and were, with one exception, the only cars unpenalised on the road section. It was a coup from which the opposing teams were never to recover and Lancia went on to dominate and win the rally. The Lancia team have tried similar tyre swaps on various Monte Carlo Rallies with varying effect, but none has ever had the complete element of surprise as that first one.

Perhaps it is in the Italian temperament, but the temptation to use all manner of tactics in order to achieve certain ends does seem to have been introduced into rallying by the Fiat and Lancia teams. Perhaps the most oblique 'interference' with the natural course of things came on the 1984 Tour de Corse when, in the closing stages of the rally, Lancia relayed information on the state of the roads and the best choice of tyres to Jean-Pierre Nicolas, who was driving the sole surviving Peugeot 205 T16. The purpose of this much appreciated gesture was to keep Nicolas in fourth place ahead of the sole surviving Audi Quattro of Stig Blomqvist, in order to maintain Lancia's points advantage over the German firm at a maximum. They already had the rally won with the Lancia 037s of Markku Alen and Miki Biasion.

Less oblique were any number of later re-arrangements of results in order to maximise prospects in one championship or another. The wholesale disqualification of the Peugeots in the course of the 1986 San Remo Rally led to Lancia stage-managing the performances of their cars on the last night so that Markku Alen ran out ahead of Miki Biasion and Dario Cerrato, both of whom had led him up to that point. The tactics eventually got them nowhere as Peugeot appealed over their ejection from the rally and FISA scrubbed the results, which had the effect of taking the World Championship crown from Alen's brow and placing it on that of Juha Kannkunen.

Indeed, one might say that as the commercial benefits to be gained from rallying have increased, so have the attempts to arrange results from behind the scenes become more blatant. It was never proved, but strongly suspected, that the Audi team on the

point before us.' Or the Saab service crew on the Arctic Rally who were summoned from their warm estate car 'to check the rear tyre pressures' only to discover that the complete rear axle of the rally car was missing. They had to fit the one from the service car, which left them warm but immobile. Sometimes the boot was on the other foot as when Ford mechanics, aware that one of their rally drivers was capable of finishing off all their rations while they worked on his car, found some remarkably good-looking dog biscuits and put them in a tin at the rear of the service car. The emptiness of the tin was only matched by the grins on the faces of the mechanics when they broke the news about the type of provisions that they had been carrying. The driver is supposed to have commented that it just proved that you could not trust anyone, but he took care to make sure of his own supplies after that incident.

As time passes, fewer and fewer rallies have secret stages, but for many years it was the big challenge for drivers to find out which roads were being used and for organisers to try to prevent them acquiring that knowledge. Where public roads are involved, road closure orders have to be proclaimed locally well in advance of the rally, so before a Circuit of Ireland, for instance, certain rally drivers would declare a great interest in a fishing holiday in Connemara and be seen reading the local press in a very thorough fashion. In Finland during the winter, the organisers used to leave the ploughing-out of the roads to be used as special stages as late as possible and then have officials out watching to see if anyone was practising. One night, a rally crew indulging in a little pace noting saw lights coming towards them on a stage. They stopped and turned out their lights. All of a sudden they could see nothing of the other car. The driver got out and casually walked forward through the snow only to bump into one of his rivals, who was equally convinced that he had come across one of the official spy cars.

The final story of this chapter must also concern characters who will remain, at least for this edition, anonymous. A rally driver in a European country was challenging for the lead of his national championship. The next round was only a week away when he received a telephone call from the Clerk of the Course who told him that he was prepared to give him all the details and locations of the special stages for this otherwise secret rally. Somewhat surprised, the driver thanked him and asked him why he had decided to reveal them to him in particular. It transpired that his rival for the championship had already obtained the stage details from the Clerk of the Course after encountering him in a certain situation with a lady who was not his wife. As he was not able entirely to right the wrong caused by his own indiscretion, the Clerk of the Course had decided to even things up by making sure that both contenders were party to the same information.

Now that was an action truly in the spirit of rallying.

1985 Ivory Coast Rally had swapped Michele Mouton's stricken Sport Quattro for a test car driven by their foreman Franz Braun. The matter was considered by the Stewards, who examined the car and found no fraud, but its subsequent retirement meant that no formal protests were ever filed. A Lancia attempt to resolve the 1976 San Remo Rally in favour of Sandro Munari's Stratos rather than the similar car of Bjorn Waldegaard backfired when Waldegaard obeyed his instructions to the letter rather than following their intent. Ford tried and succeeded in their management of the Manx International result in 1989, but that too eventually failed to achieve its aim. They slowed Mark Lovell in a Sierra Cosworth, when he was leading the rally from Russell Brookes in another Sierra, in order to further Brookes' chances in the British Rally Championship. There were several backfires from this action, first because Lovell chose to do his slowing all in one place, and that in front of the television cameras, and then when it transpired that Lovell was on Pirelli, who were supporters of the Ford works team, while Brookes was on Dunlop. It all proved to be in vain since ultimately the championship went to David Llewellin in a Toyota Celica GT4 running on Pirelli tyres, which seems to indicate that there is perhaps divine justice after all.

The most frequent stories about rallying are often to do with the interaction between the people involved. In the case of the mechanics and drivers, the possibilities for this are almost endless. A Ford service crew taking a nap at one of their points in Czechoslovakia awoke to find a note left by a rally crew which said, 'Car OK. Hope you get to the next

APPENDIX 1

WINNERS OF MAJOR RALLIES

FIA WORLD RALLY CHAMPIONSHIP

Winners of the events and championships

1973

Monte Carlo	Andruet/Petit	Alpine Renault A110
Sweden	Blomqvist/Hertz	Saab 96 V4
Portugal	Therier/Jaubert	Alpine Renault A110
Safari	Mehta/Drews	Datsun 240 Z
Morocco	Darniche/Mahé	Alpine Renault A110
Acropolis	Therier/Delferrier	Alpine Renault A110
Poland	Warmbold/Todt	Fiat Abarth 124
1000 Lakes	Makinen/Liddon	Ford Escort RS
Austria	Warmbold/Todt	BMW 2002 T Ii
San Remo	Therier/Jaubert	Alpine Renault A110
USA	Boyce/Woods	Toyota Corolla 1600
RAC Rally	Makinen/Liddon	Ford Escort RS
Corsica	Nicolas/Vial	Alpine Renault A110

WORLD CHAMPION MANUFACTURER: ALPINE RENAULT

1974

Monte Carlo	*cancelled due to fuel crisis*	
Sweden	*cancelled due to fuel crisis*	
Portugal	Pinto/Bernacchini	Fiat Abarth 124
Safari	Singh/Doig	Colt Lancer
Acropolis	*cancelled due to fuel crisis*	
1000 Lakes	Mikkola/Davenport	Ford Escort RS
San Remo	Munari/Mannucci	Lancia Stratos
Canada	Munari/Mannucci	Lancia Stratos
USA	Therier/Delferrier	Renault 17 Gordini
RAC Rally	Makinen/Liddon	Ford Escort RS
Corsica	Andruet/Petit	Lancia Stratos

WORLD CHAMPION MANUFACTURER: LANCIA

1975

Monte Carlo	Munari/Sodano	Lancia Stratos
Sweden	Waldegaard/Thorselius	Lancia Stratos
Safari	Andersson/Hertz	Peugeot 504
Acropolis	Rohrl/Berger	Opel Ascona
Morocco	Mikkola/Todt	Peugeot 504
Portugal	Alen/Kivimaki	Fiat Abarth 124
1000 Lakes	Mikkola/Aho	Toyota Corolla 1600
San Remo	Waldegaard/Thorselius	Lancia Stratos
Corsica	Darniche/Mahé	Lancia Stratos
RAC Rally	Makinen/Liddon	Ford Escort RS

WORLD CHAMPION MANUFACTURER: LANCIA

1976

Monte Carlo	Munari/Maiga	Lancia Stratos
Sweden	Eklund/Cederberg	Saab 96 V4
Portugal	Munari/Maiga	Lancia Stratos
Safari	Singh/Doig	Colt Lancer
Acropolis	Kallstrom/Andersson	Datsun Violet
Morocco	Nicolas/Gamet	Peugeot 504
1000 Lakes	Alen/Kivimaki	Fiat Abarth 131
San Remo	Waldegaard/Thorselius	Lancia Stratos
Corsica	Munari/Maiga	Lancia Stratos
RAC Rally	Clark/Pegg	Ford Escort RS

WORLD CHAMPION MANUFACTURER: LANCIA

1977

Monte Carlo	Munari/Maiga	Lancia Stratos
Sweden	Blomqvist/Sylvan	Saab 99 EMS
Portugal	Alen/Kivimaki	Fiat Abarth 131
Safari	Waldegaard/Thorselius	Ford Escort RS
New Zealand	Bachelli/Rossetti	Fiat Abarth 131
Acropolis	Waldegaard/Thorselius	Ford Escort RS
1000 Lakes	Hamalainen/Tiukkanen	Ford Escort RS
Canada	Salonen/Markkula	Fiat Abarth 131
San Remo	Andruet/Delferrier	Fiat Abarth 131
Corsica	Darniche/Mahé	Fiat Abarth 131
RAC Rally	Waldegaard/Thorselius	Ford Escort RS

WORLD CHAMPION MANUFACTURER: FIAT
FIA CUP FOR DRIVERS: SANDRO MUNARI

1978

Monte Carlo	Nicolas/Laverne	Porsche Carrera
Sweden	Waldegaard/Thorselius	Ford Escort RS
Safari	Nicolas/Lefebvre	Peugeot 504 V6 Coupé
Portugal	Alen/Kivimaki	Fiat Abarth 131
Acropolis	Rohrl/Geistdorfer	Fiat Abarth 131
1000 Lakes	Alen/Kivimaki	Fiat Abarth 131
Canada	Rohrl/Geistdorfer	Fiat Abarth 131
San Remo	Alen/Kivimaki	Lancia Stratos
Ivory Coast	Nicolas/Gamet	Peugeot 504 V6 Coupé
Corsica	Darniche/Mahé	Fiat Abarth 131
RAC Rally	Mikkola/Hertz	Ford Escort RS

WORLD CHAMPION MANUFACTURER: FIAT
FIA CUP FOR DRIVERS: MARKKU ALEN

1979

Monte Carlo	Darniche/Mahé	Lancia Stratos
Sweden	Blomqvist/Cederberg	Saab 99 Turbo
Portugal	Mikkola/Hertz	Ford Escort RS
Safari	Mehta/Doughty	Datsun 160 J
Acropolis	Waldegaard/Thorselius	Ford Escort RS
New Zealand	Mikkola/Hertz	Ford Escort RS
1000 Lakes	Alen/Kivimaki	Fiat Abarth 131
Canada	Waldegaard/Thorselius	Ford Escort RS
San Remo	'Tony'/Mannini	Lancia Stratos
Corsica	Darniche/Mahé	Lancia Stratos
RAC Rally	Mikkola/Hertz	Ford Escort RS
Ivory Coast	Mikkola/Hertz	Mercedes 450 SLC

WORLD CHAMPION MANUFACTURER: FORD
WORLD CHAMPION DRIVER: BJORN WALDEGAARD

1980

Monte Carlo	Rohrl/Geistdorfer	Fiat Abarth
Sweden	Kullang/Berglund	Opel Ascona 400
Portugal	Rohrl/Geistdorfer	Fiat Abarth 131
Safari	Mehta/Doughty	Datsun 160 J
Acropolis	Vatanen/Richards	Ford Escort RS
Argentina	Rohrl/Geistdorfer	Fiat Abarth 131
1000 Lakes	Alen/Kivimaki	Fiat Abarth 131
New Zealand	Salonen/Harjanne	Datsun 160 J
San Remo	Rohrl/Geistdorfer	Fiat Abarth 131
Corsica	Therier/Vial	Porsche 911 SC
RAC Rally	H Toivonen/White	Talbot Sunbeam Lotus
Ivory Coast	Waldegaard/Thorselius	Mercedes 500 SLC

WORLD CHAMPION MANUFACTURER: FIAT
WORLD CHAMPION DRIVER: WALTER ROHRL

1981

Monte Carlo	Ragnotti/Andrie	Renault 5 Turbo
Sweden	Mikkola/Hertz	Audi Quattro
Safari	Mehta/Doughty	Datsun Violet GT
Corsica	Darniche/Mahé	Lancia Stratos
Acropolis	Vatanen/Richards	Ford Escort RS
Argentina	Frequelin/Todt	Talbot Sunbeam Lotus
Brazil	Vatanen/Richards	Ford Escort RS
1000 Lakes	Vatanen/Richards	Ford Escort RS
San Remo	Mouton/Pons	Audi Quattro
Ivory Coast	Salonen/Harjanne	Datsun Violet GT
RAC Rally	Mikkola/Hertz	Audi Quattro

WORLD CHAMPION MANUFACTURER: TALBOT
WORLD CHAMPION DRIVER: ARI VATANEN

1982

Monte Carlo	Rohrl/Geistdorfer	Opel Ascona 400
Sweden	Blomqvist/Cederberg	Audi Quattro
Portugal	Mouton/Pons	Audi Quattro
Safari	Mehta/Doughty	Datsun Violet GT
Corsica	Ragnotti/Andrie	Renault 5 Turbo
Acropolis	Mouton/Pons	Audi Quattro
New Zealand	Waldegaard/Thorselius	Toyota Celica GT
Brazil	Mouton/Pons	Audi Quattro
1000 Lakes	Mikkola/Hertz	Audi Quattro
San Remo	Blomqvist/Cederberg	Audi Quattro
Ivory Coast	Rohrl/Geistdorfer	Opel Ascona 400
RAC Rally	Mikkola/Hertz	Audi Quattro

WORLD CHAMPION MANUFACTURER: AUDI
WORLD CHAMPION DRIVER: WALTER ROHRL

1983

Monte Carlo	Rohrl/Geistdorfer	Lancia Rally 037
Sweden	Mikkola/Hertz	Audi Quattro
Portugal	Mikkola/Hertz	Audi Quattro
Safari	Vatanen/Harryman	Opel Ascona 400
Corsica	Alen/Kivimaki	Lancia Rally 037
Acropolis	Rohrl/Geistdorfer	Lancia Rally 037
New Zealand	Rohrl/Geistdorfer	Lancia Rally 037
Argentina	Mikkola/Hertz	Audi Quattro
1000 Lakes	Mikkola/Hertz	Audi Quattro
San Remo	Alen/Kivimaki	Lancia Rally 037
Ivory Coast	Waldegaard/Thorselius	Toyota Celica Turbo
RAC Rally	Blomqvist/Cederberg	Audi Quattro

WORLD CHAMPION MANUFACTURER: LANCIA
WORLD CHAMPION DRIVER: HANNU MIKKOLA

1984

Monte Carlo	Rohrl/Geistdorfer	Audi Quattro A2
Sweden	Blomqvist/Cederberg	Audi Quattro A2
Portugal	Mikkola/Hertz	Audi Quattro A2
Safari	Waldegaard/Thorselius	Toyota Celica Turbo
Corsica	Alen/Kivimaki	Lancia Rally 037
Acropolis	Blomqvist/Cederberg	Audi Quattro A2
New Zealand	Blomqvist/Cederberg	Audi Quattro A2
Argentina	Blomqvist/Cederberg	Audi Quattro A2
1000 Lakes	Vatanen/Harryman	Peugeot 205 T16
San Remo	Vatanen/Harryman	Peugeot 205 T16
Ivory Coast	Blomqvist/Cederberg	Audi Quattro Sport
RAC Rally	Vatanen/Harryman	Peugeot 205 T16

WORLD CHAMPION MANUFACTURER: AUDI
WORLD CHAMPION DRIVER: STIG BLOMQVIST

1985

Monte Carlo	Vatanen/Harryman	Peugeot 205 T16
Sweden	Vatanen/Harryman	Peugeot 205 T16
Portugal	Salonen/Harjanne	Peugeot 205 T16
Safari	Kankkunen/Gallagher	Toyota Celica Turbo
Corsica	Ragnotti/P. Thimonier	Renault 5 Maxi Turbo
Acropolis	Salonen/Harjanne	Peugeot 205 T16
New Zealand	Salonen/Harjanne	Peugeot 205 T16
Argentina	Salonen/Harjanne	Peugeot 205 T16
1000 Lakes	Salonen/Harjanne	Peugeot 205 T16
San Remo	Rohrl/Geistdorfer	Audi Sport Quattro E2
Ivory Coast	Kankkunen/Gallagher	Toyota Celica Turbo
RAC Rally	H Toivonen/Wilson	Lancia Delta S4

WORLD CHAMPION MANUFACTURER: PEUGEOT
WORLD CHAMPION DRIVER: TIMO SALONEN

PREVIOUS PAGE Pentti Airikkala/Brian Murphy Lancia Delta HF Integrale Lombard RAC Rally 1988.

RIGHT Markku Alen/Ilkka Kivimaki Lancia Stratos HF Lombard RAC Rally 1979

1986

Monte Carlo	H Toivonen/Cresto	Lancia Delta S4
Sweden	Kankkunen/Piironen	Peugeot 205 T16
Portugal	Moutinho/Fortes	Renault 5 Maxi Turbo
Safari	Waldegaard/Gallagher	Toyota Celica Turbo
Corsica	Saby/Fauchille	Peugeot 205 T16
Acropolis	Kankkunen/Piironen	Peugeot 205 T16
New Zealand	Kankkunen/Piironen	Peugeot 205 T16
Argentina	Biasion/Siviero	Lancia Delta S4
1000 Lakes	Salonen/Harjanne	Peugeot 205 T16
Ivory Coast	Waldegaard/Gallagher	Toyota Celica Turbo
San Remo	Alen/Kivimaki	Lancia Delta S4
RAC Rally	Salonen/Harjanne	Peugeot 205 T16
USA	Alen/Kivimaki	Lancia Delta S4

WORLD CHAMPION MANUFACTURER: PEUGEOT
WORLD CHAMPION DRIVER: JUHA KANKKUNEN

1987

Monte Carlo	Biasion/Siviero	Lancia Delta HF
Sweden	Salonen/Harjanne	Mazda 323 4WD
Portugal	Alen/Kivimaki	Lancia Delta HF
Safari	Mikkola/Hertz	Audi 200 Quattro
Corsica	Béguin/Lenne	BMW M3
Acropolis	Alen/Kivimaki	Lancia Delta HF
USA	Kankkunen/Piironen	Lancia Delta HF
New Zealand	Wittmann/Pattermann	Lancia Delta HF
Argentina	Biasion/Siviero	Lancia Delta HF
1000 Lakes	Alen/Kivimaki	Lancia Delta HF
Ivory Coast	K Eriksson/Diekmann	Volkswagen Golf 16v
San Remo	Biasion/Siviero	Lancia Delta HF
RAC Rally	Kankkunen/Piironen	Lancia Delta HF

WORLD CHAMPION MANUFACTURER: LANCIA
WORLD CHAMPION DRIVER: JUHA KANKKUNEN

1988

Monte Carlo	Saby/Fauchille	Lancia Delta HF
Sweden	Alen/Kivimaki	Lancia Delta HF
Portugal	Biasion/Cassina	Lancia Delta Integrale
Safari	Biasion/Siviero	Lancia Delta Integrale
Corsica	Auriol/Occelli	Ford Sierra Cosworth
Acropolis	Biasion/Siviero	Lancia Delta Integrale
USA	Biasion/Siviero	Lancia Delta Integrale
New Zealand	Haider/Hinterleitner	Opel Kadett GSi
Argentina	Recalde/del Buono	Lancia Delta Integrale
1000 Lakes	Alen/Kivimaki	Lancia Delta Integrale
Ivory Coast	Ambrosino/Le Saux	Nissan 200 SX
San Remo	Biasion/Siviero	Lancia Delta Integrale
RAC Rally	Alen/Kivimaki	Lancia Delta Integrale

WORLD CHAMPION MANUFACTURER: LANCIA
WORLD CHAMPION DRIVER: MIKI BIASION

1989

Sweden	I Carlsson/P Carlsson	Mazda 323 4WD
Monte Carlo	Biasion/Siviero	Lancia Delta Integrale
Portugal	Biasion/Siviero	Lancia Delta Integrale
Safari	Biasion/Siviero	Lancia Delta Integrale
Corsica	Auriol/Occelli	Lancia Delta Integrale
Acropolis	Biasion/Siviero	Lancia Delta Integrale
New Zealand	I Carlsson/P Carlsson	Mazda 323 4WD
Argentina	M Eriksson/Billstam	Lancia Delta Integrale
1000 Lakes	M Eriksson/Billstam	Mitsubishi Galant VR4
Australia	Kankkunen/Piironen	Toyota Celica GT4
San Remo	Biasion/Siviero	Lancia Delta Integrale
Ivory Coast	Oreille/G Thimonier	Renault 5 GT Turbo
RAC Rally	Airikkala/McNamee	Mitsubishi Galant VR4

WORLD CHAMPION MANUFACTURER: LANCIA
WORLD CHAMPION DRIVER: MIKI BIASION

1990

Monte Carlo	Auriol/Occelli	Lancia Delta Integrale
Sweden	*Rally cancelled through lack of snow*	
Portugal	Biasion/Siviero	Lancia Delta Integrale
Safari	Waldegaard/Gallagher	Toyota Celica GT4
Corsica	Auriol/Occelli	Lancia Delta Integrale
Acropolis	Sainz/Moya	Toyota Celica GT4
New Zealand	Sainz/Moya	Toyota Celica GT4
Argentina	Biasion/Siviero	Lancia Delta Integrale
1000 Lakes	Sainz/Moya	Toyota Celica GT4
Australia	Kankkunen/Piironen	Lancia Delta Integrale
San Remo	Auriol/Occelli	Lancia Delta Integrale
Ivory Coast	Tauziac/Papin	Mitsubishi Galant VR4
RAC Rally	Sainz/Moya	Toyota Celica GT4

WORLD CHAMPION MANUFACTURER: LANCIA
WORLD CHAMPION DRIVER: CARLOS SAINZ

MONTE CARLO RALLY

Overall winners

YEAR	CREW	CAR	START TOWN
1911	H Rougier	Turcat-Méry 25hp	Paris
1912	J Beutler	Berliet 16hp	Berlin

Rally not held in 1913 and then postponed due to First World War.

1924	Ledure	Bignan 2-litre	Glasgow
1925	F Repusseau	Renault 40hp	Tunis
1926	Hon V Bruce/Brunell	Bristol AC Six	John O'Groats
1927	Lefevre/Despaux	Amilcar 1098cc	Konigsberg
1928	J Bignan	Fiat 509A 990cc	Bucharest
1929	Dr Van Eijk	Graham-Paige 4.7	Stockholm
1930	H Petit	La Licorne 905cc	Jassy
1931	Healey	Invicta 4.5	Stavanger
1932	=M Vasselle	Hotchkiss AM 2.5	Umea
	=Lavalette/	Peugeot 201	Umea
	De Cortanze		
1933	M Vasselle	Hotchkiss 620 3.5	Tallinn
1934	Gas/Trevoux	Hotchkiss 620 3.5	Athens
1935	Lahaye/Quatresous	Renault Nervasport	Stavanger
1936	Zamfirescu/Cristea	Ford V8 3.6	Athens
1937	Le Begue/Quinlin	Delahaye 135 3.5	Stavanger
1938	Bakker Schut/	Ford V8 3.6	Athens
	Karel Ton		
1939	=Trevoux/Lesurque	Hotchkiss 686 3.5	Athens
	=Paul/Contet	Delahaye 135 3.5	Athens

Rally not held due to Second World War.

1949	Trevoux/Lesurque	Hotchkiss 686 3.5	Lisbon
1950	Becquart/Secret	Hotchkiss 686 3.5	Lisbon
1951	Trevoux/Crovetto	Delahaye 175 4.5	Lisbon
1952	Allard/Warburton	Allard P 4.3	Glasgow
1953	Gatsonides/Worledge	Ford Zephyr 2.3	Monte Carlo
1954	Chiron/Basadonna	Lancia Aurelia GT	Monte Carlo
1955	Malling/Fadum	Sunbeam MKIII 2.3	Oslo
1956	Adams/Bigger	Jaguar MKVII 3.4	Glasgow
1957	*No rally due to Suez Crisis*		
1958	Monraisse/Feret	Renault Dauphine	Lisbon
1959	Coltelloni/Alexandre	Citroen ID 19	Paris
1960	Schock/Moll	Mercedes 220 SE	Warsaw
1961	Martin/Bateau	Panhard PL 17	Monte Carlo

1962	Carlsson/Haggbom	Saab 96	Oslo
1963	Carlsson/Palm	Saab 96	Stockholm
1964	Hopkirk/Liddon	Cooper S 1071	Minsk
1965	Makinen/Easter	Cooper S 1275	Stockholm
1966	P Toivonen/	Citroen DS 21	Oslo
	Mikander		
1967	Aaltonen/Liddon	Cooper S 1275	Monte Carlo
1968	Elford/Stone	Porsche 911 T	Warsaw
1969	Waldegaard/Helmer	Porsche 911	Warsaw
1970	Waldegaard/Helmer	Porsche 911 S	Oslo
1971	Andersson/Stone	Alpine Renault 110	Marrakech
1972	Munari/Manucci	Lancia Fulvia 1600	Almeria
1973	Andruet/Petit	Alpine Renault 110	Monte Carlo
1974	*No rally due to fuel crisis*		
1975	Munari/Sodano	Lancia Stratos	Monte Carlo
1976	Munari/Maiga	Lancia Stratos	Rome
1977	Munari/Maiga	Lancia Stratos	Rome
1978	Nicolas/Laverne	Porsche Carrera 3-litre	Monte Carlo
1979	Darniche/Mahé	Lancia Stratos	Paris
1980	Rohrl/Geistdorfer	Fiat Abarth 131	Frankfurt
1981	Ragnotti/Andrie	Renault 5 Turbo	Paris
1982	Rohrl/Geistdorfer	Opel Ascona 400	Bad-Homburg
1983	Rohrl/Geistdorfer	Lancia Rallye 037	Rome
1984	Rohrl/Geistdorfer	Audi Quattro	Bad-Homburg
1985	Vatanen/Harryman	Peugeot 205 Turbo 16	Paris
1986	H Toivonen/Cresto	Lancia Delta S4	Sestrière
1987	Biasion/Siviero	Lancia Delta HF 4WD	Sestrière
1988	Saby/Fauchille	Lancia Delta HF 4WD	Sestrière
1989	Biasion/Siviero	Lancia Integrale	Sestrière
1990	Auriol/Occelli	Lancia Integrale 16v	Sestrière

SWEDISH RALLY

Overall winners

The original rally was known as the **Rally to the Midnight Sun** and was organised as a summer event on gravel roads.

YEAR	CREW	CAR
1950	Cederbaum/Sohlberg	BMW 328
1951	Bengtsson/Zetterberg	Talbot Lago
1952	Persson/Norrby	Porsche 1500
1953	Nottorp/Jonsson	Porsche 1500
1954	Hammarlund/Petterson	Porsche 1500
1955	Borgefors/Gustavsson	Porsche 1500
1956	Bengtsson/Righard	VW 1200
1957	Jansson/Jansson	Volvo PV444
1958	Andersson/Jacobson	Volvo PV444
1959	Carlsson/Pavoni	Saab 93
1960	Skogh/Skogh	Saab 96
1961	Skogh/Skogh	Saab 96
1962	Soderstrom/Olsson	Mini Cooper 997
1963	Jansson/Peterson	Porsche Carrera
1964	Trana/Thermaenius	Volvo PV544

From this point onwards, the rally changed its name to the **KAK Swedish Rally** and was run as a winter event on snow-covered, forest stages.

1965	Trana/Thermaenius	Volvo PV544
1966	Ake Andersson/Svedberg	Saab 96
1967	Soderstrom/Palm	Lotus Cortina
1968	Waldegaard/Helmer	Porsche 911T
1969	Waldegaard/Helmer	Porsche 911S

LEFT Robert Droogmans/Ronny Joosten
Lancia Delta HF Integrale 16v
Lombard RAC Rally 1990

ABOVE Tom Trana/Solve Andreasson
Saab 96 V4
Swedish Rally 1968

PORTUGAL RALLY

(First eight events known as **TAP Rally**)
Overall winners

1970	Waldegaard/Helmer	Porsche 911S
1971	Blomqvist/Hertz	Saab 96 V4
1972	Blomqvist/Hertz	Saab 96 V4
1973	Blomqvist/Hertz	Saab 96 V4
1974	*Rally cancelled due to fuel crisis*	
1975	Waldegaard/Thorselius	Lancia Stratos
1976	Eklund/Cederberg	Saab 96 V4
1977	Blomqvist/Sylvan	Saab 99 EMS
1978	Waldegaard/Thorselius	Ford Escort RS
1979	Blomqvist/Cederberg	Saab 99 Turbo
1980	Kullang/Berglund	Opel Ascona 400
1981	Mikkola/Hertz	Audi Quattro A1
1982	Blomqvist/Cederberg	Audi Quattro A1
1983	Mikkola/Hertz	Audi Quattro A2
1984	Blomqvist/Cederberg	Audi Quattro A2
1985	Vatanen/Harryman	Peugeot 205 T16
1986	Kankkunen/Piironen	Peugeot 205 T16
1987	Salonen/Harjanne	Mazda 323 4WD
1988	Alen/Kivimaki	Lancia Delta HF
1989	Ingvar Carlsson/Per Carlsson	Mazda 323 4WD
1990	*Rally cancelled due to lack of snow*	

YEAR	CREW	CAR
1967	Albino/Pereira	Renault 8 Gordini
1968	Fall/Crellin	Lancia Fulvia HF
1969	Romaozinho/'Jocames'	Citroen DS 21
1970	Lampinen/Davenport	Lancia Fulvia HF
1971	Nicolas/Todt	Alpine Renault A110
1972	Warmbold/Davenport	BMW 2002 TI
1973	Therier/Jaubert	Alpine Renault A110
1974	Pinto/Bernacchini	Fiat Abarth 124
1975	Alen/Kivimaki	Fiat Abarth 124
1976	Munari/Maiga	Lancia Stratos
1977	Alen/Kivimaki	Fiat Abarth 131
1978	Alen/Kivimaki	Fiat Abarth 131
1979	Mikkola/Hertz	Ford Escort RS
1980	Rohrl/Geistdorfer	Fiat Abarth 131
1981	Alen/Kivimaki	Fiat Abarth 131
1982	Mouton/Pons	Audi Quattro A1
1983	Mikkola/Hertz	Audi Quattro A2
1984	Mikkola/Hertz	Audi Quattro A2
1985	Salonen/Harjanne	Peugeot 205 T16
1986	Moutinho/Fortes	Renault 5 Turbo
1987	Alen/Kivimaki	Lancia Delta HF
1988	Biasion/Cassina	Lancia Delta Integrale
1989	Biasion/Siviero	Lancia Delta Integrale
1990	Biasion/Siviero	Lancia Delta Integrale

EAST AFRICAN SAFARI

(Known initially as the **Coronation Safari**)
Overall winners

YEAR	CREW	CAR
1953	*No overall winner*	
	Dix/Larsen	VW 1200 (*Class A*)
	Airth/Collinge	Standard Vanguard (*Class B*)
	Marwaha/V Preston Snr	Tatra T600 (*Class C*)
	Manussis/Boyes	Chevrolet (*Class D*)
1954	Marwaha/V Preston Snr	VW 1200
1955	Marwaha/V Preston Snr	Ford Zephyr
1956	Cecil/Vickers	DKW
1957	Hofmann/Burton	VW 1200
1958	*No overall winner*	
	Brooke/Hughes	Ford Anglia (*Impala class*)
	Temple-Boreham/	Auto Union 1000 (*Leopard
	Armstrong	class*)
	A Kopperud/K Kopperud	Ford Zephyr Mk 2 (*Lion class*)
1959	Fritschy/Ellis	Mercedes 219
1960	Fritschy/Ellis	Mercedes 219
1961	Manussis/Coleridge/	Mercedes 220
	Beckett	
1962	Fjastad/Schmider	VW 1200
1963	Nowicki/Cliff	Peugeot 404
1964	Hughes/Young	Ford Cortina GT
1965	Singh/Singh	Volvo PV544
1966	Shankland/Rothwell	Peugeot 404
1967	Shankland/Rothwell	Peugeot 404
1968	Nowicki/Cliff	Peugeot 404
1969	Hillyar/Aird	Ford Taunus 20 MRS
1970	Hermann/Schuller	Darsun 1600 SSS
1971	Hermann/Schuller	Datsun 240 Z
1972	Mikkola/Palm	Ford Escort RS
1973	Mehta/Drews	Datsun 240 Z
1974	Singh/Doig	Colt Lancer
1975	Andersson/Hertz	Peugeot 504
1976	Singh/Doig	Colt Lancer
1977	Waldegaard/Thorselius	Ford Escort RS
1978	Nicolas/Lefebvre	Peugeot 504 V6 Coupé
1979	Mehta/Doughty	Datsun 160 J
1980	Mehta/Doughty	Datsun 160 J
1981	Mehta/Doughty	Datsun Violet GT
1982	Mehta/Doughty	Nissan Violet GT
1983	Vatanen/Harryman	Opel Ascona 400
1984	Waldegaard/Thorselius	Toyota Celica TC Turbo
1985	Kankkunen/Gallagher	Toyota Celica TC Turbo
1986	Waldegaard/Gallagher	Toyota Celica TC Turbo
1987	Mikkola/Hertz	Audi 200 Quattro
1988	Biasion/Siviero	Lancia Delta Integrale
1989	Biasion/Siviero	Lancia Delta Integrale
1990	Waldegaard/Gallagher	Toyota Celica GT 14

ACROPOLIS RALLY

Overall winners

YEAR	CREW	CAR
1953	Papamichael/Dimitracos	Jaguar XK 120
1954	Papadopoulos/Dimitrac	Opel Rekord
1955	Pezmazoglou/Papandreou	Opel Kapitan
1956	Schock/Moll	Mercedes 300SL
1957	Jean-Pierre Estager/	Ferrari 250 GT
	Mme. Estager	
1958	Villoresi/Basadonna	Lancia Aurelia GT
1959	Levy/Wenscher	Auto Union 1000
1960	Schock/Moll	Mercedes Benz 220SE
1961	Eric Carlsson/Walter Karlsson	Saab 96

1962	Bohringer/Lang	Mercedes Benz 220SE
1963	Bohringer/Knoll	Mercedes Benz 220SE
1964	Trana/Thermaenius	Volvo PV 544
1965	Skogh/Berggren	Volvo 122S
1966	Soderstrom/Palm	Lotus Cortina
1967	Hopkirk/Crellin	Cooper S 1275
1968	Clark/Porter	Ford Escort TC
1969	Toivonen/Kolari	Porsche 911S
1979	Therier/Callewaert	Alpine Renault A110
1971	Andersson/Hertz	Alpine Renault A110
1972	Lindberg/Eisendle	Fiat 124 Spyder
1973	Therier/Delferrier	Alpine Renault A110
1974	*Rally cancelled due to fuel crisis*	
1975	Rohrl/Berger	Opel Ascona 1.9
1976	Kallstrom/Andersson	Datson 160J
1977	Waldegaard/Thorselius	Ford Escort RS
1978	Rohrl/Geistdorfer	Fiat Abarth 131
1979	Waldegaard/Thorselius	Ford Escort RS
1980	Vatanen/Richards	Ford Escort RS
1981	Vatanen/Richards	Ford Escort RS
1982	Mouton/Pons	Audi Quattro A1
1983	Rohrl/Geistdorfer	Lancia Rally 037
1984	Blomqvist/Cederberg	Audi Quattro
1985	Salonen/Harjanne	Peugeot 205 T16
1986	Kankkunen/Piironen	Peugeot 205 T16
1987	Alen/Kivimaki	Lancia Delta HF
1988	Biasion/Siviero	Lancia Delta Integrale
1989	Biasion/Siviero	Lancia Delta Integrale
1990	Sainz/Moya	Toyota Celica 4WD

TOUR DE CORSE

Also known as **Rallye des Dix Milles Virages**
Overall winners

YEAR	CREW	CAR
1956	Thirion/Ferrier	Renault Dauphine
1957	Nicol/de Lageneste	Alfa Romeo Guilietta
1958	Monraisse/Feret	Renault Dauphine
1959	Orsini/Canonici	Renault Dauphine
1960	Strahle/Linge	Porsche SC90
1961	Trautmann/Ogier	Citroen DS 19
1962	Orsini/Canonici	Renault Dauphine
1963	Trautmann/Chabert	Citroen DS 19
1964	Vinatier/Masson	Renault 8 Gordini
1965	Orsini/Canonici	Renault 8 Gordini
1966	Piot/Jacob	Renault 8 Gordini
1967	Munari/Lombardini	Lancia Fulvia HF
1968	Andruet/Gelin	Alpine Renault A110
1969	Larrousse/Gelin	Porsche 911R
1970	Darniche/Demage	Alpine Renault A110
1971	*Rally cancelled for financial reasons*	
1972	Andruet/Petit	Alpine Renault A110
1973	Nicolas/Vial	Alpine Renault A110
1974	Andruet/Petit	Lancia Stratos
1975	Darniche/Mahé	Lancia Stratos
1976	Munari/Maiga	Lancia Stratos
1977	Darniche/Mahé	Fiat Abarth 131
1978	Darniche/Mahé	Fiat Abarth 131
1979	Darniche/Mahé	Lancia Stratos
1980	Therier/Vial	Porsche 911S
1981	Darniche/Mahé	Lancia Stratos
1982	Ragnotti/Andrie	Renault 5 Turbo
1983	Alen/Kivimaki	Lancia Rally 037
1984	Alen/Kivimaki	Lancia Rally 037
1085	Ragnotti/Thimonier	Renault Maxi 5 Turbo
1986	Saby/Fauchille	Peugeot 205 Turbo 16
1987	Beguin/Lenne	BMW M3
1988	Auriol/ Occelli	Ford Sierra Cosworth
1989	Auriol/Occelli	Lancia Delta Integrale
1990	Auriol/Occelli	Lancia Delta Integrale

1000 LAKES RALLY

Overall winners

YEAR	CREW	CAR
1951	Karlsson/Mattila	Austin Atlantic
1952	Elo/Nuortila	Peugeot 203
1953	Hietanen/Hixen	Allard
1954	Kalpala/Kalpala	Dyna Panhard
1955	Elo/Nuortila	Peugeot 403
1956	O Kalpala/E Kalpala	Donau
1957	Carlsson/Pavoni	Saab 93
1958	O Kalpala/E Kalpala	Alfa Romeo
1959	Callbo/Nurmimaa	Volvo
1960	Bremer/Lampi	Saab 96
1961	Aaltonen/Nurmimaa	Mercedes 220SE
1962	Toivonen/Kallio	Citroen DS 19
1963	Lampinen/Ahava	Saab 96
1964	Lampinen/Ahava	Saab 96
1965	Makinen/Keskitalo	Mini Cooper S
1966	Makinen/Keskitalo	Mini Cooper S
1967	Makinen/Keskitalo	Mini Cooper S
1968	Mikkola/Jarvi	Ford Escort TC
1969	Mikkola/Jarvi	Ford Escort TC
1970	Mikkola/Palm	Ford Escort TC
1971	Blomqvist/Hertz	Saab 96 V4
1972	Lampinen/Sohlberg	Saab 96 V4
1973	Makinen/Liddon	Ford Escort RS
1974	Mikkola/Davenport	Ford Escort RS
1975	Mikkola/Aho	Toyota Corolla
1976	Alen/Kivimaki	Fiat Abarth 131
1977	Hamalainen/Tiukkanen	Ford Escort RS
1978	Alen/Kivimaki	Fiat Abarth 131
1979	Alen/Kivimaki	Fiat Abarth 131
1980	Alen/Kivimaki	Fiat Abarth 131
1981	Vatanen/Richards	Ford Escort RS
1982	Mikkola/Hertz	Audi Quattro
1983	Mikkola/Hertz	Audi Quattro
1984	Vatanen/Harryman	Peugeot 205 Turbo 16
1985	Salonen/Harjanne	Peugeot 205 Turbo 16
1986	Salonen/Harjanne	Peugeot 205 Turbo 16
1987	Alen/Kivimaki	Lancia Delta HF
1988	Alen/Kivimaki	Lancia Delta Integrale
1989	M Eriksson/Billstam	Mitsubishi Galant VR4
1990	Sainz/Moya	Toyota Celica GT4

SAN REMO RALLY

The rally was originally known as the **Rallye dei Fiori** (Rally of the Flowers) after the principal trade of San Remo.

Overall winners

YEAR	CREW	CAR
1928	Urdarianu	Fiat 520
1929	Urdarianu	Fiat 521
1961	De Villa/De Villa	Alfa Romeo Giulietta TI
1962	Frescobaldi/Malinconi	Lancia Flavia
1963	Patria/Orengo	Lancia Fulvia Coupé
1064	Carlsson/Palm	Saab 96 Sport
1965	Cella/Gamenara	Lancia Fulvia
1966	Cella/Lombardini	Lancia Fulvia HF
1967	Piot/Roure	Renault R8 Gordini

The name of the rally was changed to the San Remo Rally . . .

1968	Toivonen/Tiukkanen	Porsche 911 T
1969	Kallstrom/Haggbom	Lancia Fulvia HF

. . . and then to the San Remo–Sestrière, Rally of Italy . . .

1970	Therier/Callewaert	Alpine Renault A110
1971	Andersson/Nash	Alpine Renault A110

. . . and finally back to the San Remo Rally.

1972	Ballestriere/Bernacchini	Lancia Fulvia 1600 HF
1973	Therier/Jaubert	Alpine Renault A110
1974	Munari/Manucci	Lancia Stratos
1975	Waldegaard/Thorselius	Lancia Stratos
1976	Waldegaard/Thorselius	Lancia Stratos
1977	Andruet/Delferrier	Fiat Abarth 131
1978	Alen/Kivimaki	Lancia Stratos
1979	'Tony'/Mannini	Lancia Stratos
1980	Rohrl/Geistdorfer	Fiat Abarth 131
1981	Mouton/Pons	Audi Quattro
1982	Blomqvist/Cederberg	Audi Quattro
1983	Alen/Kivimaki	Lancia Rally 037
1984	Vatanen/Harryman	Peugeot 205 Turbo 16
1985	Rohrl/Geistdorfer	Audi Sport Quattro E2
1986	Alen/Kivimaki	Lancia Delta S4
1987	Biasion/Siviero	Lancia Delta HF
1988	Biasion/Siviero	Lancia Delta Integrale
1989	Biasion/Siviero	Lancia Delta Integrale
1990	Auriol/Occelli	Lancia Delta Integrale

RIGHT Hannu Mikkola/
Arne Hertz
Mercedes 450 SLC 5-litre
Ivory Coast Rally 1980

IVORY COAST RALLY

(Also known as the **Rallye du Bandama**)

Outright winners

YEAR	CREW	CAR
1969	M Gerenthon/H Gerenthon	Renault 8 Gordini
1970	Schuller/Billstam	Datsun 1800
1971	Neyret/Terramorsi	Peugeot 504
1972	*No finishers*	
1973	Hermann/Schuller	Datsun 180B
1974	Makinen/Liddon	Peugeot 504
1975	Consten/Flocon	Peugeot 504
1976	Makinen/Liddon	Peugeot 504 Coupé V6
1977	Cowan/Syer	Mitsubishi Lancer
1978	Nicolas/M Gamet	Peugeot 504 Coupé V6
1979	Mikkola/Hertz	Mercedes-Benz 450 SLC
1980	Waldegaard/H Thorselius	Mercedes-Benz 450 SLC
1981	Salonen/Harjanne	Datsun Violet GT
1982	Rohrl/Geistdorfer	Opel Ascona 400
1983	Waldegaard/Thorselius	Toyota Celica Turbo
1984	Blomqvist/Cederberg	Audi Quattro Sport
1985	Kankkunen/Gallagher	Toyota Celica Turbo
1986	Waldegaard/Gallagher	Toyota Celica Turbo
1987	K Eriksson/Diekmann	VW Golf GTi 16v
1988	Ambrosino/Le Saux	Nissan 200 SX
1989	Oreille/G Thimonier	Renault 5 GT Turbo
1990	Tauziac/Papin	Mitsubishi Galant VR4

MANX TROPHY RALLY

Outright winners

YEAR	CREW	CAR
1963	McBride/Barrow	Ford Anglia
1964	Friswell/K Binns	Cooper S
1965	Fall/Fawcett	Cooper S
1966	Easthope/Craine	Ford Cortina GT
1967	Harvey/Vaux	Cooper S
1968	Huyton/Corrin	Ford Cortina GT
1969	Malkin/Davenport	Hillman Imp
1970	Sclater/Davenport	Ford Escort TC

Rally gained international status

YEAR	CREW	CAR
1971	Clark/Liddon	Ford Escort RS
1972	Clark/Porter	Ford Escort RS
1973	Boyd/Davenport	Ford Escort RS
1974	Curley/Fraser	Porsche Carrera RS
1975	Clark/Porter	Ford Escort RS

Rally accepted into the European Rally Championship

YEAR	CREW	CAR
1976	Vatanen/Bryant	Ford Escort RS
1977	Airikkala/Virtanen	Vauxhall Chevette
1978	Pond/Gallagher	Triumph TR8
1979	Brookes/White	Ford Escort RS
1980	Pond/Gallagher	Triumph TR8
1981	Pond/Nicholson	Vauxhall Chevette HSR
1982	McRae/Nicholson	Opel Ascona 400
1983	H Toivonen/Gallagher	Opel Manta 400
1984	McRae/Nicholson	Opel Manta 400
1985	Brookes/Broad	Opel Manta 400
1986	Pond/Arthur	MG Metro 6R4
1987	McRae/Grindrod	Ford Sierra RS
1988	Snyers/Colebunders	BMW M3
1989	Brookes/Wilson	Ford Sierra RS
1990	Brookes/Wilson	Ford Sierra RS 4×4

RAC RALLY OF GREAT BRITAIN

Rally was first held in 1932 on a national permit

YEAR	CREW	CAR
1932	*Over 1100cc*: Col AH Loughborough	Lanchester 15/18
	Up to 1100cc: VE Leverett	Riley Nine
1933	*Over 16hp*: TDW Weston	Rover Speed 20
	10hp to 16hp: Miss Brunell	AC Ace
	Up to 10hp: G Dennison	Riley Nine
1934	*Over 16hp*: TD Wynn-Weston	Rover Speed 20
	10hp to 16hp: SB Wilks	Rover 12
	Up to 10hp: FRG Spikins	Singer 9 Le Mans
1935	*No overall or class prizes – 106 Gold Awards*	
1936	AH Langley	Singer 9 Le Mans
1937	J Harrop	SS 100 Jaguar
1938	J Harrop	SS 100 Jaguar
1939	AFP Fane	Fraser-Nash BMW 328

After the Second World War and a period when petrol was severely rationed, the RAC Rally started again in 1951 as a full international.

YEAR	CREW	CAR
1951	Appleyard/Mrs Appleyard	Jaguar XJ 120
1952	Imhof/Mrs Frayling	Allard Cadillac J2
1953	Apppleyard/Mrs Appleyard	Jaguar XJ 120
1954	Wallwork/Brookes	Triumph TR2
1955	Ray/Horrocks	Standard 10
1956	Sims/Ambrose/Jones	Aston Martin DB2
1957	*Rally cancelled due to the Suez crisis*	
1958	Harper/Deane	Sunbeam Rapier Mk 1
1959	Burgess/Croft-Pearson	Ford Zephyr Mk 2
1960	E Carlsson/Turner	Saab 96
1961	E Carlsson/Brown	Saab 96
1962	E Carlsson/Stone	Saab 96
1963	Trana/Lindstrom	Volvo PV544
1964	Trana/Thermaenius	Volvo PV544
1965	Aaltonen/Ambrose	Cooper S 1275
1966	Soderstrom/Palm	Lotus Cortina Mk 1
1967	*Rally cancelled due to outbreak of Foot-and-mouth disease*	
1968	Lampinen/Davenport	Saab 96 V4
1969	Kallstrom/Haggbom	Lancia Fulvia 1.6
1970	Kallstrom/Haggbom	Lancia Fulvia 1.6
1971	Blomqvist/Hertz	Saab 96 V4
1972	Clark/Mason	Ford Escort RS
1973	Makinen/Liddon	Ford Escort RS
1974	Makinen/Liddon	Ford Escort RS
1975	Makinen/Liddon	Ford Escort RS
1976	Clark/Pegg	Ford Escort RS
1977	Waldegaard/Thorselius	Ford Escort RS
1978	Mikkola/Hertz	Ford Escort RS
1979	Mikkola/Hertz	Ford Escort RS
1980	Henri Toivonen/White	Sunbeam Talbot Lotus
1981	Mikkola/Hertz	Audi Quattro
1982	Mikkola/Hertz	Audi Quattro
1983	Blomqvist/Cederberg	Audi Quattro A1
1984	Vatanen/Harryman	Peugeot 205 T16
1985	Henri Toivonen/Wilson	Lancia Delta S4
1986	Salonen/Harjanne	Peugeot 205 T16
1987	Kankkunen/Piironen	Lancia Delta HF
1988	Alen/Kivimaki	Lancia Delta Integrale
1989	Airikkala/McNamee	Mitsubishi Galant VR-4
1990	Sainz/Moya	Toyota Celica GT4

CIRCUIT OF IRELAND

First held under the title of **Ulster Motor Rally**

Outright winners

YEAR	CREW	CAR
1931	McCaherty/Trimble	Austin 16 Saloon
1932	McMullan/McMullan	Alvis Sport Twenty
1933	Orr/'X'	Austin Seven
1934	Jones/Hamilton	Standard Ten
1935	Shaw/Drennan	Triumph Southern Cross

Rally name changed to **Circuit of Ireland**.

1936	Clarke/Adams/Holmes	Austin 16 Saloon
1937	Shaw/Johnston	Triumph Vitesse Saloon
1938	Chambers/Hicks	MG
1939	Michael/Dow	Wolseley

Rally not held due to Second World War

1946	Bell/'X'	Riley
1947	McMichael/Shilliday	MG
1948	*Rally not held due to petrol rationing*	
1949	Lindsay (alone in the car)	Ford
1950	Johnstone/Johnstone/Johnstone	Allard
1951	Hopkinson/'X'	MG TD
1952	Johnstone/Bryson	MG TD
1953	Todd/McRae	Dellow
1954	Glover/Lynn	Dellow
1955	McKinney/McKinney	Triumph TR2
1956	McKinney/McKinney	Triumph TR2
1957	*Rally cancelled due to Suez crisis*	
1958	Hopkirk/Scott	Triumph TR3A
1959	Sherry/Debarry	VW Beetle
1960	A Boyd/Johnstone	Austin Healey Sprite
1961	Hopkirk/Scott	Sunbeam Rapier
1962	Hopkirk/Scott	Sunbeam Rapier
1963	I Woodside/E Crawford	Austin Healey Sprite
1964	McCartney/Harryman	Cooper S
1965	Hopkirk/Scott	Cooper S
1966	Fall/Liddon	Cooper S
1967	Hopkirk/Harryman	Cooper S
1968	Clark/Porter	Ford Escort TC
1969	Clark/Porter	Ford Escort TC
1970	Clark/Porter	Ford Escort RS
1971	A Boyd/B Crawford	Ford Escort TC
1972	*Event not held*	
1973	Tordoff/Short	Porsche Carrera
1974	Curley/Frazer	Porsche Carrera
1975	Coleman/Phelan	Ford Escort RS
1976	Coleman/O'Sullivan	Ford Escort RS
1977	Brookes/Brown	Ford Escort RS
1978	Brookes/Brown	Ford Escort RS
1979	Airikkala/Virtanen	Vauxhall Chevette HS
1980	McRae/Nicholson	Vauxhall Chevette HSR
1981	McRae/Grindrod	Opel Ascona 400
1982	McRae/Grindrod	Opel Ascona 400
1983	Brookes/Broad	Vauxhall Chevette HSR
1984	Coleman/Morgan	Opel Manta 400
1985	McRae/Grindrod	Opel Manta 400
1986	Llewellin/Short	MG Metro 6R4
1987	McRae/Grindrod	Ford Sierra RS
1988	McRae/Arthur	Ford Sierra RS
1989	McRae/Arthur	Ford Sierra RS
1990	Llewellin/Short	Toyota Celica GT4

SCOTTISH RALLY

The Scottish Rally was the direct descendant of the Scottish Reliability Trials run by the RSAC between 1905 and 1909. It was first held in 1932, and 14 events were held between then and 1956, in which no outright winner was nominated.

Outright winners

YEAR	CREW	CAR
1957	*No rally due to Suez crisis*	
1958	Dundas/Neill	Triumph TR3
1959	Dalglish/Brass	Triumph TR3
1960	*Rally cancelled due to insufficient entries*	
1961	Melvin/Melvin	Sunbeam Alpine
1962	Cowan/Thompson	Sunbeam Rapier
1963	Cowan/Thompson	Sunbeam Rapier
1964	Clark/Porter	Ford Cortina GT
1965	Clark/Porter	Ford Cortina GT
1966	Fall/Wood	Cooper S
1967	Clark/Porter	Lotus Cortina Mk II
1968	Clark/Porter	Ford Escort TC
1969	Lampinen/Hertz	Saab 96 V4
1970	Culcheth/Syer	Triumph 2.5 PI
1971	Sclater/Davenport	Ford Escort RS
1972	Mikkola/Cardno	Ford Escort RS
1973	Clark/Porter	Ford Escort RS
1974	*Rally cancelled due to petrol tanker drivers' strike*	
1975	Clark/Porter	Ford Escort RS
1976	Brookes/Brown	Ford Escort RS
1977	Vatanen/Bryant	Ford Escort RS
1978	Mikkola/Hertz	Ford Escort RS
1979	Airikkala/Virtanen	Vauxhall Chevette HS
1980	Mikkola/Hertz	Ford Escort RS
1981	Pond/Nicholson	Vauxhall Chevette HSR
1982	Mikkola/Hertz	Audi Quattro
1983	Blomqvist/Cederberg	Audi Quattro
1984	Mikkola/Short	Audi Quattro
1985	Wilson/Harris	Audi Quattro
1986	Sundstrom/Silander	Peugeot 205 T16
1987	Llewellin/Short	Audi Coupé Quattro
1988	McRae/Arthur	Ford Sierra RS
1989	Llewellin/Short	Toyota Celica GT4
1990	Llewellin/Short	Toyota Celica GT4

WELSH RALLY

The first Welsh International Rally was due to be held in 1963 but was cancelled because of snow.

Outright winners

YEAR	CREW	CAR
1964	Williams/Griffiths	Cooper S
1965 (Jan)	Bengry/Skeffington	Ford Cortina GT
1965 (Dec)	Clark/Robson	Lotus Cortina Mk I
1966	Chappell/Llewellyn	Lotus Cortina Mk I
1967	*No event – foot and mouth epidemic*	
1968	*No event – date change*	
1969	Andersson/Palm	Ford Escort TC
1970	Sparrow/Raeburn	Cooper S
1971	Fall/Wood	Datsun 240 Z
1972	Clark/Porter	Ford Escort RS
1973	Clark/Porter	Ford Escort RS
1974	Alen/Davenport	Ford Escort RS
1975	Clark/Porter	Ford Escort RS
1976	Vatanen/Bryant	Ford Escort RS
1977	Airikkala/Francis	Vauxhall Chevette HR
1978	Mikkola/Hertz	Ford Escort RS

| 1979 | Mikkola/Hertz | Ford Escort RS |

Loss of European Championship status

1980	Vatanen/Richards	Ford Escort RS
1981	Vatanen/Richards	Ford Escort RS
1982	Waldegaard/Short	Audi Quattro
1983	Blomqvist/Cederberg	Audi Quattro
1984	Mikkola/Hertz	Audi Quattro
1985	Wilson/Harris	Audi Quattro
1986	Mikkola/Hertz	Audi Sport Quattro
1987	Brookes/Broad	Opel Manta 400
1988	Airikkala/McNamee	Mitsubishi Starion Turbo
1989	Llewellin/Short	Toyota Celica GT4
1990	Llewellin/Short	Toyota Celica GT4

POLISH RALLY

Overall winners

YEAR	CREW	CAR
1921	T Heyne	Dodge
1922	H Lorenz	Steyr
1923	H Liefeldt/V Sironcek	Austro Daimler
1924	H Liefeldt	Austro Daimler
1925	F Betagne	Austro Daimler
1927	St Szwarcsztain	Austro Daimler
1928	H Illiano	Fiat
1929	A Potocki	Austro Daimler

Between 1930 and 1959, there was no overall winner declared.
The rally was not held 1940–45, nor in 1947 or from 1949–53.

1960	W Schock/R Moll	Mercedes 220SE
1961	E Bohringer/R Aaltonen	Mercedes 220SE
1962	E Bohringer/P Lang	Mercedes 220SE
1963	D Glemser/M Braungart	Mercedes 220SE
1964	S Zasada/E Zasada	Steyr Puch 650 TR
1965	R Aaltonen/T Ambrose	Cooper S
1966	T Fall/A Krauklis	Cooper S
1967	S Zasada/E Zasada	Porsche 912
1968	K Kormonicki/Z Wisinowski	Renault 8 Gordini
1969	S Zasada/E Zasada	Porsche 911 S
1970	J-C Andruet/M Veron	Alpine Renault A110
1971	S Zasada/E Zasada	BMW 2002 RI
1972	R Pinto/L Macaluso	Fiat 124 Spyder

The Polish Rally was an inaugural round of the World
Championship.

| 1973 | A Warmbold/J Todt | Fiat Abarth 124 |

It then moved to the European Championship.

1974	K Russling/W Weiss	Porsche 911 Carrera
1975	M Verini/F Rosetti	Fiat Abarth 124
1976	A Jaroszewicz/R Zyszkowski	Lancia Stratos
1977	B Darniche/A Mahé	Lancia Stratos
1978	A Zanini/J Petisco	Fiat Abarth 131
1979	A Zanini/J Petisco	Fiat Abarth 131
1980	A Zanini/Sabater	Porsche 911 SC

The rally was not held in 1981 and 1982 due to political problems.

1983	M Bublewicz/Zyszkowski	Polonez 2000
1984	I Carlsson/B Melander	Mazda RX7
1985	B Kuzmic/R Sali	Renault 5 Turbo
1986	B Kuzmic/R Sali	Renault 5 Turbo
1987	A Ferjancz/J Tandari	Audi Coupé Quattro
1988	M Sulet/P Willem	Ford Sierra Cosworth
1989	R Droogmans/R Joesten	Ford Sierra Cosworth
1990	R Droogmans/R Joesten	Lancia Delta Integrale

TULIP RALLY

Overall winners

YEAR	CREW	CAR
1953	Van Zuylen/Worlidge	Ford Zephyr
1954	Stasse/Gendebien	Alfa Romeo
1955	Tak/Niemoller	Mercedes 300 SL
1956	R Brookes/E Brookes	Austin A 30
1957	Kreisel/Ten Hope	Renault Dauphine
1958	Kolwes/Lautmann	Volvo
1959	D Morley/E Morley	Jaguar 3.4
1960	Trautmann/Verrier	Citroen ID 19
1961	Mabbs/Griffiths	Triumph Herald Coupé
1962	Moss/Wisdom	Mini Cooper 997
1963	*Touring*: Greder/Delalande	Ford Falcon Sprint
	GT: Bakker/Umbach	Porsche 1600 S90
1964	*Touring*: Makinen/Ambrose	Cooper S 1275
	GT: D Morley/E Morley	Austin Healey 3000
1965	*Touring*: Lund/Wahlgren	Saab 96 Sport
	GT: Smith/Domleo	Hillman Imp
1966	Aaltonen/Liddon	Cooper S 1275
1967	Elford/Stone	Porsche 911 S
1968	Clark/Porter	Ford Escort TC
1969	Staepelaere/Aerts	Ford Escort TC
1970	van Grieken/Verbunt	BMW 2002 TI

Rally not held for two years.

1973	Dolk/ de Jong	Opel Ascona
1974	Rohrl/Berger	Opel Ascona
1975	*Rally not held due to organisational problems*	
1976	Lars Carlsson/de Jong	Opel Kadett GTE
1977	Staepelaere/Aerts	Ford Escort RS
1978	Brookes/Bryant	Ford Escort RS

Rally dropped from the European Championship.

1979	Danielsson/Booth	Ford Escort RS
1980	van der Marel/van Traa	Opel Kadett GTE
1981	*Rally not held*	
1982	Bak/Schoonenwolf	Porsche 911 SC
1983	Guliker/Dickhaut	Porsche 911 SC
1984	Andervang/Schoonenwolf	Ford Escort RS
1985	Bosch/Peeters	Audi Quattro
1986	Andervang/Joosten	Ford RS 200
1987	Bosch/Hodgson	Audi Quattro
1988	Bosch/Gormley	BMW M3
1989	Doctor/Barneberg	Ford Sierra RS
1990	*Rally not held*	

TOUR DE FRANCE AUTOMOBILE

Overall winners

YEAR	CREW	CAR
1899	Chevalier René de Knyff	Panhard 16 HP
1906	Barriaux	Vulpés
1908	10 cars equal on zero penalty	
1912	40 cars equal on zero penalty	
1913	10 cars equal on zero penalty	
1914	13 cars equal on zero penalty	
1922	Cesure	Peugeot
1923	19 cars equal on penalties	
1924	17 cars equal on penalties	
1925	11 cars equal on penalties	
1926	13 cars equal on penalties	
1929	16 cars equal on penalties	
1930	24 cars equal on penalties	
1931	24 cars equal on penalties	
1932	22 cars equal on penalties	
1933	38 cars equal on penalties	
1935	6 cars equal on penalties	
1936	= Mme Jourdan	La Licorne
	= Huberdeau	La Licorne
1937	Thirrot	Amilcar
Event not held due to Second World War		
1951	Pagnibon/Baraquet	Ferrari 212
1952	Gignoux/Gignoux	DB Panhard
1953	*Touring*: Condrillier/Daniel	Renault
	GT: Peron/Bertramier	Osca
1954	Pollet/Gauthier	Gordini
1955	*No event following Le Mans disaster*	
1956	De Portago/Nelson	Ferrari
1957	*Touring*: Hébert/Lauga	Alfa Romeo Giulietta
	GT: Gendebien/L Bianchi	Ferrari 250 GT
1958	*Touring*: Hébert/Consten	Alfa Romeo Giulietta
	GT: Gendebien/L Bianchi	Ferrari 250 GT
1959	*Touring*: Da Silva Ramos/Estager	Jaguar 3.4
	GT: Gendebien/L Bianchi	Ferrari 250 GT
1960	*Touring*: Consten/Renel	Jaguar 3.8
	GT: Mairesse/Berger	Ferrari 250 GT
1961	*Touring*: Consten/Renel	Jaguar 3.8
	GT: Mairesse/Berger	Ferrari 250 GT
1962	*Touring*: Consten/Renel	Jaguar 3.8
	GT: Simon/Dupeyron	Ferrari 250 GT
1963	*Touring*: Consten/Renel	Jaguar 3.8
	GT: Guichet/Behra	Ferrari GTO
1964	*Touring*: Procter/Cowan	Ford Mustang 4.7
	GT: L Bianchi/Berger	Ferrari GTO
Not held between 1965 and 1968 due to lack of sponsorship		
1969	Larrousse/Gelin	Porsche 911 R
1970	Beltoise/Todt/Depailler	Matra-Simca 650
1971	Larrousse/Rives	Matra-Simca 660
1972	Andruet/'Biche'	Ferrari 365 GTB
1973	Munari/Mannucci	Lancia Stratos
1974	Larrousse/Nicolas/Rives	Ligier JS 2
1975	Darniche/Mahé	Lancia Stratos
1976	Henry/Grobot	Porsche Carrera
1977	Darniche/Mahé	Lancia Stratos
1978	Mouton/Conconi	Fiat Abarth 131
1979	Darniche/Mahé	Lancia Stratos
1980	Darniche/Mahé	Lancia Stratos
1981	Andruet/Bouchetal	Ferrari 308 GTB
1982	Andruet/'Biche'	Ferrari 308 GTB
1983	Frequelin/Fauchille	Opel Manta 400
1984	Ragnotti/Thimonier	Renault 5 Turbo
1985	Ragnotti/Thimonier	Renault Maxi 5 Turbo
1986	Chatriot/Perin	Renault Maxi 5 Turbo

Event no longer held

LE MARATHON DE LA ROUTE

Winners of the rallies held by the Royal Motor Union of Liège under the generic title **Marathon de la Route** from 1927 until the last road event in 1964

YEAR	CREW	CAR
LIÈGE–BIARRITZ–LIÈGE		
1927	Six cars equal on zero penalties	
LIÈGE–MADRID–LIÈGE		
1928	Minsart/Havelange	Bugatti 44 3000cc
1929	Nine cars equal on zero penalties	
1930	Minsart/Reynaertz	Bugatti
LIÈGE–ROME–LIÈGE		
1931	Toussaint/Evrard	Bugatti 49 3300cc
1932	Orban/Havelange	Bugatti 46 5300cc
1933	= Georges/Collon	FN 3.2-litre
	Von Guillaume/Bahr	Adler 2-litre
1934	= Evrard/Trasenster	Bugatti
	Peeters/Collon	Bugatti
	Lahaye/Quatresous	Renault
	Bahr/Von Guillaume	Imperia
	Van Naemen/Canciani	Lancia
	Thirion/Bouriano	Bugatti
	Bernet/Sailer	Mercedes Benz
1935	= Trasenster/Breyre	Bugatti
	Lahaye/Quatresous	Renault
1936	*Rally not held due to date dispute with Belgian authorities*	
1937	Haeberle/Glockler	Hanomag
1938	Trasenster/Breyre	Bugatti
1939	= Trasenster/Breyre	Bugatti
	Trevoux/Lesurque	Hotchkiss

Rally not held between 1940 and 1949 due to Second World War

YEAR	CREW	CAR
1950	Dubois/De Cortanze	Peugeot Special 1490cc
1951	Claes/Ickx	Jaguar XK 120 3442cc
1952	Polensky/Schlutter	Porsche 356 1486cc
1953	Claes/Trasenster	Lancia Aurelia GT 2500cc
1954	Polensky/Linge	Porsche 356 1486cc
1955	Gendebien/Stasse	Mercedes Benz 300 SL
1956	Mairesse/Genin	Mercedes Benz 300 SL
1957	Storez/Buchet	Porsche 356 1498cc
1958	Hébert/Consten	Alfa Romeo Giulietta
1959	Buchet/Strahle	Porsche Carrera 1598cc
1960	Moss/Wisdom	Austin Healey 3000
LIÈGE–SOFIA–LIÈGE		
1961	Bianchi/Harris	Citroen DS 19
1962	Bohringer/Eger	Mercedes 220 SEB
1963	Bohringer/Kaiser	Mercedes 230 SL
1964	Aaltonen/Ambrose	Austin Healey 3000

The name **Marathon de la Route** was then applied to an event held at the Nurburgring and run for a period of 84 hours.

1965	Greder/Rives	Ford Mustang 4.7-litre
1966	Vernaeve/Hedges	MGB GT 1798cc
1967	Herrmann/Neerpasch/Elford	Porsche 911 2-litre
1968	Linge/Glemser/Kauhsen	Porsche 911 2-litre
1969	Kallstrom/Barbasio/Fall	Lancia Fulvia HF 1600

COUPE DES ALPES

Winners of Coupe des Alpes in the French International rally organised by the *A.C. de Marseille Provence* from 1946 to the last such event in 1971.

YEAR	DRIVER	CAR
1947	Clermont	Lancia
	Descollas	Bugatti
1948	Appleyard	Jaguar SS 100
	Potter	Allard K1
	Murray-Frame	Sunbeam Talbot
	Gautruche	Lancia
	Claude	Lancia
	Descollas	Lancia
	Richard	HRG 1500
	Auriach	Simca 8 Coupé
1949	Gautruche	Citroen
1950	Appleyard	Jaguar XK 120
	Lapchin	Panhard Dyna 4CV
	Colas	Panhard Dyna 4CV
	Masset	Panhard Dyna 4CV
	Grosogeat	Panhard Dyna 4CV
	Burgerhout	Panhard Dyna 4CV
	Signoret	Panhard Dyna 4CV
1951	Landon	Renault
	Anglevin	Simca
	Gott	HRG 1500
	Duff	Frazer Nash
	Piodi	Lancia
	Wisdom	Aston Martin
	Wadsworth	Healey
	Appleyard	Jaguar XK 120
	Habisreutinger	Jaguar XK 120
	Imhof	Allard J2
1952	De Regibus	Renault
	Fabre	Panhard Dyna 5CV
	Picon	Renault
	Von Falkenhausen	BMW 328
	Gatta	Lancia
	Murray-Frame	Sunbeam Talbot
	M Hawthorn	Sunbeam Talbot
	S Moss	Sunbeam Talbot
	M Gatsonides	Jaguar XK 120
	I Appleyard	Jaguar XK 120
1953	Polenski	Porsche
	Sauerwein	Porsche
	Herzet	Ferrari
	Zeller	Porsche
	I Appleyard	Jaguar XK 120
	Von Falkenhausen	Frazer Nash
	Von Hoesch	Porsche
	Gatta	Lancia
	J Lurani	Lancia
	Fraikin	Jaguar
	Stempert	Panhard
	Bulto-Marques	Porsche
	Fabregas	Lancia
	S Moss	Sunbeam Talbot
	Schwob d'Hericourt	Panhard
	De Carlat	Porsche
	Cheiusse	Panhard
	Murray-Frame	Sunbeam Talbot
	Persoglio	Renault
	Fitch	Sunbeam Talbot
	Poletti	Simca
	Mansbridge	Jaguar
	Asso	Alfa Romeo
	S Van Damm	Sunbeam Talbot

YEAR	DRIVER	CAR
	Marion	Citroen

COUPE D'OR: I Appleyard (1951, 1952 & 1953)

YEAR	DRIVER	CAR
1954	Lesur	Renault 4CV
	J Redele	Renault 4CV
	Meier	DKW
	Guiraud	Peugeot 203
	Barbier	Peugeot 203
	Denzel	Denzel
	O'Hara-Moore	Frazer Nash
	M. Gatsonides	Triumph TR2
	S Moss	Sunbeam Talbot
	Rauch	Salmson
	A Burton	Aston Martin

COUPE D'OR: S Moss (1952, 1953 & 1954)

YEAR	DRIVER	CAR
1955	*Rally not held in wake of Le Mans accident*	
1956	P David	Peugeot 203 Coupé
	M Lauga	Denzel
	M Collanfe	Alfa Romeo
	P Strahle	Porsche
	R Buchet	Porsche
	W Rickert	Porsche
	P Hopkirk	Triumph TR2
	M Gatsonides	Triumph TR2
	J Kat	Triumph TR2
	J Griffiths	Triumph TR2
1957	*Rally not held due to Suez crisis*	
1958	B Consten	Alfa Romeo Giulietta SV
	Clarou	Alfa Romeo Giulietta
	Riess	Alfa Romeo Giulietta
	K Ballisat	Triumph TR3
	E Harrison	Ford Zephyr
	P Harper	Sunbeam Rapier Mk I
	W Shepherd	Austin Healey 100-6
1959	Rey	DB Panhard
	P Condriller	Renault Dauphine
	Kuhne	DKW 1000
	P Hopkirk	Sunbeam Rapier Mk II
	P Riley	Ford Zephyr
	P Jopp	Sunbeam Rapier Mk II
	E Harrison	Ford Zephyr
	T Lewis	Triumph TR3
1960	R de Lageneste	Alfa Romeo Giulietta SZ
	P Moss	Austin Healey 3000
	J Behra	Jaguar
	E Bohringer	Mercedes 220 SE
	B Parkes	Jaguar
	R Trautmann	Citroen ID 19
1961	D Morley	Austin Healey 3000
1962	D Morley	Austin Healey 3000
	H Walter	Porsche
	P Moss	Austin Healey 3000
	M Sutcliffe	Triumph TR3
	R Trautmann	Citroen ID 19
1963	J Rolland	Alfa Romeo Zagato
	R Aaltonen	Cooper S
	H Taylor	Ford Cortina GT
	D Seigle-Morris	Ford Cortina GT
	R Trautmann	Citroen DS 19
	P Mayman	Cooper S

COUPE D'ARGENT: R Trautmann (1960, 1962 & 1963)

YEAR	DRIVER	CAR
1964	J Rolland	Alfa Romeo Zagato
	D Morley	Austin Healey 3000
	J Rey	Porsche
	R Aaltonen	Cooper S
	J Wadsworth	Cooper S
	V Elford	Ford Cortina GT
	E Carlsson	Saab 96 Sport

COUPE D'ARGENT: D Morley (1961, 1962 & 1964)

YEAR	DRIVER	CAR
1965	R Trautmann	Lancia Flavia Zagato
	T Makinen	Cooper S

ABOVE Jean-François Piot/Jim Porter   Ford Escort RS 1800   Coupe des Alpes 1971

H Taylor	Ford Lotus Cortina
P Hopkirk	Cooper S
J-F Piot	Renault R8 Gordini
J Vinatier	Renault R8 Gordini
J-C Ogier	Citroen DS 21
T Fall	Cooper S

COUPE D'ARGENT: P Hopkirk (1956, 1959 & 1965)

1966	J Rolland	Alfa Romeo GTA
	R Clark	Ford Lotus Cortina
	J-F Piot	Renault R8 Gordini
	H Greder	Ford Lotus Cortina
	N Labaune	Alfa Romeo GTA
	L Bianchi	Citroen DS 21
	J-P Nicolas	Renault R8 Gordini
1967	P Hopkirk	Cooper S
	B Consten	Alfa Romeo GTA
1968	J Vinatier	Alpine Renault A110
1969	J Vinatier	Alpine Renault A110
1970	*Rally not held due to lack of sponsorship*	
1971	B Darniche	Alpine Renault A110
	J Vinatier	Alpine Renault A110

COUPE D'OR: J Vinatier (1968, 1969 & 1971)

BOUCLES DE SPA

Outright winners

YEAR	CREW	CAR
1953	Richard/X	Volkswagen
1954	Gendebien/Wascher	Aston Martin
1955	*No finishers – all competitors out of time*	
1956	Evrard/ Collignon	Ford Anglia
1962	Sander/Sander	Daf 33
1963	*Event cancelled due to date problems*	
1964	Staepaelere/Meeuwissen	Lotus Cortina
1965	Mombaerts/Mosbeux	Lotus Elan
1966	Staepaelere/Christiaens	Ford Cortina GT
1967	Haxhe/Tricot	Lotus Elan
1968	Jacquemin/Chavan	Renault 8 Gordini
1969	Jacquemin/Demey	Alpine A110
1970	Chavan/Van Gutshoven	Alfa Romeo Duetto
1971	Pedro/'Jimmy'	BMW 2002 T Ii

1972	Adriensens/Daemers	BMW 2002 TIi
1973	Haxhe/C Delferrier	Daf 66
1974	Brink/'Idel'	Porsche Carrera
1975	Staepaelere/Vaillant	Ford Escort RS
1976	Blomqvist/Sylvan	Saab 99
1977	Pond/Gallagher	Triumph TR7
1978	Dumont/Materne	Opel Kadett GTE
1979	Kleint/Wanger	Opel Ascona 1.9
1980	Blomqvist/Cederberg	Saab 99 Turbo
1981	Snyers/Symens	Ford Escort RS
1982	Colsoul/Lopes	Opel Ascona 400
1983	Duez/Lux	Audi Quattro
1984	Capone/Cresto	Lancia Rallye 037
1985	Waldegaard/H Thorselius	Audi Quattro A2
1986	Probst/De Canck	Ford Sierra 4×4
1987	Snyers/Colebunders	Lancia Delta HF
1988	Snyers/Colebunders	BMW M3
1989	Snyers/Colebunders	Toyota Celica 4WD
1990	Saby/Grateloup	Lancia Delta Integrale

LONDON–SYDNEY

YEAR	CREW	CAR
1968	A Cowan/C Malkin/B Coyle	Hillman Hunter
1977	A Cowan/C Malkin/M Broad	Mercedes 300 SE

LONDON–MEXICO (WORLD CUP RALLY)

YEAR	CREW	CAR
1970	H Mikkola/G Palm	Ford Escort Mk I

LONDON–MUNICH (WORLD CUP RALLY)

YEAR	CREW	CAR
1974	A Welinski/K Tubman/J Reddix	Citroen DS 23

PARIS–DAKAR

Outright winners of the automobile event

YEAR	CREW	CAR
1979	Genestier/Lemordant/Tierbault	Range Rover
1980	F Kottulinsky/Luffelmann	Volkswagen Iltis
1981	R Metge/B Giroux	Range Rover
1982	Marreau/Marreau	Renault 20 Turbo
1983	J Ickx/C Brasseur	Mercedes 280 GE
1984	R Metge/D Lemoyne	Porsche 911
1985	P Zanirolli/da Silva	Mitsubishi Pajero
1986	R Metge/D Lemoyne	Porsche 959
1987	A Vatanen/B Giroux	Peugeot 205 T 16
1988	J Kankkunen/J Piironen	Peugeot 205 T 16
1989	A Vatanen/B Berglund	Peugeot 405 T 16
1990	A Vatanen/B Berglund	Peugeot 405 T 16
1991	A Vatanen/B Berglund	Citroen ZX Rallye Raid

AUSTRALIAN SAFARI

Outright winners of the automobile event

YEAR	CREW	CAR
1985	A Cowan/F Gocentas	Mitsubishi Pajero
1986	A Cowan/F Gocentas	Mitsubishi Pajero
1987	D Stewart/F Gocentas	Mitsubishi Pajero
1988	R Dunkerton/S McKinnie	Mitsubishi Pajero
1989	D Officer/R Runnals	Mitsubishi Pajero
1990	K Shinozuka/H Magne	Mitsubishi Prototype

ARGENTINA RALLY

Outright winners

YEAR	CREW	CAR
1979	Guichet/Todt	Peugeot 504
1980	Rohrl/Geistdorfer	Fiat Abarth 131
1981	Frequelin/Todt	Talbot Sunbeam Lotus
1982	*Rally not held*	
1983	Mikkola/Hertz	Audi Quattro A1
1984	Blomqvist/Cederberg	Audi Quattro A2
1985	Salonen/Harjanne	Peugeot 205 T16
1986	Biasion/Siviero	Lancia Delta S4
1987	Biasion/Siviero	Lancia Delta HF
1988	Recalde/del Buono	Lancia Delta Integrale
1989	Eriksson/Billstam	Lancia Delta Integrale
1990	Biasion/Siviero	Lancia Delta Integrale

RALLY OF AUSTRALIA

YEAR	CREW	CAR
1988	I Carlsson/P Carlsson	Mazda 323 4WD
1989	I Carlsson/P Carlsson	Mazda 323 4WD
1990	Kankkunen/Piironen	Lancia Delta Integrale

NEW ZEALAND RALLY

Outright winners

YEAR	CREW	CAR
1969	G Thompson/R Rimmer	Holden Monaro
1970	P Adams/D Fenwick	BMW 2002 TI
1971	B Hodgson/M Mitchell	Ford Lotus Cortina
1972	A Cowan/J Scott	Mini 1275 GT
1973	H Mikkola/J Porter	Ford Escort RS
1974	*Rally not held due to lack of sponsorship*	
1975	M Marshall/A McWatt	Ford Escort RS
1976	A Cowan/J Scott	Hillman Avenger
1977	F Bacchelli/F Rosetti	Fiat Abarth 131
1978	R Brookes/C Porter	Ford Escort RS
1979	H Mikkola/A Hertz	Ford Escort RS
1980	T Salonen/S Harjanne	Datsun 160J
1981	J Donald/K Lancaster	Ford Escort RS
1982	B Waldegaard/H Thorselius	Toyota Celica
1983	W Rohrl/C Geistdorfer	Lancia Rallye 037
1984	S Blomqvist/B Cederberg	Audi Quattro A2
1985	T Salonen/S Harjanne	Peugeot 205 T16
1986	J Kankkunen/J Piironen	Peugeot 205 T16
1987	F Wittmann/J Pettermann	Lancia Delta HF
1988	J Haider/F Hinterleitner	Opel Kadett GSi
1989	I Carlsson/P Carlsson	Mazda 323 4WD
1990	C Sainz/L Moya	Toyota Celica GT4

APPENDIX 2 RESULTS FOR TOP DRIVERS

RAUNO AALTONEN

YEAR	EVENT	CAR	CO-DRIVER	POS.
1959	1000 Lakes	Saab 93	P Siutala	11th
1960	1000 Lakes	Mercedes 220 SE	P Siutala	7th
1961	1000 Lakes	Mercedes 220 SE	V Nurmimaa	1st
1961	FINNISH CHAMPION RALLY DRIVER			
1962	RAC	Mini Cooper	T Ambrose	5th
1963	Monte Carlo	Mini Cooper	T Ambrose	3rd
1963	Swedish	Chrysler Valiant	R Skogh	10th
1963	Alpine Rally	Cooper S	T Ambrose	2nd
1963	1000 Lakes	Saab 96	V Nurmimaa	3rd
1964	Swedish	Saab 96	R Skogh	6th
1964	1000 Lakes	Saab 96	V Nurmimaa	3rd
1964	Liège	Healey 3000	T Ambrose	1st
1965	Geneva	Cooper S	T Ambrose	1st
1965	Alpine	Cooper S	T Ambrose	14th
1965	Czechoslovakia	Cooper S	T Ambrose	1st
1965	Polish	Cooper S	T Ambrose	1st
1965	1000 Lakes	Cooper S	A Jarvi	2nd
1965	3 Cities	Cooper S	T Ambrose	1st
1965	RAC	Cooper S	T Ambrose	1st
1965	EUROPEAN AND FINNISH CHAMPION RALLY DRIVER			
1966	Tulip	Cooper S	H Liddon	1st
1966	Czechoslovakia	Cooper S	H Liddon	1st
1966	1000 Lakes	Cooper S	V Nurmimaa	3rd
1966	Alpine Rally	Cooper S	H Liddon	3rd
1966	RAC	Cooper S	H Liddon	4th
1967	Monte Carlo	Cooper S	H Liddon	1st
1967	Swedish	Cooper S	H Liddon	3rd
1967	Tulip	Cooper S	H Liddon	3rd
1968	Monte Carlo	Cooper S	H Liddon	3rd
1968	Acropolis	Cooper S	H Liddon	5th
1968	Corsica	Lancia Fulvia	H Liddon	2nd
1969	San Remo	Lancia Fulvia	H Liddon	2nd
1969	Safari	Lancia Fulvia	H Liddon	9th
1969	Corsica	BMW 2002 TI	T Ambrose	7th
1970	London/Mexico	Ford Escort	H Liddon	3rd
1970	RAC	Datsun 240 Z	P Easter	7th
1971	Monte Carlo	Datsun 240 Z	P Easter	5th
1971	Safari	Datsun 240 Z	P Easter	7th
1972	Monte Carlo	Datsun 240 Z	J Todt	3rd
1972	Safari	Datsun 240 Z	T Fall	6th
1973	Monte Carlo	Datsun 240 Z	P Easter	18th
1973	Acropolis	Fiat Abarth 124	R Turvey	2nd
1974	Safari	Datsun 1800	W Stiller	6th
1974	RAC	Fiat Abarth 124	P Easter	12th
1976	Portugal	Opel Ascona	C Billstam	4th
1977	Safari	Datsun Violet	L Drews	2nd
1977	Australia	Datsun Violet		1st
1978	Safari	Datsun 160J	L Drews	3rd
1979	Safari	Datsun 160J	L Drews	5th
1980	Safari	Datsun 160J	L Drews	2nd
1981	Safari	Datsun Violet GT	L Drews	2nd
1984	Safari	Opel Manta 400	L Drews	2nd

MARKKU ALEN

YEAR	EVENT	CAR	CO-DRIVER	POS.
1971	1000 Lakes	Volvo 142	J Toivonen	3rd
1972	Arctic	Volvo 142	J Toivonen	2nd
1972	1000 Lakes	Volvo 142	J Toivonen	3rd
1972	RAC	Volvo 142	A Aho	12th
1973	1000 Lakes	Volvo 142	J Toivonen	2nd
1973	RAC	Ford Escort RS	I Kivimaki	3rd
1974	Arctic	Ford Escort RS	I Kivimaki	4th
1974	Portugal	Fiat Abarth 124	I Kivimaki	3rd
1974	Welsh	Ford Escort RS	J Davenport	1st
1974	1000 Lakes	Fiat Abarth 124	I Kivimaki	3rd
1974	USA	Fiat Abarth 124	I Kivimaki	2nd
1975	Monte Carlo	Fiat Abarth 124	I Kivimaki	3rd
1975	Swedish	Fiat Abarth 124	I Kivimaki	6th
1975	Portugal	Fiat Abarth 124	I Kivimaki	1st
1976	Monte Carlo	Fiat Abarth 124	I Kivimaki	6th
1976	Elba	Fiat Abarth 124	I Kivimaki	1st
1976	Tulip	Fiat Abarth 124	I Kivimaki	3rd
1976	Morocco	Fiat Abarth 124	I Kivimaki	12th
1976	1000 Lakes	Fiat Abarth 131	I Kivimaki	1st
1977	Portugal	Fiat Abarth 131	I Kivimaki	1st
1977	New Zealand	Fiat Abarth 131	I Kivimaki	3rd
1978	Sweden	Fiat Abarth 131	I Kivimaki	3rd
1978	Portugal	Fiat Abarth 131	I Kivimaki	1st
1978	Acropolis	Fiat Abarth 131	I Kivimaki	2nd
1978	1000 Lakes	Fiat Abarth 131	I Kivimaki	1st
1978	Canada	Fiat Abarth 131	I Kivimaki	2nd
1978	San Remo	Lancia Stratos	I Kivimaki	1st
1978	Giro d'Italia	Lancia Stratos	I Kivimaki	1st
1978	WINNER FIA DRIVER'S CUP			
1979	Monte Carlo	Fiat Abarth 131	I Kivimaki	3rd
1979	Sweden	Fiat Abarth 131	I Kivimaki	4th
1979	Hankirally	Fiat Abarth 131	I Kivimaki	1st
1979	Safari	Fiat Abarth 131	I Kivimaki	3rd
1979	Brazil	Fiat Abarth 131	I Kivimaki	1st
1979	1000 Lakes	Fiat Abarth 131	I Kivimaki	1st
1979	San Remo	Fiat Abarth 131	I Kivimaki	6th
1979	RAC	Lancia Stratos	I Kivimaki	5th
1980	Portugal	Fiat Abarth 131	I Kivimaki	2nd
1980	Acropolis	Fiat Abarth 131	I Kivimaki	3rd
1980	1000 Lakes	Fiat Abarth 131	I Kivimaki	1st
1981	Monte Carlo	Fiat Abarth 131	I Kivimaki	7th
1981	Costa Smeralda	Fiat Abarth 131	I Kivimaki	1st
1981	Portugal	Fiat Abarth 131	I Kivimaki	1st
1981	Acropolis	Fiat Abarth 131	I Kivimaki	2nd
1981	1000 Lakes	Fiat Abarth 131	I Kivimaki	2nd
1981	San Remo	Fiat Abarth 131	I Kivimaki	9th
1982	Corsica	Lancia Rallye 037	I Kivimaki	9th
1982	RAC	Lancia Rallye 037	I Kivimaki	4th
1983	Monte Carlo	Lancia Rallye 037	I Kivimaki	2nd
1983	Portugal	Lancia Rallye 037	I Kivimaki	4th
1983	Corsica	Lancia Rallye 037	I Kivimaki	1st
1983	Acropolis	Lancia Rallye 037	I Kivimaki	2nd
1983	Argentina	Lancia Rallye 037	I Kivimaki	5th
1983	1000 Lakes	Lancia Rallye 037	I Kivimaki	3rd
1983	San Remo	Lancia Rallye 037	I Kivimaki	1st
1984	Monte Carlo	Lancia Rallye 037	I Kivimaki	8th
1984	Portugal	Lancia Rallye 037	I Kivimaki	2nd
1984	Safari	Lancia Rallye 037	I Kivimaki	4th
1984	Corsica	Lancia Rallye 037	I Kivimaki	1st
1984	Acropolis	Lancia Rallye 037	I Kivimaki	3rd
1984	New Zealand	Lancia Rallye 037	I Kivimaki	2nd
1984	1000 Lakes	Lancia Rallye 037	I Kivimaki	2nd
1985	1000 Lakes	Lancia Rallye 037	I Kivimaki	3rd
1985	San Remo	Lancia Rallye 037	I Kivimaki	4th
1985	RAC	Lancia Delta S4	I Kivimaki	2nd
1986	Swedish	Lancia Delta S4	I Kivimaki	2nd
1986	Safari	Lancia Rallye 037	I Kivimaki	3rd
1986	New Zealand	Lancia Delta S4	I Kivimaki	2nd
1986	Argentina	Lancia Delta S4	I Kivimaki	2nd
1986	1000 Lakes	Lancia Delta S4	I Kivimaki	3rd
1986	RAC	Lancia Delta S4	I Kivimaki	2nd
1986	USA	Lancia Delta S4	I Kivimaki	1st
1987	Swedish	Lancia Delta HF	I Kivimaki	5th
1987	Portugal	Lancia Delta HF	I Kivimaki	1st
1987	Acropolis	Lancia Delta HF	I Kivimaki	1st
1987	USA	Lancia Delta HF	I Kivimaki	3rd
1987	1000 Lakes	Lancia Delta HF	I Kivimaki	1st
1987	RAC	Lancia Delta HF	I Kivimaki	5th
1988	Sweden	Lancia Delta HF	I Kivimaki	1st

1988	Portugal	Lancia Delta Int.	I Kivimaki	6th
1988	Acropolis	Lancia Delta Int.	I Kivimaki	4th
1988	1000 Lakes	Lancia Delta Int.	I Kivimaki	1st
1988	San Remo	Lancia Delta Int.	I Kivimaki	4th
1988	RAC	Lancia Delta Int.	I Kivimaki	1st
1989	Portugal	Lancia Delta Int.	I Kivimaki	2nd
1989	Australia	Lancia Delta Int.	I Kivimaki	3rd
1990	1000 Lakes	Subaru Legacy	I Kivimaki	4th

OVE ANDERSSON

YEAR	EVENT	CAR	CO-DRIVER	POS.
1963	Swedish	Mini Cooper	G Wiman	5th
1964	Acropolis	Saab 96 Sport	T Aman	10th
1964	Swedish	Saab 96 Sport	T Aman	5th
1964	1000 Lakes	Saab 96 Sport	T Aman	7th
1965	Monte Carlo	Saab 96 Sport	T Aman	13th
1965	Swedish	Saab 96 Sport	T Aman	6th
1965	1000 Lakes	Saab 96 Sport	S Svedberg	11th
1966	Monte Carlo	Lancia Flavia	R Dahlgren	3rd
1966	San Remo	Lancia Fulvia	R Dahlgren	3rd
1966	Acropolis	Lancia Fulvia	R Dahlgren	4th
1966	RAC	Lancia Fulvia	J Davenport	7th
1967	Monte Carlo	Lancia Fulvia	J Davenport	2nd
1967	San Remo	Lancia Fulvia	J Davenport	3rd
1967	Acropolis	Lancia Fulvia	J Davenport	2nd
1967	Gulf London	Lotus Cortina Mk2	J Davenport	1st
1967	Spain	Lancia Fulvia	J Davenport	1st
1967	1000 Lakes	Lotus Cortina Mk2	A Norlund	4th
1968	Monte Carlo	Lancia Fulvia	J Davenport	6th
1968	San Remo	Ford Escort TC	J Davenport	3rd
1968	Sestrière	Lancia Fulvia	J Davenport	4th
1968	Tulip	Ford Escort TC	J Davenport	2nd
1969	Sestrière	Ford Escort TC	L Nystrom	2nd
1970	Acropolis	Ford Escort TC	J Porter	3rd
1971	Monte Carlo	Alpine A110	D Stone	1st
1971	San Remo	Alpine A110	T Nash	1st
1971	Austrian	Alpine A110	A Hertz	1st
1971	Acropolis	Alpine A110	A Hertz	1st
1972	Swedish	Renault R12G	J Davenport	15th
1972	Safari	Datsun 180B	J Davenport	12th
1972	RAC	Toyota Celica	G Phillips	9th
1973	Monte Carlo	Alpine A110	J Todt	2nd
1973	Safari	Peugeot 504	J Todt	3rd
1973	Austria	Toyota Celica	G Haggbom	8th
1973	RAC	Toyota Celica	G Phillips	12th
1974	Wiesbaden	Toyota Corolla	A Hertz	3rd
1974	Portugal	Toyota Corolla	A Hertz	4th
1974	Total	Toyota Celica	A Hertz	1st
1975	Safari	Peugeot 504	A Hertz	1st
1975	Portugal	Toyota Corolla	A Hertz	3rd
1975	Total SA	Toyota Corolla	A Hertz	3rd
1976	Portugal	Toyota Celica	A Hertz	2nd
1976	RAC	Toyota Corolla	M Holmes	5th
1977	Portugal	Toyota Celica	H Liddon	3rd
1977	Ireland	Toyota Celica	P Phelan	3rd
1978	Portugal	Toyota Celica	H Liddon	4th
1979	Portugal	Toyota Celica	H Liddon	3rd
1979	Ivory Coast	Toyota Celica	H Liddon	5th
1980	Portugal	Toyota Celica	H Liddon	6th
1980	Acropolis	Toyota Celica	H Liddon	6th

PREVIOUS PAGE The road to the top culminates in scenes like this for Carlos Sainz on the 1990 Lombard RAC Rally.

JEAN-CLAUDE ANDRUET

YEAR	EVENT	CAR	CO-DRIVER	POS.
1967	Alpine	Alpine A110	M Gelin	5th
1968	Lyon–Char	Alpine A110	M Gelin	1st
1968	Corsica	Alpine A110	M Gelin	1st
1969	Alpine	Alpine A110	P Ecot	2nd
1969	Crit. Alpin	Alpine A110	P Ecot	1st
1970	Lyon–Char	Alpine A110	D Stone	1st
1970	Lorraine	Alpine A110		1st
1970	Corsica	Alpine A110	M Vial	2nd
1970	Geneva	Alpine A110	M Veron	1st
1970	3 Cities	Alpine A110	M Veron	1st
1970	Polish	Alpine A110	M Veron	1st
1970	EUROPEAN CHAMPION RALLY DRIVER			
1971	Monte Carlo	Alpine A110	M Vial	=3rd
1972	Lyon–Char	Alpine A110	M Vial	1st
1972	Cevenole	Alpine A110		1st
1972	Tour de France	Ferrari GTB		1st
1972	Corsica	Alpine A110	M Petit	1st
1973	Monte Carlo	Alpine A110	M Petit	1st
1974	Neige et Glace	Lancia Stratos	M Petit	1st
1974	Corsica	Lancia Stratos	M Petit	1st
1974	Tour de France	Lancia Stratos		3rd
1975	Elba	Alfa Romeo GT	M Petit	4th
1975	Corsica	Alfa Romeo GT	Y Jouanny	3rd
1977	Monte Carlo	Fiat Abarth 131	M Petit	2nd
1977	Antibes	Fiat Abarth 131	M Petit	1st
1977	San Remo	Fiat Abarth 131	C Delferrier	1st
1978	Lorraine	Fiat Abarth 131	M Petit	2nd
1978	Limousin	Fiat Abarth 131	M Petit	1st
1978	Corsica	Fiat Abarth 131	M Petit	2nd
1979	Tour de France	Fiat Abarth 131	J Lienard	2nd
1980	Cevennes	Fiat Abarth 131	D Emmanuelli	1st
1980	Var	Fiat Abarth 131	D Emmanuelli	1st
1981	Targa Florio	Ferrari 308 GTB	'Tilber'	1st
1981	4 Regions	Ferrari 308 GTB	D Emmanuelli	1st
1981	Ypres	Ferrari 308 GTB	D Emmanuelli	1st
1981	Tour de France	Ferrari 308 GTB	F Bouchetal	1st
1982	Tour de France	Ferrari 308 GTB	M Petit	1st
1983	Ypres	Lancia Rallye 037	A Sappey	2nd
1984	Corsica	Lancia Rallye 037	M Rick	6th
1984	Tour de France	Lancia Rallye 037	A Peuvergne	2nd
1984	Garrigues	Lancia Rallye 037	M Rick	1st
1984	Tour de France	Lancia Rallye 037	A Peuvergne	2nd
1986	Sweden	Citroen BX4 TC	A Peuvergne	6th

MIKI BIASION

YEAR	EVENT	CAR	CO-DRIVER	POS.
1980	Targa Florio	Opel Ascona	T Siviero	5th
1980	San Marino	Opel Ascona	T Siviero	9th
1981	Targa Florio	Opel Ascona 400	T Siviero	7th
1981	Costa Smeralda	Opel Ascona 400	T Siviero	5th
1981	4 Regions	Opel Ascona 400	T Siviero	4th
1981	San Marino	Opel Ascona 400	T Siviero	4th
1982	Targa Florio	Opel Ascona 400	T Siviero	3rd
1982	Elba	Opel Ascona 400	T Siviero	4th
1982	4 Regions	Opel Ascona 400	T Siviero	3rd
1982	Della Lana	Opel Ascona 400	'Rudy'	1st
1982	San Remo	Opel Ascona 400	T Siviero	8th
1982	San Marino	Opel Ascona 400	T Siviero	2nd
1983	Costa Brava	Lancia Rallye 037	T Siviero	1st
1983	Spanish	Lancia Rallye 037	T Siviero	1st
1983	Costa Smeralda	Lancia Rallye 037	T Siviero	1st
1983	4 Regions	Lancia Rallye 037	T Siviero	1st

1983	Della Lana	Lancia Rallye 037	T Siviero	2nd	1987	San Remo	Lancia Delta HF	T Siviero	1st
1983	Ypres	Lancia Rallye 037	T Siviero	1st	1988	Portugal	Lancia Delta Int	C Cassina	1st
1983	Madeira	Lancia Rallye 037	T Siviero	1st	1988	Safari	Lancia Delta Int	T Siviero	1st
1983	San Remo	Lancia Rallye 037	T Siviero	5th	1988	Acropolis	Lancia Delta Int	T Siviero	1st
1983	San Marino	Lancia Rallye 037	T Siviero	1st	1988	USA	Lancia Delta Int	T Siviero	1st
1983	EUROPEAN CHAMPION RALLY DRIVER				1988	Argentina	Lancia Delta Int	T Siviero	2nd
1984	Monte Carlo	Lancia Rallye 037	T Siviero	6th	1988	San Remo	Lancia Delta Int	T Siviero	1st
1984	Corsica	Lancia Rallye 037	T Siviero	2nd	1988	WORLD CHAMPION RALLY DRIVER			
1894	San Remo	Lancia Rallye 037	T Siviero	3rd	1989	Monte Carlo	Lancia Delta Int	T Siviero	1st
1985	Costa Brava	Lancia Rallye 037	T Siviero	1st	1989	Portugal	Lancia Delta Int	T Siviero	1st
1985	Portugal	Lancia Rallye 037	T Siviero	2nd	1989	Safari	Lancia Delta Int	T Siviero	1st
1985	Spain	Lancia Rallye 037	T Siviero	1st	1989	Acropolis	Lancia Delta Int	T Siviero	1st
1985	Elba	Lancia Rallye 037	T Siviero	2nd	1989	1000 Lakes	Lancia Delta Int	T Siviero	6th
1985	Halkidikis	Lancia Rallye 037	T Siviero	1st	1989	San Remo	Lancia Delta Int	T Siviero	1st
1986	Acropolis	Lancia Delta S4	T Siviero	2nd	1989	WORLD CHAMPION RALLY DRIVER			
1986	New Zealand	Lancia Delta S4	T Siviero	3rd	1990	Monte Carlo	Lancia Delta Int	T Siviero	3rd
1986	Argentina	Lancia Delta S4	T Siviero	1st	1990	Portugal	Lancia Delta Int	T Siviero	1st
1987	Monte Carlo	Lancia Delta HF	T Siviero	1st	1990	Acropolis	Lancia Delta Int	T Siviero	3rd
1987	Corsica	Lancia Delta Hf	T Siviero	3rd	1990	Argentina	Lancia Delta Int	T Siviero	1st
1987	USA	Lancia Delta HF	T Siviero	2nd	1990	RAC	Lancia Delta Int	T Siviero	3rd
1987	Argentina	Lancia Delta HF	T Siviero	1st					

STIG BLOMQVIST

YEAR	EVENT	CAR	CO-DRIVER	POS.
1967	Swedish	Saab 96 V4	L Blomqvist	9th
1968	Swedish	Saab 96 V4	B Reinicke	9th
1969	Swedish	Saab 96 V4	B Moreus	8th
1970	Swedish	Saab 96 V4	B Reinicke	2nd
1971	Swedish	Saab 96 V4	A Hertz	1st
1971	Hankirally	Saab 96 V4	A Hertz	1st
1971	Safari	Saab 96 V4	A Hertz	13th
1971	1000 Lakes	Saab 96 V4	A Hertz	1st
1971	RAC	Saab 96 V4	A Hertz	1st
1972	Swedish	Saab 96 V4	A Hertz	1st
1972	RAC	Saab 96 V4	A Hertz	2nd
1973	Swedish	Saab 96 V4	A Hertz	1st
1973	Cyprus	Saab 96 V4	A Hertz	1st
1974	Arctic	Saab 96 V4	H Sylvan	2nd
1974	RAC	Saab 96 V4	H Sylvan	2nd
1975	Swedish	Saab 96 V4	H Sylvan	2nd
1975	Arctic	Saab 96 V4	H Sylvan	2nd
1976	Spa	Saab 99 EMS	H Sylvan	1st
1976	Swedish	Saab 96 V4	H Sylvan	2nd
1976	RAC	Saab 99 EMS	H Sylvan	2nd
1977	Swedish	Saab 99 EMS	H Sylvan	1st
1978	Swedish	Lancia Stratos	H Sylvan	4th
1979	Swedish	Saab 99 Turbo	B Cederberg	1st
1979	Mintex	Saab 99 Turbo	B Cederberg	1st
1979	South Swedish	Saab 99 Turbo	B Cederberg	1st
1980	Swedish	Saab 99 Turbo	B Cederberg	2nd
1980	Costa Smeralda	Saab 99 Turbo	B Cederberg	2nd
1981	Swedish	Saab 99 Turbo	B Cederberg	5th
1981	Hankirally	Saab 99 Turbo	O Grondahl	4th
1981	South Swedish	Sunbeam Lotus	L Gustavsson	2nd
1981	1000 Lakes	Sunbeam Lotus	B Cederberg	8th
1981	RAC	Sunbeam Lotus	B Cederberg	3rd
1982	Swedish	Audi Quattro	B Cederberg	1st
1982	Hankirally	Audi Quattro	B Cederberg	1st
1982	Welsh	Sunbeam Lotus	B Cederberg	3rd
1982	South Swedish	Audi Quattro	B Cederberg	1st
1982	1000 Lakes	Audi Quattro	B Cederberg	2nd
1982	San Remo	Audi Quattro	B Cederberg	1st
1982	RAC	Sunbeam Lotus	B Cederberg	8th
1983	Monte Carlo	Audi Quattro	B Cederberg	3rd
1983	Swedish	Audio 80 Quattro	B Cederberg	2nd
1983	Acropolis	Audi Quattro	B Cederberg	3rd
1983	Argentina	Audi Quattro	B Cederberg	2nd
1983	1000 Lakes	Audi Quattro	B Cederberg	2nd
1983	RAC	Audi Quattro	B Cederberg	1st
1984	Monte Carlo	Audi Quattro	B Cederberg	2nd
1984	Sweden	Audi Quattro	B Cederberg	1st
1984	Corsica	Audi Quattro	B Cederberg	5th
1984	Acropolis	Audi Quattro	B Cederberg	1st
1984	New Zealand	Audi Quattro	B Cederberg	1st
1984	Argentina	Audi Quattro	B Cederberg	1st
1984	1000 Lakes	Audi Quattro	B Cederberg	4th
1984	Ivory Coast	Audi Sport Quattro	B Cederberg	1st
1984	WORLD CHAMPION RALLY DRIVER			
1985	Swedish	Audi Sport Quattro	B Cederberg	2nd
1985	Acropolis	Audi Sport Quattro	B Cederberg	2nd
1985	1000 Lakes	Audi Sport Quattro	B Cederberg	2nd
1986	South Swedish	Ford RS 200	B Berglund	1st
1986	Argentina	Peugeot 205 T 16	B Berglund	3rd
1986	HK–Peking	Audi Quattro	B Berglund	1st
1987	1000 Lakes	Ford Sierra RS	B Berglund	3rd
1987	RAC	Ford Sierra RS	B Berglund	2nd
1989	Safari	VW Golf GTi 16v	B Cederberg	3rd

LEFT Jean-Claude Andruet/Michelle Petit
Alpine Renault A110 1.3   Coupe des Alpes 1968

EUGEN BOHRINGER

YEAR	EVENT	CAR	CO-DRIVER	POS.
1960	Monte Carlo	Mercedes 220 SE	H Socher	2nd
1961	Polish	Mercedes 220 SE	R Aaltonen	1st
1961	Liège	Mercedes 220 SE	R Aaltonen	4th
1961	German	Mercedes 220 SE	R Aaltonen	2nd
1962	Monte Carlo	Mercedes 220 SE	P Lang	2nd
1962	Acropolis	Mercedes 220 SE	P Lang	1st
1962	Polish	Mercedes 220 SE	P Lang	1st
1962	Liège	Mercedes 220 SE	H Eger	1st
1962	German	Mercedes 220 SE	P Lang	2nd
1962	EUROPEAN CHAMPION RALLY DRIVER			
1963	Monte Carlo	Mercedes 220 SE	P Lang	11th
1963	Acropolis	Mercedes 300 SE	R Knoll	1st
1963	Argentina	Mercedes 230 SL	K Kaiser	1st
1963	Liège	Mercedes 230 SL	K Kaiser	1st
1963	German	Mercedes 300 SE	K Kaiser	1st
1964	Monte Carlo	Mercedes 300 SE	K Kaiser	8th
1964	Lyon–Charbon.	Mercedes 300 SE	K Kaiser	8th
1964	Argentina	Mercedes 230 SL	K Kaiser	1st
1964	Portugal	Mercedes 300 SE	K Kaiser	4th
1964	Liège	Mercedes 230 SL	K Kaiser	3rd
1965	Monte Carlo	Porsche 904	R Wutherlich	2nd

JOHN BUFFUM

YEAR	EVENT	CAR	CO-DRIVER	POS.
1969	Monte Carlo	Porsche 911	S Behr	12th
1973	USA	Ford Escort RS	W Zitkus	4th
1975	CDN Winter	Porsche 911	V Buffum	1st
1975	Canada	Porsche 911	V Buffum	1st
1975	SCCA RALLY CHAMPION			
1976	Olympus	Porsche 911	V Buffum	1st
1977	Canada	Triumph TR7	V Buffum	4th
1977	SCCA RALLY CHAMPION			
1978	Olympus	Triumph TR7	D Shepherd	1st
1978	POR	Triumph TR7	D Shepherd	1st
1978	SCCA RALLY CHAMPION			
1979	SCCA RALLY CHAMPION			
1980	SCCA RALLY CHAMPION			
1981	Haspengouw	Triumph TR7 V8	Molkenboer	8th
1982	Costa Smeralda	Sunbeam Lotus	N Wilson	8th
1982	Olympus	Audi Quattro	D Shepherd	1st
1982	POR	Audi Quattro	D Shepherd	1st
1982	RAC	Audi Quattro	N Wilson	12th
1982	SCCA RALLY CHAMPION			
1983	Sachs Winter	Audi Quattro	A Fischer	1st
1983	Olympus	Audi Quattro	Fellows	2nd
1983	RAC	Audi Quattro	N Wilson	6th
1983	SCCA RALLY CHAMPION			
1984	Acropolis	Audi Quattro	F Gallagher	5th
1984	Hunsruck	Audi Quattro	N Wilson	4th
1984	Cyprus	Audi Quattro	F Gallagher	1st
1984	SCCA RALLY CHAMPION			
1985	Olympus	Audi Quattro	N Wilson	1st
1985	SCCA RALLY CHAMPION			
1986	USA	Audi Sport Quattro	N Wilson	3rd
1986	POR	Audi Sport Quattro	T Grimshaw	1st
1986	SCCA RALLY CHAMPION			
1987	POR	Audi Sport Quattro	T Grimshaw	1st
1987	SCCA RALLY CHAMPION			
1988	USA	Audi Coupé Quattro	J Bellefleur	3rd

ERIK CARLSSON

YEAR	EVENT	CAR	CO-DRIVER	POS.
1955	Rikspokalen	Saab 92	S Helm	1st
1957	1000 Lakes	Saab 93	M Pavoni	1st
1958	1000 Lakes	Saab 93	M Pavoni	8th
1959	Tulip	Saab 93	E Svensson	5th
1959	Swedish	Saab 93	M Pavoni	1st
1959	Adriatic	Saab 93	E Svensson	2nd
1959	1000 Lakes	Saab 93	M Pavoni	4th
1959	Norway	Saab 93	M Pavoni	2nd
1959	German	Saab 93	M Pavoni	1st
1960	Acropolis	Saab 96	W Karlsson	2nd
1960	1000 Lakes	Saab 96	L Simonsson	2nd
1960	RAC	Saab 96	S Turner	1st
1961	Acropolis	Saab 96	W Karlsson	1st
1961	RAC	Saab 96	J Brown	1st
1962	Monte Carlo	Saab 96	G Haggbom	1st
1962	Safari	Saab 96	E Svensson	7th
1962	Acropolis	Saab 96	E Svensson	2nd
1962	Swedish	Saab 96	G Haggbom	3rd
1962	1000 Lakes	Saab 96	G Haggbom	3rd
1962	Geneva	Saab 96	G Haggbom	2nd
1962	RAC	Saab 96	D Stone	1st
1963	Monte Carlo	Saab 96	G Palm	1st
1963	Swedish	Saab 96 Sport	G Palm	2nd
1963	Liège	Saab 96 Sport	G Palm	2nd
1963	RAC	Saab 96 Sport	G Palm	3rd
1964	Monte Carlo	Saab 96 Sport	G Palm	3rd
1964	San Remo	Saab 96 Sport	G Palm	1st
1964	Safari	Saab 96 Sport	G Palm	2nd
1964	Tulip	Saab 96 Sport	G Palm	5th
1964	Acropolis	Saab 96 Sport	G Palm	13th
1964	Polish	Saab 96 Sport	G Palm	2nd
1064	Alpine	Saab 96 Sport	G Palm	2nd
1964	Liège	Saab 96 Sport	G Palm	2nd
1964	Geneva	Saab 96 Sport	G Palm	3rd
1964	RAC	Saab 96 Sport	G Palm	7th
1965	Monte Carlo	Saab 96 Sport	G Palm	16th
1965	Acropolis	Saab 96 Sport	T Aman	2nd
1965	BP Australian	Saab 96 Sport	T Aman	2nd
1965	Polish	Saab 96 Sport	T Aman	3rd
1965	RAC	Saab 96 Sport	T Aman	4th
1967	Czech	Saab 96 V4	T Aman	1st

ROGER CLARK

YEAR	EVENT	CAR	CO-DRIVER	POS.
1961	Ireland	Renault Dauphine	J Porter	51st
1961	RAC	Morris Mini 850	J Porter/ J Oldham	52nd
1962	Ireland	Mini Cooper	J Porter	4th
1963	Scottish	Mini Cooper	H Patton	2nd
1963	Alpine	Reliant Sabre 6	B Aston	6th
1964	Acropolis	Rover 3-litre P5	R Martin-Hurst	9th
1964	Scottish	Ford Cortina GT	J Porter	1st
1965	Monte Carlo	Rover 2000 P6	J Porter	6th
1965	Ireland	Ford Cortina GT	J Porter	3rd
1965	Scottish	Ford Cortina GT	J Porter	1st
1965	Gulf London	Ford Cortina GT	J Porter	1st
1965	Alpine	Rover 2000 P6	J Porter	10th
1965	RAC	Rover 2000 P6	J Porter	14th
1965	Welsh	Lotus Cortina	G Robson	1st
1966	Canada	Lotus Cortina	R Edwardes	3rd
1966	Acropolis	Lotus Cortina	B Melia	2nd
1966	Polish	Lotus Cortina	B Melia	4th
1966	Alpine	Lotus Cortina	B Melia	2nd

ABOVE Perhaps the most determined British rally driver of the last two decades has been Roger Clark. He has had multiple wins on all the major rallies in the United Kingdom, but has never really been offered a major programme in Europe, though whenever he has competed away from home, it has usually provided a good result.

1967	Canada	Lotus Cortina	J Peters	1st
1967	Scottish	Lotus Cortina	J Porter	1st
1968	Ireland	Ford Escort TC	J Porter	1st
1968	Tulip	Ford Escort TC	J Porter	1st
1968	Acropolis	Ford Escort TC	J Porter	1st
1968	Scottish	Ford Escort TC	J Porter	1st
1969	San Remo	Ford Escort TC	J Porter	10th
1969	Ireland	Ford Escort TC	J Porter	1st
1969	Acropolis	Ford Escort TC	J Porter	2nd
1969	RAC	Ford Escort TC	J Porter	6th
1970	Monte Carlo	Ford Escort TC	J Porter	5th
1970	Ireland	Ford Escort RS	J Porter	1st
1971	Manx	Ford Escort RS	H Liddon	1st
1971	RAC	Ford Escort RS	J Porter	11th
1972	Welsh	Ford Escort RS	J Porter	1st
1972	Scottish	Ford Escort RS	J Porter	2nd
1972	Manx	Ford Escort RS	J Porter	1st
1972	RAC	Ford Escort RS	T Mason	1st
1973	San Remo	Ford Escort RS	J Porter	10th
1973	Welsh	Ford Escort RS	J Porter	1st
1973	Scottish	Ford Escort RS	J Porter	1st
1973	RAC	Ford Escort RS	T Mason	2nd
1974	Tour Britain	Ford Escort 2000	J Porter	1st
1974	Total SA	Ford Escort RS	S Pegg	1st
1974	Manx	Ford Escort RS	J Porter	3rd
1974	RAC	Ford Escort RS	T Mason	7th
1975	Welsh	Ford Escort RS	J Porter	1st
1975	Scottish	Ford Escort RS	J Porter	1st
1975	Total SA	Ford Escort RS	S Pegg	1st
1975	Manx	Ford Escort RS	J Porter	1st
1975	RAC	Ford Escort RS	T Mason	2nd
1976	Monte Carlo	Ford Escort RS	J Porter	5th
1976	Welsh	Ford Escort RS	J Porter	3rd

1976	Scottish	Ford Escort RS	J Porter	2nd
1976	Total SA	Ford Escort RS	S Pegg	2nd
1976	RAC	Ford Escort RS	S Pegg	1st
1977	Acropolis	Ford Escort RS	J Porter	2nd
1977	Canada	Ford Escort RS	J Porter	3rd
1977	RAC	Ford Escort RS	S Pegg	4th
1978	Welsh	Ford Escort RS	J Porter	2nd
1978	Scottish	Ford Escort RS	J Porter	3rd
1978	Cyprus	Ford Escort RS	J Porter	1st
1980	Scottish	Triumph TR7 V8	J Porter	9th
1980	Cyprus	Ford Escort RS	N Wilson	1st
1981	Manx	Ford Escort RS	J Porter	5th
1981	RAC	Ford Escort RS	C Serle	10th

ANDREW COWAN

YEAR	EVENT	CAR	CO-DRIVER	POS.
1962	Scottish	Sunbeam Rapier	Thompson	1st
1963	Scottish	Sunbeam Rapier	Thompson	1st
1964	Tour de France	Ford Mustang	P Procter	1st
1964	RAC	Sunbeam Rapier	B Coyle	20th
1965	Monte Carlo	Sunbeam Tiger	R Turvey	11th
1965	Alpine	Rover 2000 P6	B Coyle	3rd
1967	Alpine	Hillman Imp	B Coyle	9th
1968	Monte Carlo	Hillman Imp	B Coyle	22nd
1968	Gulf London	Hillman Imp	B Coyle	7th
1968	London/Sydney	Hillman Hunter	C Malkin/ B Coyle	1st
1969	Scottish	Hillman Imp	B Coyle	2nd
1969	Southern Cross	Austin 1800	J Bryson	1st
1970	RAC	Alpine A110	H Cardno	5th
1971	Monte Carlo	Cooper S	J Syer	21st
1971	RAC	Ford Escort RS	J Syer	13th
1972	Scottish	Ford Escort RS	B Coyle	6th
1972	New Zealand	Cooper S	J Scott	1st
1972	Southern Cross	Mitsubishi Galant	J Bryson	1st
1973	Scottish	Ford Escort RS	J Syer	3rd
1973	Southern Cross	Mitsubishi Lancer	J Bryson	1st
1974	World Cup	Ford Escort RS	J Syer	15th
1974	Tour Britain	Vauxhall Magnum	R Finlay	7th
1974	Total SA	Dodge Colt	G Phillips	7th
1974	Southern Cross	Mitsubishi Lancer	F Gocentas	1st
1974	CDN Winter	Dodge Colt	B Crawford	3rd
1975	Safari	Mitsubishi Lancer	J Mitchell	4th
1975	Southern Cross	Mitsubishi Lancer	F Gocentas	1st
1975	Total SA	Dodge Avenger	G Phillips	8th
1976	Safari	Mitsubishi Lancer	J Syer	3rd
1976	New Zealand	Hillman Avenger	J Scott	1st
1976	Southern Cross	Mitsubishi Lancer	F Gocentas	1st
1977	Safari	Mitsubishi Lancer	P White	4th
1977	London/Sydney	Mercedes 280 E	C Malkin/ M Broad	1st
1977	Ivory Coast	Mitsubishi Lancer	J Syer	1st
1978	Volta SA	Mercedes 450 SLC	C Malkin	1st
1979	Safari	Mercedes 280 E	J Syer	4th
1979	Scottish	Ford Escort RS	J Syer	5th
1979	Ivory Coast	Mercedes 450 SLC	K Kaiser	3rd
1980	Safari	Mercedes 450 SLC	K Kaiser	6th
1980	Scottish	Ford Escort RS	J Syer	6th
1980	Cyprus	Mitsubishi Lancer	J Syer	3rd
1983	Scottish	Audi 80 Quattro	A Douglas	7th
1985	Aus. Safari	Mitsubishi Pajero	F Gocentas	1st
1986	Paris–Dakar	Mitsubishi Pajero	J Syer	2nd
1986	Aus. Safari	Mitsubishi Pajero	F Gocentas	1st
1987	Paris–Dakar	Mitsubishi Pajero	J Syer	8th
1989	Paris–Dakar	Mitsubishi Pajero	C Delferrier	5th
1990	Paris–Dakar	Mitsubishi Pajero	C Delferrier	4th

BERNARD DARNICHE

YEAR	EVENT	CAR	CO-DRIVER	POS.
1969	Cevennes	NSU 1300	B Demange	2nd
1969	Var	NSU 1300	B Demange	1st
1970	Corsica	Alpine A110	B Demange	1st
1970	Austria	Alpine A110	A Mahé	5th
1970	Spanish	Alpine A110	M Callewaert	3rd
1971	Monte Carlo	Alpine A110	J Robertet	8th
1971	San Remo	Alpine A110	A Mahé	4th
1971	Alpine	Alpine A110	A Mahé	1st
1971	Mont Blanc	Alpine A110	A Mahé	2nd
1971	Var	Alpine A110	A Mahé	1st
1971	Cevennes	Alpine A110	A Mahé	1st
1972	Monte Carlo	Alpine A110	A Mahé	25th
1972	Neige et Glace	Alpine A110	A Mahé	1st
1972	Lyon–Char	Alpine A110	A Mahé	2nd
1972	Portugal	Alpine A110	A Mahé	2nd
1972	Corsica	Alpine A110	A Mahé	4th
1973	Monte Carlo	Alpine A110	A Mahé	10th
1973	Morocco	Alpine A110	A Mahé	1st
1973	Austria	Alpine A110	A Mahé	2nd
1974	Tour de France	Ligier JS2	A Mahé	2nd
1974	USA	Renault 17 G	A Mahé	6th
1975	Neige et Glace	Fiat X1/9		2nd
1975	Corsica	Lancia Stratos	A Mahé	1st
1975	Tour de France	Lancia Stratos	A Mahé	1st
1976	Monte Carlo	Lancia Stratos	A Mahé	3rd
1976	Corsica	Lancia Stratos	A Mahé	2nd
1976	Lyon–Char	Lancia Stratos	A Mahé	1st
1976	4 Regions	Lancia Stratos	A Mahé	1st
1976	Antibes	Lancia Stratos	A Mahé	1st
1976	San Martino	Lancia Stratos	A Mahé	1st
1976	Baltic	Lancia Stratos	A Mahé	1st
1976	Spanish	Lancia Stratos	A Mahé	2nd
1976	EUROPEAN CHAMPION RALLY DRIVER			
1977	Corsica	Fiat Abarth 131	A Mahé	1st
1977	Sicily	Lancia Stratos	A Mahé	1st
1977	Elba	Lancia Stratos	A Mahé	1st
1977	Firestone	Lancia Stratos	A Mahé	1st
1977	Crit. Alpin	Lancia Stratos	A Mahé	1st
1977	4 Regions	Lancia Stratos	A Mahé	1st
1977	Ypres	Lancia Stratos	A Mahé	1st
1977	Polish	Lancia Stratos	A Mahé	1st
1977	Tour de France	Lancia Stratos	A Mahé	1st
1977	EUROPEAN CHAMPION RALLY DRIVER			
1978	Monte Carlo	Fiat Abarth 131	A Mahé	5th
1978	Corsica	Fiat Abarth 131	A Mahé	1st
1979	Monte Carlo	Lancia Stratos	A Mahé	1st
1979	Tour de France	Lancia Stratos	A Mahé	1st
1980	Monte Carlo	Lancia Stratos	A Mahé	2nd
1980	Tour de France	Lancia Stratos	A Mahé	1st
1981	Monte Carlo	Lancia Stratos	A Mahé	6th
1981	Corsica	Lancia Stratos	A Mahé	1st
1981	Touraine	Lancia Stratos	A Mahé	1st
1981	Tour de France	Lancia Stratos	A Mahé	2nd
1983	Tour de France	Lancia Rallye 037	A Mahé	3rd
1983	San Remo	Audi Quattro	A Mahé	9th
1984	Tour de France	Audi Quattro	A Mahé	4th

PADDY HOPKIRK

YEAR	EVENT	CAR	CO-DRIVER	POS.
1958	Ireland	Triumph TR3A	J Scott	1st
1959	Alpine	Sunbeam Rapier	J Scott	3rd
1961	Ireland	Sunbeam Rapier	J Scott	1st
1962	Monte Carlo	Sunbeam Rapier	J Scott	3rd
1962	Ireland	Sunbeam Rapier	J Scott	1st
1962	RAC	Austin Healey 3000	J Scott	2nd
1963	Monte Carlo	Mini Cooper	J Scott	6th
1963	Tulip	Mini Cooper	H Liddon	2nd
1963	Tour de France	Cooper S 1071	H Liddon	3rd
1963	Liège	Austin Healey 3000	H Liddon	6th
1963	RAC	Cooper S 1071	H Liddon	4th
1964	Monte Carlo	Cooper S 1071	H Liddon	1st
1964	Austria	Austin Healey 3000	H Liddon	1st
1965	Monte Carlo	Cooper S 1275	H Liddon	26th
1965	Ireland	Cooper S 1275	T Harryman	1st
1965	1000 Lakes	Cooper S 1275	K Ruutsalo	6th
1966	Acropolis	Cooper S 1275	R Crellin	3rd
1967	San Remo	Cooper S 1275	R Crellin	2nd
1967	Ireland	Cooper S 1275	T Harryman	1st
1967	Acropolis	Cooper S 1275	R Crellin	1st
1967	Alpine	Cooper S 1275	R Crellin	1st
1968	Monte Carlo	Cooper S 1275	R Crellin	5th
1968	Portugal	Cooper S 1275	T Nash	2nd
1968	London/Sydney	BMC 1800	T Nash/A Poole	2nd
1969	Ireland	Cooper S 1275	T Nash	2nd
1970	Scottish	Mini Clubman 1275	T Nash	2nd
1970	London/Mexico	Triumph 2500	T Nash/ N Johnstone	4th
1977	London/Sydney	Citroen CX 2400	Taylor/Riley	3rd
1982	RAC Golden 50	Cooper S 1275	B Culcheth	1st

HARRY KALLSTROM

YEAR	EVENT	CAR	CO-DRIVER	POS.
1963	RAC	VW 1500 S	G Haggbom	2nd
1963	Norway	VW 1200	N Bjorck	6th
1964	Swedish	Cooper S	R Hakansson	2nd
1964	1000 Lakes	Cooper S	R Hakansson	18th
1966	RAC	Cooper S	R Hakansson	2nd
1967	Alpine	Renault R8 G	G Haggbom	4th
1967	1000 Lakes	Renault R8 G	K Lyxell	11th
1968	San Remo	Lancia Fulvia	G Haggbom	4th
1968	999 Minutes	Lancia Fulvia	G Haggbom	1st
1968	Acropolis	Lancia Fulvia	G Haggbom	6th
1969	Mediterranée	Lancia Fulvia	G Haggbom	1st
1969	Sweden	Lancia Fulvia	G Haggbom	6th
1969	Sestrière	Lancia Fulvia	G Haggbom	3rd
1969	San Remo	Lancia Fulvia	G Haggbom	1st
1969	Austria	Lancia Fulvia	G Haggbom	2nd
1969	Czech	Lancia Fulvia	G Haggbom	2nd
1969	Poland	Lancia Fulvia	G Haggbom	3rd
1969	Spain	Lancia Fulvia	G Haggbom	1st
1969	Corsica	Lancia Fulvia	G Haggbom	9th
1969	RAC	Lancia Fulvia	G Haggbom	1st
1969	EUROPEAN CHAMPION RALLY DRIVER			
1970	San Remo	Lancia Fulvia	G Haggbom	2nd
1970	Austria	Lancia Fulvia	G Haggbom	9th
1970	RAC	Lancia Fulvia	G Haggbom	1st
1971	Sweden	Lancia Fulvia	G Haggbom	3rd
1971	Safari	Lancia Fulvia	G Haggbom	8th
1971	RAC	Lancia Fulvia	G Haggbom	8th
1972	Sweden	Lancia Fulvia	G Haggbom	3rd
1972	Elba	Lancia Fulvia	G Haggbom	3rd
1972	RAC	Lancia Fulvia	G Haggbom	4th

1973	Monte Carlo	Lancia Fulvia	G Haggbom	8th
1973	Swedish	Lancia Fulvia	G Haggbom	4th
1973	Safari	Datsun 1800	C Billstam	2nd
1973	Austria	VW 1302 S	C Billstam	11th
1973	RAC	Datsun 240Z	C Billstam	14th
1974	Portugal	Datsun 240Z	C Billstam	5th
1974	Safari	Datsun 260Z	C Billstam	4th
1974	1000 Lakes	Datsun 160J	C Billstam	21st
1974	RAC	Datsun Violet	C Billstam	15th
1974	Ivory Coast	Datsun 180 B	C Billstam	3rd
1975	Total SA	Datsun 160J	L Drews	5th
1975	RAC	Datsun Violet	M Steyt	11th
1976	Safari	Datsun Violet	L Lindqvist	7th
1976	Acropolis	Datsun 710	C-G Andersson	1st
1977	Acropolis	Datsun 160J	C Billstam	3rd
1977	Australia	Datsun Violet	C Billstam	2nd
1978	Acropolis	Datsun 160J	C Billstam	4th
1978	Qatar	Datsun 160J	C Billstam	1st
1979	Acropolis	Datsun 160J	C Billstam	3rd
1979	Bahrain	Datsun 160J	C Billstam	1st

JUHA KANKKUNEN

YEAR	EVENT	CAR	CO-DRIVER	POS.
1979	1000 Lakes	Ford Escort RS	T Hantunen	14th
1983	Spa	Opel Manta GTE	J Piironen	6th
1983	1000 Lakes	Toyota Celica TCT	S Pettersson	6th
1983	RAC	Toyota Celica TCT	J Piironen	7th
1984	1000 Lakes	Toyota Celica TCT	F Gallagher	5th
1985	Safari	Toyota Celica TCT	F Gallagher	1st
1985	Ivory Coast	Toyota Celica TCT	F Gallagher	1st
1985	RAC	Toyota Celica TCT	F Gallagher	5th
1986	Monte Carlo	Peugeot 205 T16	J Piironen	5th
1986	Swedish	Peugeot 205 T16	J Piironen	1st
1986	Safari	Peugeot 205 T16	J Piironen	5th
1986	Acropolis	Peugeot 205 T16	J Piironen	1st
1986	New Zealand	Peugeot 205 T16	J Piironen	1st
1986	1000 Lakes	Peugeot 205 T16	J Piironen	2nd
1986	RAC	Peugeot 205 T16	J Piironen	3rd
1986	USA	Peugeot 205 T16	J Piironen	2nd
1986	WORLD CHAMPION RALLY DRIVER			
1987	Monte Carlo	Lancia Delta HF	J Piironen	2nd
1987	Swedish	Lancia Delta HF	J Piironen	3rd
1987	Portugal	Lancia Delta HF	J Piironen	4th
1987	Acropolis	Lancia Delta HF	J Piironen	2nd
1987	USA	Lancia Delta HF	J Piironen	1st
1987	1000 Lakes	Lancia Delta HF	J Piironen	5th
1987	RAC	Lancia Delta HF	J Piironen	1st
1987	WORLD CHAMPION RALLY DRIVER			
1988	Safari	Toyota Supra Turbo	J Piironen	5th
1989	Monte Carlo	Toyota Celica GT4	J Piironen	5th
1989	Corsica	Toyota Celica GT4	J Piironen	3rd
1989	Australia	Toyota Celica GT4	J Piironen	1st
1989	San Remo	Toyota Celica GT4	J Piironen	5th
1989	RAC	Toyota Celica GT4	J Piironen	3rd
1990	Portugal	Lancia Delta Int.	J Piironen	3rd
1990	Safari	Lancia Delta Int	J Piironen	2nd
1990	Acropolis	Lancia Delta Int	J Piironen	2nd
1990	1000 Lakes	Lancia Delta Int	J Piironen	5th
1990	Australia	Lancia Delta Int	J Piironen	1st
1990	San Remo	Lancia Delta Int	J Piironen	2nd

SIMO LAMPINEN

YEAR	EVENT	CAR	CO-DRIVER	POS.
1961	1000 Lakes	Jaguar 3.4 Mk II	E Vainio	44th
1962	1000 Lakes	Saab 96	J Ahava	4th
1963	1000 Lakes	Saab 96 Sport	J Ahava	1st
1963	FINNISH CHAMPION RALLY DRIVER			
1964	1000 Lakes	Saab 96 Sport	J Ahava	1st
1964	FINNISH CHAMPION RALLY DRIVER			
1965	1000 Lakes	Saab 96 Sport	J Ahava	4th
1965	Monte Carlo	Triumph Spitfire	J Ahava	24th
1966	Swedish	Saab 96 Sport	B Olsson	2nd
1966	1000 Lakes	Saab 96 Sport	K Sohlberg	5th
1967	Swedish	Saab 96 V4	T Palm	2nd
1967	1000 Lakes	Saab 96 V4	K Sohlberg	2nd
1967	FINNISH CHAMPION RALLY DRIVER			
1968	Scottish	Saab 96 V4	T Palm	4th
1968	Czech	Saab 96 V4	T Palm	2nd
1968	1000 Lakes	Saab 96 V4	K Sohlberg	2nd
1968	RAC	Saab 96 V4	J Davenport	1st
1969	Austrian	Saab 96 V4	A Hertz	4th
1969	Scottish	Saab 96 V4	A Hertz	1st
1969	1000 Lakes	Saab 96 V4	K Sohlberg	2nd
1970	1000 Lakes	Lancia Fulvia	J Davenport	3rd
1970	Portugal	Lancia Fulvia	J Davenport	1st
1970	1000 Minutes	Lancia Fulvia	M Mannucci	1st
1971	Monte Carlo	Lancia Fulvia	J Davenport	6th
1971	Acropolis	Lancia Fulvia	J Davenport	3rd
1971	4 Regions	Lancia Fulvia	J Davenport	1st
1971	Portugal	Lancia Fulvia	J Davenport	2nd
1971	RAC	Lancia Fulvia	J Davenport	6th
1972	Monte Carlo	Lancia Fulvia	S Andreasson	4th
1972	Morocco	Lancia Fulvia	S Andreasson	1st
1972	Acropolis	Lancia Fulvia	B Reinicke	2nd
1972	1000 Lakes	Saab 96 V4	K Sohlberg	1st
1972	RAC	Lancia Fulvia	S Andreasson	5th
1973	Romania	Lancia Fulvia	S Andreasson	2nd
1973	1000 Lakes	Saab 96 V4	J Davenport	4th
1973	San Remo	Lancia Fulvia	P Sodano	8th
1974	Arctic	Saab 96 V4	J Markkanen	5th
1974	Total SA	Mazda RX2	H Liddon	6th
1974	1000 Lakes	Saab 96 V4	J Markkanen	5th
1974	Canada	Lancia Beta Coupé	J Davenport	2nd
1974	USA	Lancia Beta Coupé	J Davenport	4th
1974	RAC	Lancia Beta Coupé	S Andreasson	10th
1975	Swedish	Lancia Beta Coupé	S Andreasson	3rd
1975	Arctic	Saab 96 V4	J Markkanen	1st
1975	Hankirally	Saab 96 V4	J Markkanen	1st
1975	1000 Lakes	Saab 96 V4	J Markkanen	2nd
1975	RAC	Lancia Beta Coupé	P Sodano	10th
1976	Swedish	Lancia Stratos	A Hertz	4th
1976	Safari	Peugeot 504	A Hertz	5th
1976	Morocco	Peugeot 504	A Aho	2nd
1976	1000 Lakes	Saab 96 V4	J Markkanen	5th
1977	Sweden	Fiat Abarth 131	S Andreasson	4th
1977	New Zealand	Fiat Abarth 131	S Andreasson	4th
1977	Acropolis	Fiat Abarat 131	S Andreasson	4th
1977	Canada	Fiat Abarth 131	S Andreasson	2nd
1977	RAC	Fiat Abarth 131	S Andreasson	7th
1978	Safari	Peugeot 504	H Liddon	5th
1978	1000 Lakes	Fiat Abarth 131	J Markkanen	5th
1978	Ivory Coast	Peugeot 504 V6	A Aho	4th

LEFT Harry Kallstrom/Gunnar Haggbom
Lancia Fulvia Coupé HF 1.6
Monte Carlo Rally 1973

TIMO MAKINEN

YEAR	EVENT	CAR	CO-DRIVER	POS.
1959	1000 Lakes	Triumph TR3	H Makinen	38th
1961	1000 Lakes	Morris Mini 850	K Ruutsalo	24th
1963	Monte Carlo	Austin Healey 3000	C Carlisle	13th
1963	1000 Lakes	Mini Cooper	K Ruutsalo	9th
1963	RAC	Austin Healey 3000	M Wood	5th
1964	Monte Carlo	Cooper S	P Vanson	4th
1964	Tulip	Cooper S	T Ambrose	1st
1964	1000 Lakes	Cooper S	P Keskitalo	4th
1964	RAC	Austin Healey 3000	D Barrow	2nd
1965	Monte Carlo	Cooper S	P Easter	1st
1965	Tulip	Cooper S	P Easter	6th
1965	Alpine	Cooper S	P Easter	2nd
1965	1000 Lakes	Cooper S	P Keskitalo	1st
1965	RAC	Austin Healey 3000	P Easter	2nd
1966	Tulip	Cooper S	P Easter	9th
1966	Czech	Cooper S	P Easter	3rd
1966	Polish	Cooper S	P Easter	2nd
1966	1000 Lakes	Cooper S	P Keskitalo	1st
1966	3 Cities	Cooper S	P Easter	1st
1966	FINNISH CHAMPION RALLY DRIVER			
1967	Tulip	Cooper S	P Easter	2nd
1967	1000 Lakes	Cooper S	P Keskitalo	1st
1969	1000 Lakes	Saab 96 V4	P Keskitalo	4th
1969	Corsica	Lancia Fulvia F&M	P Easter	11th
1970	Monte Carlo	Ford Escort TC	H Liddon	7th
1970	London/Mexico	Ford Escort	G Staepelaere	5th
1970	1000 Lakes	Ford Escort TC	H Liddon	2nd
1971	Safari	Ford Escort TC	H Liddon	20th
1971	RAC	Ford Escort TC	H Liddon	5th
1972	Safari	Ford Escort RS	H Liddon	8th
1972	Hong Kong	Ford Escort RS	H Liddon	1st
1972	1000 Lakes	Ford Escort RS	H Liddon	2nd
1973	Monte Carlo	Ford Escort RS	H Liddon	11th
1973	Arctic	Ford Escort RS	E Salonen	1st
1973	Hong Kong	Ford Escort RS	H Liddon	7th
1973	1000 Lakes	Ford Escort RS	H Liddon	1st
1973	RAC	Ford Escort RS	H Liddon	1st
1974	Arctic	Ford Escort RS	E Salonen	3rd
1974	1000 Lakes	Ford Escort RS	H Liddon	2nd
1974	RAC	Ford Escort RS	H Liddon	1st
1974	Ivory Coast	Peugeot 504	H Liddon	1st
1975	Morocco	Peugeot 504	H Liddon	5th
1975	Scottish	Ford Escort RS	H Liddon	5th
1975	1000 Lakes	Ford Escort RS	H Liddon	3rd
1975	RAC	Ford Escort RS	H Liddon	1st
1976	1000 Lakes	Ford Escort RS	H Liddon	4th
1976	Firestone	Ford Escort RS	H Liddon	2nd
1976	Ivory Coast	Peugeot 504 V6	H Liddon	1st
1978	Ivory Coast	Peugeot 504 V6	J Todt	2nd
1980	1000 Lakes	Triumph TR7 V8	E Salonen	22nd

SHEKHAR MEHTA

YEAR	EVENT	CAR	CO-DRIVER	POS.
1971	Safari	Datsun 240Z	M Doughty	2nd
1971	RAC	Datsun 240Z	L Drews	19th
1972	Acropolis	Datsun 240Z	P Easter	6th
1972	Kenya 2000	Datsun 240Z	L Drews	1st
1973	Safari	Datsun 240Z	L Drews	1st
1973	New Zealand	Datsun 180 B	W Jones	3rd
1973	RAC	Datsun Sunny	K Wood	37th
1974	Safari	Lancia Fulvia	M Doughty	11th
1974	San Remo	Lancia Beta Coupé	M Holmes	4th
1975	Portugal	Datsun Violet	Y Pratt	7th
1975	Morocco	Datsun Violet	B Bean	6th
1975	New Caledonia	Datsun 160J	Y Pratt	1st
1976	Acropolis	Datsun Violet	H Liddon	3rd
1976	Southern Cross	Datsun 710	A Mortimer	3rd
1976	Darma Putra	Mazda 616	Y Pratt	1st
1976	Cyprus	Datsun Violet	Y Pratt	1st
1978	Acropolis	Datsun 160 J	Y Mehta	3rd
1979	Kuwait	Datsun 160J	Y Mehta	1st
1979	Safari	Datsun 160J	M Doughty	1st
1980	Bahrain	Datsun 160J	Y Mehta	1st
1980	Kuwait	Datsun 160J	Y Mehta	1st
1980	Safari	Datsun 160J	M Doughty	1st
1980	Argentina	Datsun 160J	Y Mehta	4th
1980	Himalayan	Opel Ascona 400	L Drews	1st
1981	Safari	Datsun Violet GT	M Doughty	1st
1981	Acropolis	Datsun 160J	Y Mehta	5th
1981	Argentina	Datsun Violet GT	Y Mehta	2nd
1981	Ivory Coast	Datsun Violet GT	M Doughty	3rd
1982	Safari	Nissan Violet GT	M Doughty	1st
1982	Acropolis	Nissan Violet GT	Y Mehta	4th
1983	Acropolis	Nissan 240 RS	Y Mehta	6th
1983	New Zealand	Nissan 240 RS	Y Mehta	4th
1983	Argentina	Audi Quattro	Y Mehta	4th
1983	Halkidikis	Nissan 240 RS	Y Mehta	2nd
1984	Monte Carlo	Subaru EAB5	Y Mehta	14th
1984	Safari	Nissan 240 RS	R Combes	5th
1984	Acropolis	Nissan 240 RS	Y Mehta	7th
1984	Halkidikis	Nissan 240 RS	Y Mehta	2nd
1984	Corte Ingles	Nissan 240 RS	Y Mehta	5th
1984	Lucky Strike	Nissan 240 RS	Y Mehta	1st
1984	Ivory Coast	Nissan 240 RS	R Combes	3rd
1984	RAC	Nissan 240 RS	Y Mehta	8th
1985	Acropolis	Nissan 240 RS	Y Mehta	4th
1985	Hong Kong	Nissan 240 RS	Y Mehta	5th
1985	Argentina	Nissan 240 RS	Y Mehta	4th
1986	Paris–Dakar	Peugeot 205 T16	M Doughty	5th
1986	Safari	Peugeot 206 T16	R Combes	8th
1986	Morocco	Nissan 240 RS	Y Mehta	1st
1987	Olympus	Nissan 200 SX	Y Mehta	8th
1987	Ivory Coast	Nissan 200 SX	R Combes	2nd

HANNU MIKKOLA

YEAR	EVENT	CAR	CO-DRIVER	POS.
1967	1000 Lakes	Volvo 122 S	A Jarvi	3rd
1968	Monte Carlo	Datsun Fairlady	A Jarvi	9th
1968	Austrian	Lancia Fulvia	A Jarvi	2nd
1968	1000 Lakes	Ford Escort TC	A Jarvi	1st
1968	FINNISH CHAMPION RALLY DRIVER			
1969	Monte Carlo	Ford Escort TC	J Porter	32nd
1969	Austrian	Ford Escort RS	M Wood	1st
1969	1000 Lakes	Ford Escort TC	A Jarvi	1st
1970	Arctic Rally	Ford Escort TC	A Jarvi	1st
1970	1000 Lakes	Ford Escort TC	G Palm	1st
1970	World Cup	Ford Escort	G Palm	1st
1972	Safari	Ford Escort RS	G Palm	1st
1972	Scottish	Ford Escort RS	H Cardno	1st
1972	Corsica	Peugeot 304	A Aho	18th
1973	Monte Carlo	Ford Escort RS	J Porter	4th
1973	Scottish	Ford Escort RS	J Davenport	2nd
1973	New Zealand	Ford Escort RS	J Porter	1st
1974	Total SA	Peugeot 504	J Davenport	4th
1974	1000 Lakes	Ford Escort RS	J Davenport	1st
1975	Monte Carlo	Fiat Abarth 124	J Todt	2nd
1975	Arctic	Fiat Abarth 124	J Todt	7th
1975	Morocco	Peugeot 504	J Todt	1st
1975	Portugal	Fiat Abarth 124	J Todt	2nd

ABOVE Shekhar Mehta/Rob Combes
Nissan 240 RS   Safari Rally 1984

1975	1000 Lakes	Toyota Corolla	A Aho	1st
1975	Total SA	Peugeot 504	J Todt	4th
1976	1000 Lakes	Toyota Celica	A Hertz	3rd
1976	Corsica	Peugeot 104 ZS	J Todt	10th
1977	RAC	Toyota Celica	A Hertz	2nd
1978	Swedish	Ford Escort RS	A Hertz	2nd
1978	Portugal	Ford Escort RS	A Hertz	2nd
1978	RAC	Ford Escort RS	A Hertz	1st
1979	Portugal	Ford Escort RS	A Hertz	1st
1979	Safari	Mercedes 450 SLC	A Hertz	2nd
1979	Welsh	Ford Escort RS	A Hertz	1st
1979	New Zealand	Ford Escort RS	A Hertz	1st
1979	RAC	Ford Escort RS	A Hertz	1st
1979	Ivory Coast	Mercedes 450 SLC	A Hertz	1st
1980	Mintex	Ford Escort RS	A Hertz	1st
1980	Argentina	Mercedes 450 SLC	A Hertz	2nd
1980	New Zealand	Mercedes 500 SLC	A Hertz	3rd
1980	San Remo	Ford Escort RS	A Hertz	3rd
1980	RAC	Ford Escort RS	A Hertz	2nd
1981	Swedish	Audi Quattro	A Hertz	1st
1981	1000 Lakes	Audi Quattro	A Hertz	3rd
1981	RAC	Audi Quattro	A Hertz	1st
1982	Monte Carlo	Audi Quattro	A Hertz	2nd
1982	Ireland	Audi Quattro	A Hertz	6th
1982	Scottish	Audi Quattro	A Hertz	1st
1982	1000 Lakes	Audi Quattro	A Hertz	1st
1982	San Remo	Audi Quattro	A Hertz	2nd
1982	RAC	Audi Quattro	A Hertz	1st

1983	Sweden	Audi Quattro	A Hertz	1st
1983	Portugal	Audi Quattro	A Hertz	1st
1983	Safari	Audi Quattro	A Hertz	2nd
1983	Argentina	Audi Quattro	A Hertz	1st
1983	1000 Lakes	Audi Quattro	A Hertz	1st
1983	USA	Audi Quattro	F Pons	1st
1983	Ivory Coast	Audi Quattro	A Hertz	2nd
1983	RAC	Audi Quattro	A Hertz	2nd
1983	WORLD CHAMPION RALLY DRIVER			
1984	Monte Carlo	Audi Quattro	A Hertz	3rd
1984	Portugal	Audi Quattro	A Hertz	1st
1984	Safari	Audi Quattro	A Hertz	3rd
1984	Welsh	Audi Quattro	A Hertz	1st
1984	Acropolis	Audi Quattro	A Hertz	2nd
1984	Scottish	Audi Quattro	A Hertz	1st
1984	New Zealand	Audi Quattro	A Hertz	3rd
1984	Argentina	Audi Quattro	A Hertz	2nd
1984	Ivory Coast	Audi Quattro	A Hertz	2nd
1984	RAC	Audi Quattro	A Hertz	2nd
1986	Monte Carlo	Audi Sport Quattro	A Hertz	3rd
1987	Safari	Audi 200 Quattro	A Hertz	1st
1987	Acropolis	Audi 200 Quattro	A Hertz	3rd
1988	Portugal	Mazda 323 4WD	C Geistdorfer	4th
1989	Monte Carlo	Mazda 323 4WD	C Geistdorfer	4th
1990	Portugal	Mazda 323 4WD	A Hertz	6th

PAT MOSS

YEAR	EVENT	CAR	CO-DRIVER	POS.
1957	Liège	Morris Minor 1000	A Wisdom	23rd
1958	RAC	Morris Minor 1000	A Wisdom	4th
1958	Ireland	Riley 1.5	A Wisdom	20th
1958	Tulip	Riley 1.5	A Wisdom	19th
1958	Alpine	Austin Healey 100	A Wisdom	8th
1958	Liège	Austin Healey 100	A Wisdom	4th
1959	Monte Carlo	Austin A40	A Wisdom	10th
1959	Sestrière	Riley 1.5	A Wisdom	21st
1959	German	Austin Healey 3000	A Wisdom	2nd
1960	Geneva	Austin Healey 3000	A Wisdom	8th
1960	Tulip	Austin Healey 3000	A Wisdom	8th
1960	Alpine	Austin Healey 3000	A Wisdom	2nd
1960	Liège	Austin Healey 3000	A Wisdom	1st
1961	Tulip	Austin Healey 3000	A Wisdom	11th
1961	RAC	Austin Healey 3000	A Wisdom	2nd
1961	Corsica	Austin Healey 3000	A Wisdom	16th
1962	Safari	Saab 96	A Wisdom	3rd
1962	Tulip	Mini Cooper	A Wisdom	1st
1962	Acropolis	Austin Healey 3000	P Mayman	8th
1962	Alpine	Austin Healey 3000	P Mayman	3rd
1962	Polish	Austin Healey 3000	P Mayman	2nd
1962	German	Mini Cooper	P Mayman	1st
1962	Geneva	Mini Cooper	P Mayman	3rd
1962	RAC	Austin Healey 3000	P Mayman	3rd
1963	Tulip	Ford Cortina GT	J Nadin	12th
1963	Acropolis	Ford Cortina GT	A Riley	6th
1963	RAC	Ford Cortina GT	J Nadin	7th
1964	Monte Carlo	Saab 96 Sport	U Wirth	5th
1964	San Remo	Saab 96 Sport	V Domleo	2nd
1964	Safari	Saab 96 Sport	J Mayers	9th
1964	Tulip	Saab 96 Sport	L Nystrom	11th
1964	Acropolis	Saab 96 Sport	V Domleo	3rd
1964	Polish	Saab 96 Sport	L Nystrom	3rd
1964	Geneva	Saab 96 Sport	L Nystrom	7th
1964	Liège	Saab 96 Sport	L Nystrom	4th
1964	RAC	Saab 96 Sport	L Nystrom	4th
1965	Monte Carlo	Saab 96 Sport	L Nystrom	3rd
1965	London	Saab 96 Sport	L Nystrom	5th
1965	RAC	Saab 96 Sport	L Nystrom	10th
1966	Czech	Saab 96 Sport	L Nystrom	5th
1967	Czech	Saab 96 V4	L Nystrom	3rd
1968	Monte Carlo	Lancia Fulvia	L Nystrom	14th
1968	San Remo	Lancia Fulvia	L Nystrom	2nd
1968	Sestrière	Lancia Fulvia	L Nystrom	1st
1968	Acropolis	Lancia Fulvia	L Nystrom	8th
1968	Corsica	Lancia Fulvia	L Nystrom	7th
1969	999 Minuti	Lancia Fulvia	S Seigle-Morris	3rd
1972	Monte Carlo	Alpine A110	L Crellin	10th

MICHÉLE MOUTON

YEAR	EVENT	CAR	CO-DRIVER	POS.
1974	Rouerge	Alpine A110	Furia	2nd
1974	Corsica	Alpine A110	A Arrii	12th
1975	Corsica	Alpine A110	F Conconi	5th
1975	EUROPEAN LADIES RALLY CHAMPION			
1976	Monte Carlo	Alpine 110	F Conconi	11th
1976	Crit. Alpin	Alpine A310	D Emmanuelli	2nd
1976	Nice	Alpine A310	F Conconi	3rd
1976	Cevenole	Alpine A310		4th
1977	Crit. Alpin	Fiat Abarth 131	F Conconi	4th
1977	Antibes	Fiat Abarth 131	F Conconi	2nd
1977	Tour de France	Fiat Abarth 131	F Conconi	2nd
1977	Corsica	Fiat Abarth 131	F Conconi	8th
1977	Spain	Porsche Carrera	F Conconi	1st
1977	EUROPEAN LADIES RALLY CHAMPION			
1978	Monte Carlo	Lancia Stratos	F Conconi	7th
1978	Crit. Alpin	Fiat Abarth 131	F Conconi	3rd
1978	Lorraine	Fiat Abarth 131	F Conconi	4th
1978	Antibes	Fiat Abarth 131	F Conconi	3rd
1978	Tour de France	Fiat Abarth 131	F Conconi	1st
1978	Giro d'Italia	Fiat Abarth 131	F Conconi	4th
1978	Corsica	Fiat Abarth 131	F Conconi	5th
1978	EUROPEAN LADIES RALLY CHAMPION			
1979	Monte Carlo	Fiat Abarth 131	F Conconi	7th
1979	Lyon–Charbonn.	Fiat Abarth 131	F Conconi	1st
1979	Antibes	Fiat Abarth 131	F Conconi	2nd
1979	Tour de France	Fiat Abarth 131	F Conconi	3rd
1979	Corsica	Fiat Abarth 131	F Conconi	5th
1979	Chataigne	Fiat Abarth 131	F Conconi	2nd
1979	EUROPEAN LADIES RALLY CHAMPION			
1980	Monte Carlo	Fiat Abarth 131	A Arrii	7th
1980	Spa	Fiat Abarth 131	A Arrii	4th
1980	Tour de France	Fiat Abarth 131	A Arrii	3rd
1980	Corsica	Fiat Abarth 131	A Arrii	5th
1980	EUROPEAN LADIES RALLY CHAMPION			
1981	Portugal	Audi Quattro	A Arrii	4th
1981	Garrigues	Audi Quattro	A Arrii	1st
1981	San Remo	Audi Quattro	F Pons	1st
1982	Sweden	Audi Quattro	F Pons	5th
1982	Portugal	Audi Quattro	F Pons	1st
1982	Corsica	Audi Quattro	F Pons	7th
1982	Acropolis	Audi Quattro	F Pons	1st
1982	Brazil	Audi Quattro	F Pons	1st
1982	San Remo	Audi Quattro	F Pons	4th
1982	RAC	Audi Quattro	F Pons	2nd
1982	RUNNER-UP IN WORLD CHAMPIONSHIP FOR RALLY DRIVERS			
1983	Swedish	Audi Quattro	F Pons	4th
1983	Portugal	Audi Quattro	F Pons	2nd
1983	Safari	Audi Quattro	F Pons	3rd
1983	Argentina	Audi Quattro	F Pons	3rd
1983	1000 Lakes	Audi Quattro	F Pons	16th
1983	San Remo	Audi Quattro	F Pons	7th
1984	Swedish	Audi Quattro	F Pons	2nd
1984	RAC	Audi Sport Quattro	F Pons	4th
1985	Welsh	Audi Quattro	F Pons	2nd
1986	Kohl und Stahl	Peugeot 205 T16	T Harryman	1st
1986	Vorderpfalz	Peugeot 205 T16	T Harryman	1st
1986	Hessen	Peugeot 205 T16	T Harryman	1st
1986	German	Peugeot 205 T16	T Harryman	1st
1986	Baltic	Peugeot 205 T16	T Harryman	1st
1986	3 Cities	Peugeot 205 T16	T Harryman	1st
1986	GERMAN RALLY CHAMPION			

SANDRO MUNARI

YEAR	EVENT	CAR	CO-DRIVER	POS.
1966	Monte Carlo	Lancia Flavia	G Harris	35th
1967	Monte Carlo	Lancia Fulvia	G Harris	5th
1967	Geneva	Lancia Fulvia	G Harris	2nd
1967	Spain	Lancia Fulvia	L Lombardini	2nd
1967	Corsica	Lancia Fulvia	L Lombardini	1st
1967	ITALIAN RALLY CHAMPION			
1968	Nurburg 84 hrs	Lancia Fulvia	H Kallstrom/ R Pinto	1st
1968	Alpi Orientali	Lancia Fulvia	O Druetto	1st
1969	Sestrière	Lancia Fulvia	J Davenport	1st
1969	Alpi Orientali	Lancia Fulvia	J Davenport	1st
1969	Corsica	Lancia Fulvia F&M	J Davenport	13th
1969	ITALIAN RALLY CHAMPION			
1970	Portugal	Lancia Fulvia	M Mannucci	2nd
1971	Semperit	Lancia Fulvia	M Mannucci	1st

1971	San Martino	Lancia Fulvia	M Mannucci	1st
1971	1000 Minuti	Lancia Fulvia	M Mannucci	1st
1971	Spain	Lancia Fulvia	M Mannucci	6th
1971	RAC	Lancia Fulvia	M Mannucci	9th
1972	Targa Florio	Ferrari 312P	A Merzario	1st
1973	Costa Brava	Lancia Stratos	M Mannucci	1st
1973	Firestone	Lancia Stratos	M Mannucci	1st
1973	Targa Florio	Lancia Stratos	J-C Andruet	2nd
1973	Czech	Lancia Fulvia	M Mannucci	2nd
1973	Danube	Lancia Fulvia	M Mannucci	3rd
1973	San Martino	Lancia Fulvia	M Mannucci	1st
1973	Tour de France	Lancia Stratos	M Mannucci	1st
1973	EUROPEAN RALLY CHAMPION DRIVER			
1974	Safari	Lancia Fulvia	L Drews	3rd
1974	4 Regions	Lancia Stratos	M Mannucci	1st
1974	San Remo	Lancia Stratos	M Mannucci	1st
1974	Canada	Lancia Stratos	M Mannucci	1st
1974	RAC	Lancia Stratos	P Sodano	3rd
1975	Monte Carlo	Lancia Stratos	M Mannucci	1st
1975	Safari	Lancia Stratos	L Drews	2nd
1975	4 Regions	Lancia Stratos	M Mannucci	1st
1976	Monte Carlo	Lancia Stratos	S Maiga	1st
1976	Portugal	Lancia Stratos	S Maiga	1st
1976	Morocco	Lancia Stratos	S Maiga	3rd
1976	San Remo	Lancia Stratos	S Maiga	2nd
1976	Corsica	Lancia Stratos	S Maiga	1st
1976	RAC	Lancia Stratos	S Maiga	4th
1977	Monte Carlo	Lancia Stratos	S Maiga	1st
1977	Safari	Lancia Stratos	P Sodano	3rd
1977	Total SA	Lancia Stratos	P Sodano	1st
1977	San Martino	Lancia Stratos	P Sodano	1st
1977	WINNER FIA CUP FOR RALLY DRIVERS			
1978	Corsica	Fiat Abarth 131	M Mannucci	3rd
1979	Safari	Fiat Abarth 131	S Maiga	10th

JEAN-PIERRE NICOLAS

YEAR	EVENT	CAR	CO-DRIVER	POS.
1967	Corsica	Renault R8 G	C Roure	7th
1968	Morocco	Renault R8 G	de Alexandris	1st
1969	Alpine	Alpine A110		6th
1970	Spanish	Alpine A110	D Stone	1st
1970	Geneva	Alpine A110	D Stone	2nd
1970	Acropolis	Alpine A110	F Veron	6th
1970	3 Cities	Alpine A110	D Stone	2nd
1971	San Remo	Alpine A110	M Vial	6th
1971	Geneva	Alpine A110	M Vial	1st
1971	Lyon–Charbon.	Alpine A110	M Vial	1st
1971	Spanish	Alpine A110	M Vial	1st
1971	Acropolis	Alpine A110	M Vial	2nd
1971	Portugal	Alpine A110	J Todt	1st
1971	FRENCH RALLY CHAMPION			
1972	Firestone	Alpine A110	J Todt	1st
1972	Olympia	Alpine A110	J Todt	1st
1972	Corsica	Alpine A110	M Callewaert	6th
1973	Monte Carlo	Alpine A110	M Vial	3rd
1973	Swedish	Renault 12 G	M Vial	14th
1973	Portugal	Alpine A110	M Vial	2nd
1973	Morocco	Alpine A110	M Vial	5th
1973	Acropolis	Alpine A110	M Vial	3rd
1973	Austria	Alpine A110	M Vial	5th
1973	San Remo	Alpine A110	M Vial	3rd
1973	Corsica	Alpine A110	M Vial	1st
1973	RAC	Alpine A110	C Roure	5th
1974	Antibes	Alpine A110	C Roure	1st
1974	Morocco	Alpine A110	C Delferrier	1st
1974	Antibes	Alpine A110	A Mahé	1st
1974	Ypres	Alpine A110	C Delferrier	4th

1974	Tour de France	Ligier JS2	G Larrousse/ J Rives	1st
1974	USA	Renault 17 G	G Phillips	3rd
1974	Corsica	Alpine A110	V Laverne	2nd
1975	Neige et Glace	Renault 17 G		3rd
1975	Antibes	Alpine A110	V Laverne	1st
1975	Crit. Alpin	Alpine A110	V Laverne	1st
1975	Corsica	Alpine A110	V Laverne	2nd
1976	Morocco	Peugeot 504	M Gamet	1st
1976	Safari	Peugeot 504	J-C Lefèbvre	9th
1976	Ivory Coast	Peugeot 504	J-C Lefèbvre	2nd
1977	Chamonix Ice	Peugeot 104 ZS		1st
1978	Monte Carlo	Porsche 911	V Laverne	1st
1978	Safari	Peugeot 504 V6	J-C Lefèbvre	1st
1978	Portugal	Ford Escort RS	J-C Lefèbvre	3rd
1978	Ivory Coast	Peugeot 504 V6	M Gamet	1st
1978	Corsica	Opel Kadett	V Laverne	7th
1979	Monte Carlo	Porsche 911	J Todt	6th
1980	Safari	Opel Ascona 400	H Liddon	5th
1984	Corsica	Peugeot 205 T16	C Pasquier	4th
1984	San Remo	Peugeot 205 T16	C Pasquier	5th

JEAN RAGNOTTI

YEAR	EVENT	CAR	CO-DRIVER	POS.
1970	Monte Carlo	Opel Kadett	P Thimonier	11th
1970	Tulip	Opel Kadett	P Thimonier	2nd
1970	Spanish	Opel Kadett	P Thimonier	7th
1972	Olympia	Opel Ascona	J-C Rouget	3rd
1973	Monte Carlo	Renault 12 G	J Jaubert	15th
1976	Corsica	Alpine A310	J Jaubert	4th
1978	Monte Carlo	Renault 5 Alpine	J-M Andrie	2nd
1978	Ivory Coast	Renault 5 Alpine	J-M Andrie	3rd
1979	Acropolis	Renault 5 Alpine	J-M Andrie	4th
1979	Mille Pistes	Sunbeam Lotus	J Todt	5th
1979	Corsica	Renault 5 Alpine	J-M Andrie	2nd
1980	Lyon–Charbonn.	Renault 5 Alpine	J-M Andrie	1st
1980	Mont Blanc	Renault 5 Alpine	J-M Andrie	1st
1981	Monte Carlo	Renault 5 Turbo	J-M Andrie	1st
1981	Du Vin	Renault 5 Turbo	J-M Andrie	2nd
1981	RAC	Renault 5 Turbo	M Holmes	5th
1982	Crit. Alpin	Renault 5 Turbo	J-M Andrie	3rd
1982	Corsica	Renault 5 Turbo	J-M Andrie	1st
1984	Portugal	Renault 5 Turbo	P Thimonier	5th
1984	Corsica	Renault 5 Turbo	P Thimonier	3rd
1984	Crit. Alpin	Renault 5 Turbo	P Thimonier	1st
1984	Antibes	Renault 5 Turbo	P Thimonier	4th
1984	Tour de France	Renault 5 Turbo	P Thimonier	1st
1985	Corsica	Renault Maxi Turbo	P Thimonier	1st
1985	Ypres	Renault Maxi Turbo	P Thimonier	1st
1985	Tour de France	Renault Maxi Turbo	P Thimonier	1st
1986	Corsica	Renault 11 Turbo	P Thimonier	5th
1986	Var	Renault 11 Turbo	P Thimonier	2nd
1987	Monte Carlo	Renault 11 Turbo	P Thimonier	8th
1987	Portugal	Renault 11 Turbo	P Thimonier	2nd
1987	Corsica	Renault 11 Turbo	P Thimonier	4th
1987	Acropolis	Renault 11 Turbo	P Thimonier	5th
1987	San Remo	Renault 11 Turbo	P Thimonier	3rd

WALTER RÖHRL

YEAR	EVENT	CAR	CO-DRIVER	POS.
1971	Wiesbaden	Ford Capri RS	H Maracek	1st
1972	Polish	Ford Capri RS	H Maracek	2nd
1973	Semperit	Opel Ascona	J Berger	2nd
1973	Czechoslovakia	Opel Ascona	J Berger	1st
1973	Danube	Opel Ascona	J Berger	1st
1973	Three Cities	Opel Ascona	J Berger	1st
1974	Firestone	Opel Ascona	J Berger	1st
1974	Tulip	Opel Ascona	J Berger	1st
1974	Hessen	Opel Ascona	J Berger	1st
1974	Ypres	Opel Ascona	L Carlsson	8th
1974	Czechoslovakia	Opel Ascona	J Berger	1st
1974	Danube	Opel Ascona	J Berger	1st
1974	RAC	Opel Ascona	J Berger	5th
1974	EUROPEAN CHAMPION RALLY DRIVER			
1975	Costa Brava	Opel Ascona	J Berger	4th
1975	Acropolis	Opel Ascona	J Berger	1st
1976	Monte Carlo	Opel Kadett GT/E	J Berger	4th
1976	Hessen	Opel Kadett GT/E	J Berger	2nd
1976	Ypres	Opel Kadett GT/E	W-P Pitz	1st
1976	San Martino	Opel Kadett GT/E	J Berger	5th
1978	Acropolis	Fiat Abarth 131	C Geistdorfer	1st
1978	Saarland	Lancia Stratos	C Geistdorfer	1st
1978	Hunsruck	Lancia Stratos	C Geistdorfer	1st
1978	Quebec	Fiat Abarth 131	C Geistdorfer	1st
1979	Sachs Winter	Fiat Abarth 131	C Geistdorfer	1st
1979	Hunsruck	Fiat Abarth 131	C Geistdorfer	1st
1979	Metz	Fiat Abarth 131	C Geistdorfer	1st
1979	San Remo	Fiat Abarth 131	C Geistdorfer	2nd
1980	Monte Carlo	Fiat Abarth 131	C Geistdorfer	1st
1980	Portugal	Fiat Abarth 131	C Geisdorfer	1st
1980	Trifels	Fiat Abarth 131	C Geistdorfer	1st
1980	Rheinhessen	Fiat Abarth 131	C Geistdorfer	1st
1980	Argentina	Fiat Abarth 131	C Geistdorfer	1st
1980	New Zealand	Fiat Abarth 131	C Geistdorfer	2nd
1980	San Remo	Fiat Abarth 131	C Geistdorfer	1st
1980	Corsica	Fiat Abarth 131	C Geistdorfer	2nd
1980	WORLD CHAMPION RALLY DRIVER			
1981	Hessen	Porsche 924 GTS	C Geistdorfer	1st
1981	Vorderpfalz	Porsche 924 GTS	C Geistdorfer	1st
1982	Monte Carlo	Opel Ascona 400	C Geistdorfer	1st
1982	Swedish	Opel Ascona 400	C Geistdorfer	3rd
1982	Safari	Opel Ascona 400	C Geistdorfer	2nd
1982	Acropolis	Opel Ascona 400	C Geistdorfer	2nd
1982	New Zealand	Opel Ascona 400	C Geistdorfer	3rd
1982	Brazil	Opel Ascona 400	C Geistdorfer	2nd
1982	San Remo	Opel Ascona 400	C Geistdorfer	3rd
1982	Ivory Coast	Opel Ascona 400	C Geistdorfer	1st
1982	WORLD CHAMPION RALLY DRIVER			
1983	Monte Carlo	Lancia Rallye 037	C Geistdorfer	1st
1983	Portugal	Lancia Rallye 037	C Geistdorfer	3rd
1983	Corsica	Lancia Rallye 037	C Geistdorfer	2nd
1983	Acropolis	Lancia Rallye 037	C Geistdorfer	1st
1983	New Zealand	Lancia Rallye 037	C Geistdorfer	1st
1983	San Remo	Lancia Rallye 037	C Geistdorfer	2nd
1984	Monte Carlo	Audi Quattro	C Geistdorfer	1st
1984	Portugal	Audi Quattro	C Geistdorfer	6th
1984	Ulster	Audi Sport Quattro	C Geistdorfer	1st
1985	Monte Carlo	Audi Sport Quattro	C Geistdorfer	2nd
1985	Portugal	Audi Sport Quattro	C Geistdorfer	3rd
1985	New Zealand	Audi Sport Quattro	C Geistdorfer	3rd
1985	San Remo	Audi Sport Quattro	C Geistdorfer	1st
1987	Monte Carlo	Audi 200 Quattro	C Geistdorfer	3rd
1987	Safari	Audi 200 Quattro	C Geistdorfer	2nd

CARLOS SAINZ

YEAR	EVENT	CAR	CO-DRIVER	POS.
1984	Catalunya	Opel Manta 400	Orozco	2nd
1986	Costa Brava	Renault Maxi 5 T	A Boto	2nd
1986	Corte Ingles	Renault Maxi 5 T	A Boto	1st
1986	Asturias	Renault Maxi 5 T	A Boto	2nd
1986	Catalunya	Renault Maxi 5 T	A Boto	2nd
1987	Corsica	Ford Sierra RS	A Boto	7th
1987	Asturias	Ford Sierra RS	A Boto	1st
1987	RAC	Ford Sierra RS	A Boto	8th
1987	SPANISH RALLY CHAMPION			
1988	Catalunya	Ford Sierra RS	L Rodriguez	2nd
1988	Corsica	Ford Sierra RS	L Moya	5th
1988	1000 Lakes	Ford Sierra RS	L Moya	6th
1988	Asturias	Ford Sierra RS	L Rodriguez	2nd
1988	San Remo	Ford Sierra RS	L Moya	5th
1988	Corte Ingles	Ford Sierra RS	L Rodriguez	1st
1988	RAC	Ford Sierra RS	L Moya	7th
1988	SPANISH RALLY CHAMPION			
1989	1000 Lakes	Toyota Celica GT4	L Moya	3rd
1989	San Remo	Toyota Celica GT4	L Moya	3rd
1989	RAC	Toyota Celica GT4	L Moya	2nd
1990	Monte Carlo	Toyota Celica GT4	L Moya	2nd
1990	Safari	Toyota Celica GT4	L Moya	4th
1990	Corsica	Toyota Celica GT4	L Moya	2nd
1990	Acropolis	Toyota Celica GT4	L Moya	1st
1990	New Zealand	Toyota Celica GT4	L Moya	1st
1990	Argentina	Toyota Celica GT4	L Moya	2nd
1900	1000 Lakes	Toyota Celica GT4	L Moya	1st
1990	Australia	Toyota Celica GT4	L Moya	2nd
1990	San Remo	Toyota Celica GT4	L Moya	3rd
1990	RAC	Toyota Celica GT4	L Moya	1st
1990	WORLD CHAMPION RALLY DRIVER			

TIMO SALONEN

YEAR	EVENT	CAR	CO-DRIVER	POS.
1974	1000 Lakes	Mazda 1300	S Harjanne	22nd
1975	1000 Lakes	Datsun Violet	J Markkula	6th
1976	Hankirally	Datsun Violet	J Markkula	5th
1976	1000 Lakes	Datsun 160J	J Markkula	6th
1977	Hankirally	Fiat Abarth 131	J Markkula	2nd
1977	1000 Lakes	Fiat Abarth 131	J Markkula	2nd
1977	Quebec	Fiat Abarth 131	J Markkula	1st
1978	Hankirally	Fiat Abarth 131	J Markkula	3rd
1978	1000 Lakes	Fiat Abarth 131	E Nyman	2nd
1979	Acropolis	Datsun 160J	S Harjanne	2nd
1979	Quebec	Datsun 160J	S Harjanne	2nd
1979	RAC	Datsun 160J	S Harjanne	3rd
1980	Swedish	Datsun 160J	S Harjanne	7th
1980	Acropolis	Datsun 160J	S Harjanne	2nd
1980	New Zealand	Datsun 160J	S Harjanne	1st
1981	Safari	Datsun Silvia	S Harjanne	4th
1981	1000 Lakes	Datsun Violet GT	S Harjanne	4th
1981	Ivory Coast	Datsun Violet GT	S Harjanne	1st
1982	Arctic	Datsun Violet GT	S Harjanne	1st
1982	New Zealand	Nissan Violet GTS	S Harjanne	4th
1982	1000 Lakes	Nissan Silvia T	S Harjanne	4th
1983	New Zealand	Nissan 240 RS	S Harjanne	2nd
1983	1000 Lakes	Nissan 240 RS	S Harjanne	8th
1984	Monte Carlo	Nissan 240 RS	S Harjanne	10th
1984	Safari	Nissan 240 RS	S Harjanne	7th
1984	Acropolis	Nissan 240 RS	S Harjanne	7th
1984	New Zealand	Nissan 240 RS	S Harjanne	4th
1984	RAC	Nissan 240 RS	S Harjanne	6th
1985	Monte Carlo	Peugeot 205 T16	S Harjanne	3rd

1985	Swedish	Peugeot 205 T16	S Harjanne	3rd
1985	Portugal	Peugeot 205 T16	S Harjanne	1st
1985	Acropolis	Peugeot 205 T16	S Harjanne	1st
1985	New Zealand	Peugeot 205 T16	S Harjanne	1st
1985	Argentina	Peugeot 205 T16	S Harjanne	1st
1985	1000 Lakes	Peugeot 205 T16	S Harjanne	1st
1985	San Remo	Peugeot 205 T16	S Harjanne	2nd
1985	WORLD CHAMPION RALLY DRIVER			
1986	Monte Carlo	Peugeot 205 T16	S Harjanne	2nd
1986	1000 Lakes	Peugeot 205 T16	S Harjanne	1st
1986	RAC	Peugeot 205 T16	S Harjanne	1st
1987	Swedish	Mazda 323 4WD	S Harjanne	1st
1988	Monte Carlo	Mazda 323 4WD	S Harjanne	5th
1988	1000 Lakes	Mazda 323 4WD	S Harjanne	4th
1988	RAC	Mazda 323 4WD	V Silander	2nd
1989	1000 Lakes	Mazda 323 4WD	V Silander	2nd
1989	RAC	Mazda 323 4WD	V Silander	6th

JEAN-LUC THERIER

YEAR	EVENT	CAR	CO-DRIVER	POS.
1969	Monte Carlo	Renault R8 G	M Callewaert	5th
1970	San Remo	Alpine A110	M Callewaert	1st
1970	Acropolis	Alpine A110	M Callewaert	1st
1971	Monte Carlo	Alpine A110	M Callewaert	2nd
1972	Corsica	Alpine A110	M Callewaert	5th
1972	Cevennes	Alpine A110	M Callewaert	1st
1973	Monte Carlo	Alpine A110	M Callewaert	5th
1973	Sweden	Alpine A110	M Callewaert	3rd
1973	Portugal	Alpine A110	J Jaubert	1st
1973	Morocco	Alpine A110	C Delferrier	7th
1973	Acropolis	Alpine A110	C Delferrier	1st
1973	Cevenole	Alpine A110		1st
1973	San Remo	Alpine A110	J Jaubert	1st
1973	Corsica	Alpine A110	M Callewaert	3rd
1974	Morocco	Renault 17 G	M Vial	2nd
1974	USA	Renault 17 G	C Delferrier	1st
1974	Corsica	Alpine A310	M Vial	3rd
1975	San Remo	Alpine A110	M Vial	3rd
1978	Mille Pistes	Toyota Celica	M Vial	1st
1979	Mistral	Toyota Celica	M Vial	1st
1979	Bordeaux	Autobianchi 1500	M Vial	1st
1979	Mille Pistes	Toyota Celica	M Vial	1st
1980	Quercy	Toyota Celica	M Vial	1st
1980	Hunsruck	VW Golf GTi	M Vial	5th
1980	Corsica	Porsche 911	M Vial	1st
1981	Hunsruck	VW Golf GTi	M Vial	4th

1981	Jamt	Toyota Celica	M Vial	1st
1982	Monte Carlo	Porsche 911	M Vial	3rd
1982	Crit. Alpin	Renault 5 Turbo	M Vial	1st
1982	Mille Pistes	Renault 5 Turbo	M Vial	1st
1982	Tour de France	Renault 5 Turbo	M Vial	2nd
1982	Antibes	Renault 5 Turbo	M Vial	4th
1983	Antibes	Renault 5 Turbo	M Vial	1st
1984	Monte Carlo	Renault 5 Turbo	M Vial	4th

HENRI TOIVONEN

YEAR	EVENT	CAR	CO-DRIVER	POS.
1977	1000 Lakes	Chrysler Avenger	A Linqvist	5th
1978	Arctic	Chrysler Avenger	M Tiukkanen	2nd
1978	Hankirally	Chrysler Avenger	J Korhonen	8th
1978	RAC	Chrysler Avenger	J Korhonen	9th
1979	Welsh	Ford Escort RS	B Harris	6th
1980	Arctic	Sunbeam Lotus	A Lindqvist	1st
1980	Welsh	Sunbeam Lotus	P White	4th
1980	Scottish	Sunbeam Lotus	N Wilson	13th
1980	San Remo	Sunbeam Lotus	A Lindqvist	5th
1980	RAC	Sunbeam Lotus	P White	1st
1981	Monte Carlo	Sunbeam Lotus	F Gallagher	5th
1981	Arctic	Sunbeam Lotus	F Gallagher	3rd
1981	Portugal	Sunbeam Lotus	F Gallagher	2nd
1981	San Remo	Sunbeam Lotus	F Gallagher	2nd
1982	Ireland	Opel Ascona 400	F Gallagher	3rd
1982	Welsh	Opel Ascona 400	F Gallagher	2nd
1982	Acropolis	Opel Ascona 400	F Gallagher	3rd
1982	Scottish	Opel Ascona 400	F Gallagher	3rd
1982	RAC	Opel Ascona 400	F Gallagher	3rd
1983	Monte Carlo	Opel Ascona 400	F Gallagher	6th
1983	Manx	Opel Ascona 400	F Gallagher	1st
1983	San Remo	Opel Manta 400	F Gallagher	4th
1984	Garrigues	Porsche 911 SC	J Piironen	3rd
1984	Crit. Alpin	Porsche 911 SC	J Piironen	2nd
1984	Costa Smeralda	Porsche 911 SC	J Piironen	1st
1984	Bulgaria	Porsche 911 SC	I Grindrod	2nd
1984	Ypres	Porsche 911 SC	I Grindrod	1st
1984	Madeira	Porsche 911 SC	J Piironen	1st
1984	1000 Lakes	Lancia Rallye 037	J Piironen	3rd
1985	Monte Carlo	Lancia Rallye 037	J Piironen	6th
1985	1000 Lakes	Lancia Rallye 037	J Piironen	4th
1985	San Remo	Lancia Rallye 037	J Piironen	3rd
1985	RAC	Lancia Delta S4	N Wilson	1st
1986	Monte Carlo	Lancia Delta S4	S Cresto	1st
1986	Costa Smeralda	Lancia Delta S4	S Cresto	1st

RIGHT Henri Toivonen/
Sergio Cresto
Lancia Delta S4
Costa Smeralda Rally
1986

ARI VATANEN

YEAR	EVENT	CAR	CO-DRIVER	POS.
1975	Scottish	Opel Ascona	D Richards	8th
1976	Welsh	Ford Escort RS	P Bryant	1st
1976	Tour Britain	Ford Escort 2000	P Bryant	1st
1976	Manx	Ford Escort RS	P Bryant	1st
1977	Arctic	Ford Escort RS	A Aho	1st
1977	Welsh	Ford Escort RS	P Bryant	2nd
1977	Scottish	Ford Escort RS	P Bryant	1st
1977	Hunsruck	Ford Escort RS	P Bryant	4th
1977	New Zealand	Ford Escort RS	J Scott	2nd
1978	Arctic	Ford Escort RS	A Aho	1st
1978	Swedish	Ford Escort RS	A Aho	5th
1978	Donegal	Ford Escort RS	P Bryant	1st
1978	Madeira	Ford Escort RS	H Liddon	1st
1978	Cork 20	Ford Escort RS	A Hertz	1st
1979	Monte Carlo	Ford Escort RS	D Richards	10th
1979	New Zealand	Ford Escort RS	D Richards	3rd
1979	1000 Lakes	Ford Escort RS	D Richards	2nd
1979	Quebec	Ford Escort RS	D Richards	3rd
1979	Cyprus	Ford Escort RS	D Richards	1st
1979	RAC	Ford Escort RS	D Richards	4th
1980	Ireland	Ford Escort RS	D Richards	2nd
1980	Welsh	Ford Escort RS	D Richards	1st
1980	Acropolis	Ford Escort RS	D Richards	1st
1980	Scottish	Ford Escort RS	D Richards	2nd
1980	Spain	Ford Escort RS	D Richards	2nd
1980	1000 Lakes	Ford Escort RS	D Richards	2nd
1980	Manx	Ford Escort RS	D Richards	2nd
1980	San Remo	Ford Escort RS	D Richards	2nd
1981	Sweden	Ford Escort RS	D Richards	2nd
1981	Lubeck	Ford Escort RS	D Richards	1st
1981	Spain	Ford Escort RS	D Richards	2nd
1981	Acropolis	Ford Escort RS	D Richards	1st
1981	Brazil	Ford Escort RS	D Richards	1st
1981	1000 Lakes	Ford Escort RS	D Richards	1st
1981	San Remo	Ford Escort RS	D Richards	7th
1981	Ivory Coast	Ford Escort RS	D Richards	9th
1981	RAC	Ford Escort RS	D Richards	2nd
1981	WORLD CHAMPION RALLY DRIVER			
1982	Sweden	Ford Escort RS	T Harryman	2nd
1982	Ireland	Ford Escort RS	N Wilson	7th
1983	Monte Carlo	Opel Ascona 400	T Harryman	5th
1983	Sweden	Opel Ascona 400	T Harryman	6th
1983	Safari	Opel Ascona 400	T Harryman	1st
1983	Acropolis	Opel Ascona 400	T Harryman	4th
1983	ITA	Opel Ascona 400	R Vatanen	1st
1983	Manx	Opel Ascona 400	T Harryman	2nd
1984	1000 Lakes	Peugeot 205 T16	T Harryman	1st
1984	San Remo	Peugeot 205 T16	T Harryman	1st
1984	RAC	Peugeot 205 T16	T Harryman	1st
1985	Monte Carlo	Peugeot 205 T16	T Harryman	1st
1985	Swedish	Peugeot 205 T16	T Harryman	1st
1985	New Zealand	Peugeot 205 T16	T Harryman	2nd
1987	Paris–Dakar	Peugeot 205 T16	B Giroix	1st
1987	Safari	Subaru Coupé	'Tilber'	10th
1987	1000 Lakes	Ford Sierra RS	T Harryman	2nd
1989	Paris–Dakar	Peugeot 405 T16	B Berglund	1st
1989	RAC	Mitsubishi VR4	B Berglund	5th
1990	Paris–Dakar	Peugeot 405 T16	B Berglund	1st
1990	1000 Lakes	Mitsubishi VR-4	B Berglund	2nd

BJORN WALDEGAARD

YEAR	EVENT	CAR	CO-DRIVER	POS.
1965	Swedish	VW 1500 S	L Helmer	3rd
1965	1000 Lakes	VW 1500 S	L Nystrom	12th
1966	1000 Lakes	VW 1600 TL	L Helmer	16th
1967	Tulip	Porsche 911	L Helmer	4th
1967	1000 Lakes	Porsche 911	L Helmer	12th
1968	Monte Carlo	Porsche 911 T	L Helmer	10th
1968	Swedish	Porsche 911 T	L Helmer	1st
1969	Monte Carlo	Porsche 911	L Helmer	1st
1969	Swedish	Porsche 911	L Helmer	1st
1970	Monte Carlo	Porsche 911 S	L Helmer	1st
1970	Swedish	Porsche 911 S	L Helmer	1st
1970	Austria	Porsche 911 S	L Nystrom	1st
1970	Portugal	Porsche 911 S	B Thorselius	3rd
1971	Monte Carlo	Porsche 914/6	H Thorselius	=3rd
1971	RAC	Porsche 911 S	L Nystrom	2nd
1972	Swedish	Porsche 911 S	L Helmer	2nd
1972	Portugal	Citroen SM	H Thorselius	3rd
1973	Swedish	VW 1302 S	H Thorselius	6th
1973	Morocco	Fiat Abarth 124	F Sager	6th
1973	RAC	BMW 2002 TI	H Thorselius	7th
1974	Safari	Porsche 911 S	H Thorselius	2nd
1974	Total SA	Toyota 2000 GL	H Thorselius	8th
1974	1000 Lakes	Opel Ascona	A Hertz	10th
1975	Swedish	Lancia Stratos	H Thorselius	1st
1975	Safari	Lancia Stratos	H Thorselius	3rd
1975	Total SA	Toyota Corolla	H Thorselius	2nd
1975	San Remo	Lancia Stratos	H Thorselius	1st
1976	Monte Carlo	Lancia Stratos	H Thorselius	2nd
1976	San Remo	Lancia Stratos	H Thorselius	1st
1976	RAC	Ford Escort RS	H Thorselius	3rd
1977	Portugal	Ford Escort RS	H Thorselius	2nd
1977	Safari	Ford Escort RS	H Thorselius	1st
1977	Acropolis	Ford Escort RS	H Thorselius	1st
1977	1000 Lakes	Ford Escort RS	C Billstam	3rd
1977	San Remo	Ford Escort RS	H Thorselius	5th
1977	RAC	Ford Escort RS	H Thorselius	1st
1978	Swedish	Ford Escort RS	H Thorselius	1st
1978	Safari	Porsche 911 SC	H Thorselius	4th
1978	RAC	Ford Escort RS	H Thorselius	2nd
1979	Monte Carlo	Ford Escort RS	H Thorselius	2nd
1979	Swedish	Ford Escort RS	H Thorselius	2nd
1979	Portugal	Ford Escort RS	H Thorselius	2nd
1979	Safari	Mercedes 450 SL	H Thorselius	6th
1979	Acropolis	Ford Escort RS	H Thorselius	1st
1979	1000 Lakes	Ford Escort RS	C Billstam	3rd
1979	Quebec	Ford Escort RS	H Thorselius	1st
1979	RAC	Ford Escort RS	H Thorselius	9th
1979	Ivory Coast	Mercedes 450 SL	H Thorselius	2nd
1979	WORLD CHAMPION RALLY DRIVER			
1980	Monte Carlo	Fiat Abarth 131	H Thorselius	3rd
1980	Swedish	Fiat Abarth 131	H Thorselius	3rd
1980	Ivory Coast	Mercedes 500 SLC	H Thorselius	1st
1981	Portugal	Toyota Celica	H Thorselius	3rd
1981	1000 Lakes	Toyota Celica	H Thorselius	9th
1982	South Swedish	Toyota Celica	H Thorselius	3rd
1982	New Zealand	Toyota Celica	H Thorselius	1st
1982	Ivory Coast	Toyota Celica	H Thorselius	3rd
1983	1000 Lakes	Toyota Celica TCT	H Thorselius	12th
1983	Ivory Coast	Toyota Celica TCT	H Thorselius	1st
1984	Safari	Toyota Celica TCT	H Thorselius	1st
1985	Safari	Toyota Celica TCT	H Thorselius	2nd
1985	1000 Lakes	Toyota Celica TCT	H Thorselius	7th
1985	Ivory Coast	Toyota Celica TCT	H Thorselius	2nd
1986	Safari	Toyota Celica TCT	F Gallagher	1st
1986	Ivory Coast	Toyota Celica TCT	F Gallagher	1st
1987	HK–Peking	Toyota Supra 3.0i	F Gallagher	1st
1988	Safari	Toyota Supra Turbo	F Gallagher	7th
1988	Hunsruck	Toyota Celica GT4	F Gallagher	2nd
1988	Cyprus	Toyota Celica GT4	F Gallagher	1st
1988	RAC	Toyota Celica GT4	F Gallagher	3rd
1990	Paris–Dakar	Peugeot 405 T16	Fenouil	2nd
1990	Safari	Toyota Celica GT4	F Gallagher	1st

PICTURE ACKNOWLEDGEMENTS

Action-Plus: p 63

Agence France–Presse: p 200

Allsport: pp 2–3, 30, 38–9, 47, 50–1, 94, 107(bottom), 110(bottom), 123(top), 158–9, 166, 166–7, 186–7, 190, 202–3

Allsport/Agence Vandystadt: pp 103, 114–5, 134, 135(top), 138, 138–9, 139, 143, 151, 155, 219

Author's collection: pp 4, 6(left), 6–7, 12, 18, 29(bottom), 33(top), 40, 41, 42, 42–3, 43, 44(bottom), 52(top), 54, 55, 58–9, 61(bottom), 62, 73, 74, 76, 78(both), 81, 94–5, 101(top), 102, 109, 111, 128, 149, 153, 157, 161(top), 164, 169, 172, 184, 185, 189, 192, 206, 208

Hugh Bishop: pp 22–3, 30–1, 31, 34, 34–5, 79, 90–1, 95, 98–9, 106, 122, 122–3, 176, 178, 182, 183(both), 213, 217

BMC: p 69(bottom)

Central Press: p 112

Edition Automobile: pp 19(bottom), 22

Mary Evans Picture Library: pp 15, 16, 19(top)

Explorer Archives: p 14

Ford Motor Company: pp 108, 116, 161(bottom)

Gamma: pp 130–1, 140, 142, 144, 168

Graham Gauld: p 48

Peter Gilbert: p 129

Ralph Hardwick: p 100(top)

Martin Holmes: pp 8–9, 33(bottom), 45, 46, 56, 62–3, 66–7, 70, 71(both), 75, 80, 82, 83(both), 86, 87(top), 100(bottom), 123(bottom), 145, 146–7, 150, 154, 162, 170, 174–5, 179

Hulton Picture Company: pp 17, 20(both), 21, 24, 36, 37, 107(top), 132, 136, 137(both), 148

Lehtikuva Oy: pp 85, 125, 162–3, 177

Kevin Mashiter: p 60

Morelli/Bertier: pp 96, 210

National Motor Museum: pp 13, 26, 27, 28, 29(top), 32, 44(top), 56–7, 64, 69(top), 97, 110(top), 117

Tony North: p 105

John Overton: p 173

Photo-Leisure: p 5

Pirelli: pp 180–1

Popperfoto: pp 25, 48–9, 52(bottom), 53, 61(top), 77, 84, 88, 92–3, 113, 120(both), 133, 156, 181

Professional Sport: pp 10–1, 87(bottom), 118–19, 126–7

Professional Sport/Presse–Sport: pp 135(bottom), 171

Maurice Selden: pp 154–5

Colin Taylor: pp 93, 104, 160, 165, 194

Topical Press: p 72